Marching to the promised land

Marching to the promised land

Has the church a future?

Ian Bradley

John Murray

First published in 1992
by John Murray (Publishers) Ltd.,
50 Albemarle Street, London W1X 4BD

A catalogue record for this book is available from the British Library

ISBN 0-7195-4995 7

Set in 11½/13 pt Times
Printed and set in Great Britain by Butler & Tanner Limited, Frome, Somerset

Contents

Preface

What is happening to the church? The statistics suggest terminal decline, or at the very least, change and decay. Yet it is certainly not slipping quietly away, unnoticed and unmourned. For a supposedly secular and post-Christian society we seem to have an abiding interest in and affection for an institution with which increasingly few of us are actually involved. Hardly a day goes by without newspapers focusing on some new ecclesiastical crisis or theological dispute. Issues like women's ordination, the loss of the Prayer Book, new styles of church music and worship and charging for entry to cathedrals arouse strong passions far beyond the ranks of committed church-goers.

This book attempts to assess the present state and the future prospects of the churches in Britain and to examine some of the main issues which they are facing at the end of the twentieth century. I should make clear at the outset its scope. It covers those churches and Christian communities which subscribe to an orthodox Trinitarian faith. I do not attempt to deal with groups like the Church of Jesus Christ of Latter Day Saints, better known as the Mormons, or the Jehovah's Witnesses, which while numerically significant, and growing in size and influence, do not subscribe to the historic creeds and shared beliefs of the universal church.

The main focus of the book is on England and Scotland. These are the two church communities with which I am familiar, and I have deemed it better not to risk misrepresentation by trying to cover in detail the other parts of the United Kingdom. While there is a certain amount about Wales, I have not attempted to describe church life in Northern Ireland. It is, of course, by far the strongest and most vigorous Christian community, with 70 per cent of the population being church members, as against 30 per cent in Scotland, 17 per cent in Wales and 11 per cent in England. But its particular complexities and tragic divisions really demand a separate study and I do not feel competent to unravel them here.

I should also perhaps declare my own church allegiance at this stage. I was baptized in the Church of Scotland, grew up and was confirmed in the Church of England, and am now back in the Church of Scotland as a minister. I have to confess that denominational differences sit fairly lightly on my shoulders. I rejoice in the fact that my ordination was into the one universal catholic and apostolic church. I also rejoice in the rich diversity of branches of this one church which exist in this country, each of which has something important to offer to the whole.

The idea of writing a book on the state of the churches in Britain in the 1990s was put to me on a car journey through central Scotland by Hugo Brunner, who has been a consistent supporter and friend throughout its period of gestation. I have also benefited much from the suggestions and support of Grant McIntyre and other members of the editorial and production staff at John Murray.

I would also like to record my thanks to the many people in many different churches and organizations who have put up with my questions and queries during the period that this book was being researched and written. I hope that when they read it they will still feel able to count me among their friends.

Introduction

Churches feature prominently in the British landscape of popular sentiment and romantic nostalgia. Along with the pub, the parish church is a central feature of the English village scene as depicted in *The Archers*, the tourist board brochures, and the minds of the urban and suburban majority clinging to an idealized vision of what constitutes the real heart of their country. With one place of worship for every 1,200 people, there are, in fact, more churches than pubs in England. They are probably more loved if less often patronized. Many Scots have a similarly romantic attachment to the wee kirk in the glen and an even stronger sense than their southern neighbours of the role played by the church in forging and preserving a distinctive national identity.

Churchmen too, on the face of it, enjoy a high status and command strong affection in contemporary Britain. The Archbishop of Canterbury ranks in precedence before the Lord Chancellor and the Prime Minister in England, while in Scotland only the Queen and the Duke of Edinburgh rank before the Lord High Commissioner to the General Assembly of the Church. Twenty-six bishops sit in the House of Lords. Television comedy series perpetuate the image of the clergy as essentially lovable and decent souls, if inclined to be slightly dithery, rather plummy-voiced and often a little eccentric.

The reality, however, is rather different. Church buildings may exist in our villages, but often they are used for worship only occasionally and some are kept open simply for the benefit of tourists. In terms of attendance and of the value that is placed on them, churches are no longer the focal point of the community.

Other temples have risen to take their place: it is through the automatic sliding doors and down the wide aisles of hypermarkets and superstores that most of us now prefer to make our Sunday morning pilgrimage. Instead of going up to the sanctuary to receive bread and wine, we now queue at the cash dispensers, waiting to tap out our personal code to instant salvation and insert our little plastic cards to appease the great god consumption.

In a society where Mammon is so clearly the main object of worship, those who devote their lives to the pursuit of the spiritual and the service of the church tend to be dismissed as irrelevant and eccentric. The clerical profession in Britain may still retain some vestigial privileges and affection but in reality it is overworked, badly paid, demoralized and downtrodden. The gentle spirituality and painstaking pastoral care of the clergy go largely unnoticed while every small peccadillo and every disagreement on doctrine is seized upon by a popular press that seems to find nothing quite as scintillating as a story about an errant vicar or a trendy bishop.

Judged in terms of regular participation in public worship, Britain is one of the most secular countries in the world. Admittedly there are considerable variations between different parts of the United Kingdom. In Northern Ireland nearly 40 per cent of the adult population still go to church every week. In Scotland the figure is around 17 per cent and in Wales 13 per cent. England comes bottom, with fewer than one in ten adults regularly attending any place of worship, although again there are significant regional differences: in South Yorkshire the figure is just 6 per cent, while in Cumbria and the Roman Catholic strongholds of Lancashire and Merseyside it is over 13 per cent. Overall, only Scandinavia comes below us in the European league table for church attendance.

Christianity and churches play a smaller part in our national life than in that of many other European countries. There is no specifically Christian political party here as there is in Germany or the Low Countries. Issues like abortion and contraception do not assume the same public and political importance as in Roman Catholic nations like Italy and the Irish Republic. It is hard to imagine Christianity ever playing the central role in Britain that it has over the last few years in Eastern Europe, where the churches have been the primary focus for anti-Communist feeling and among the principal agents of resistance to oppressive regimes.

The comparison with the rest of the world beyond Europe is even more marked. Europe is the only continent where the Christian church is in decline. Everywhere else in the world it is growing faster than at any time in its history. North Americans, used to much higher levels of church-going and to a much higher public profile for Christianity, are surprised at the extent of secularization in Britain. Many Christians in the developing world, especially in the Commonwealth, also look askance at the lack of religious observance in the country that for centuries sent out missionaries to convert them. At the beginning of this century we were still confidently singing hymns about the Africans and Indians calling on us to deliver their lands from error's chain – lands where the heathens in their blindness bowed down to wood and stone. Nowadays the churches of Africa, Asia and Latin America, the fastest-growing areas for Christianity, could well claim that it is Western Europe in general, and Britain in particular, which is in the grip of heathenism and in need of missionary outreach. Indeed, to some extent this is already happening. One of the most successful recent evangelists in this country has been Luis Palau from Argentina, while the songs and chants of African and Asian Christians are increasingly in demand to enliven the worship of churches in Britain.

The 1990s have been declared a decade of evangelization by the Pope and a decade of evangelism by the bishops of the Anglican communion. These could well be seen as fairly desperate last-minute attempts to recover some of the ground that has steadily been lost by the churches throughout the twentieth century. The omens do not look good for stemming, let along reversing, the steady decline in both church membership and attendance which has gone on for so long and which has been particularly marked over the last 30 years. In 1960 there were still ten million church members in the United Kingdom. Now there are fewer than seven million. The loss has been particularly pronounced in the main national churches. The Church of England's membership has dropped from around 2.5 million (7 per cent of the adult population) in 1960 to just over 1.5 million (4 per cent) 30 years later. Over the same period the Church of Scotland has suffered an even worse decline, though from a much higher base, dropping from 1.3 million members (38 per cent of the adult population) to 786,000 (20 per cent) in 1990. The decline in church-going has been equally spectacular. According to a detailed survey carried out by MARC Europe at the end of 1989 and published in early 1991, attendance at Sunday services in English churches has fallen at the rate of a thousand people a week over the last ten years – a net loss of over half a million worshippers over the decade, nearly 90 per cent of whom are under the age of 30. By contrast, it has been estimated that in Argentina church-going is increasing at the staggering rate of 8,000 people a day.

There is some evidence that the decline in church-going in Britain may at last be bottoming out. The MARC survey found that while weekly adult church attendance in England dropped by 7 per cent between 1979 and 1985, it fell by only 1 per cent over the following four years. Figures released by the Church of England for 1988 show the first year-on-year rise in church attendance since such statistics were first collected more than 20 years ago. Not too much should be read into these figures – the increase in church-going is among older people, and amounts to only 0.3 per cent over the previous year. What is more significant is the steady decline in the number of young people either belonging to or attending churches. Nearly all experts are agreed in predicting that, as older members die off, churches will continue to empty throughout the 1990s at the rate of about 50,000 lost members each year.

We have become used to the idea that we live in a secular society. The phrase was coined by sociologists in the mid 1960s with books like Bryan Wilson's *Religion in a Secular Society* and Harvey Cox's *The Secular City*. The other fashionable phrases used by academics to describe the religious complexion of contemporary Britain are 'post-Christian' or 'pluralist' – there is also much talk of ours now being a 'multi-faith' society. Certainly the growth and vigour of non-Christian faiths is in striking contrast with the decline of the main Christian denominations. While churches and chapels are closing at the rate of one a week, four or five new mosques and temples are being opened every month. Indeed, redundant Christian churches quite often find a new life as places of worship for other faiths; the Congregational Chapel in the centre of Leicester has been transformed at a cost of £1.3 million into the first temple in the west for one of the world's oldest religions, Jainism. The Muslim population in Britain has almost doubled over the last ten years and now numbers nearly a million – more than the combined strength of the historic Free Churches (Methodist, Baptist, Congregationalist and United Reformed). There are about half a million Hindus and Sikhs – more than there are Methodists – while the combined strength of Mormons and Jehovah's Witnesses (around 240,000) exceeds that of the Baptists.

It is easy to be misled by figures like these into overestimating the hold of non-Christian religions in Britain – they still represent a minority, but it is a growing minority and their expansion and fervour is in marked contrast to the general state of the mainstream Christian churches. It is also very easy to be dominated by the statistics of decline, and to fail to recognize that despite them church-going is still a very major activity in Britain. Every Sunday throughout the year nearly six million people attend a place of Christian worship. That is vastly more than the number who regularly watch live sporting events or who take part in political activities. It is even more than the number of people who go fishing, supposedly the most popular recreational activity in contemporary Britain.

It is also a mistake to put too much reliance on statistics of church membership and attendance when assessing the overall health and influence of Christianity. There are many reasons why people do or do not go to church. Robert Runcie recalled in one of his last major speeches as Archbishop of Canterbury that when he started as a priest in Newcastle in the early 1950s, 'there was nothing open on a Sunday. If you are absolutely realistic, there were a lot of people in the church for that very reason.' We need to be very careful about drawing the conclusion from the declining numbers at church on Sunday morning that there has been a corresponding decline in religious faith. Indeed, there is much other evidence to suggest that we may even be entering a new post-secular age where interest in spiritual matters is increasing.

One of the most perceptive commentators on the spiritual state of our society is the Chief Rabbi, Jonathan Sacks. In his 1990 Reith Lectures he observed, 'Perhaps the most unexpected fact about contemporary Britain is that the overwhelming majority of the population has not stopped being Christian. It may not be reflected in church-going or religious observance. But it answers the question increasingly unanswerable in other terms. The question: Who am I? ... What has become clear, if paradoxical, is that religious identity can go hand in hand with a decline among all measurable axes of religious behaviour. We practise the rituals of faith less often. We go to places of worship rarely. We can be, it seems, religious and secular at the same time.' (*The Listener*, 3 January 1991.)

Certainly, if opinion polls are to be believed, religious belief in modern Britain remains remarkably strong and generally Christian in focus. If anything, younger people express a stronger and more orthodox religious faith than the middle-aged. An extensive poll carried out in 1989 for the book *Britain under the MORIscope* found that more than three-quarters of those interviewed said they believed in God (other recent polls have put the number as high as 80 per cent), more than two-thirds testified to the existence of a soul, and 60 per cent believed in heaven. Perhaps even more surprisingly, over a third accepted the existence of the devil and only slightly fewer believed in hell. Nearly two-thirds of those interviewed in another recent survey agreed with the proposition that Jesus is the son of God – a rather bigger vote of confidence in the Incarnation than I suspect would be obtained if the same question were put to theologians. In a poll carried out in 1986 by Gallup on behalf of the Alister Hardy Research Centre which studies religious experience, more than half the respondents claimed that they had had some kind of religious experience in their lives, a significantly higher figure than when the same question was asked ten years earlier and only 36 per cent responded positively.

Of course, this growing interest in matters spiritual does not necessarily betoken an increasing commitment to Christianity. For some it leads to an espousal of the so-called 'New Age' movement associated with the astrological transition from the Age of Pisces to the Age of Aquarius. Others find their spiritual cravings fulfilled in Buddhism, Hinduism or other Eastern traditions of meditation, deep ecology and nature worship, or in various kinds of mysticism. A small minority, more disturbingly, turn to devil-worship and black magic. All these forms of religious belief are on the increase in Britain, as they are throughout the Western world. They may not put more bottoms on church pews – indeed, perhaps their growth indicates the unattractiveness of the institutional church to many who are seeking spiritual sustenance – but they do point to the inadequacy of scientific materialism and rationalism as satisfying food for contemporary minds and souls.

Those who predicted the coming of the secular or post-Christian society in the 1960s made much of the extent to which faith in science and technological progress had made both the supernatural explanations and the psychological crutch provided by religion largely redundant. Since then, growing concern about the environment and the capacity of human beings and technology to poison and pollute the planet has led to a marked loss of faith in science, and to a serious questioning of the belief in progress and unaided human resourcefulness that has held sway in the West since the Enlightenment. There is now much more willingness to see humans as frail and dependent rather than masterful, to view the world as a mystery to be approached in awe and wonder rather than an object that can be quantified and described in theorems and equations. This radical shift in thinking at the very least makes Christianity a much more credible creed than it was a generation or even a few years ago.

Indeed, to a greater extent than is often acknowledged, the Christian churches have already been the beneficiaries of this reaction against rationalism and scientific materialism. Although some young people may have taken up 'New Age' cults or Eastern religions, a good number have been attracted to a distinctively Christian form of spirituality as it is expressed in comparatively new movements like the communities at Taizé and Iona. There is a booming market in books on Celtic Christianity, on medieval mystics like Dame Julian of Norwich and Hildegaard of Bingen, and on the spiritual exercises of Ignatius Loyola. Monastic and other religious communities which offer facilities for retreats and periods of contemplation are inundated with bookings. Indeed, there is even a 'good retreat' guide, *Away from it all*, which helps people find the best place for their spiritual refreshment and renewal.

Nor is the revival of interest in Christianity simply expressing itself in an escapist retreat into a comforting and cocooning spirituality. There is also evidence of much more debate and discussion about the substance of faith and doctrine. Popular interest in theology and what the churches have to say is almost certainly greater than at any time this century. One would need to go back to the great set-piece debate in Oxford in 1860 between Bishop Wilberforce and Professor Huxley on the subject of evolution to find as much newspaper coverage of theological issues as that generated by the Bishop of Durham's comments in the late 1980s on the doctrines of the Resurrection and the Virgin Birth. The pronouncements of bishops and the debates in the synods and assemblies of the major churches receive far more column inches in the press and far more air time on radio and television than the levels of their membership could possibly justify. It is true that a number of particularly sensational and divisive issues, such as women priests, homosexual clergy and the ill-fated *Crockford's* affair, have provided especially juicy fare for the media over the last few years and have meant that the internal agonies of the Church of England in particular have been paraded across the front pages of the tabloid press. But in less sensational and more edifying ways, there is clear evidence through the media of widespread public interest in religious matters and of a real hunger for spiritual food.

As someone who has recently been professionally involved in religious broadcasting, I find particularly significant and heartening the vote of confidence recently given by the Radio 4 audience to the *Thought for the Day* slot on the *Today* programme. There had been some muttering among senior BBC executives about the anachronism of having a self-consciously religious slot, and more often than not an avowedly Christian homily, in the middle of a secular current affairs programme. Several senior figures in the news and current affairs directorate were also protesting that the daily pause for reflection and meditation interrupted the punchy flow of their fast-moving news programme. But a representative poll among the six million or so people who tune into *Today* at some point in the week found that, far from being a little-regarded and superfluous part of the programme, *Thought for the Day* was rated higher than several of the newsier items, including the financial news, the sports reports and the highlights of the previous day's debates in Parliament. Equally striking are the enormous audiences regularly gained by *Songs of Praise* and *Highway* on television. Often as much as a quarter of the entire population chooses to spend the early part of every Sunday evening watching hymn singing and listening to people talking about their faith.

The continuing popularity of these programmes is just one example of the hold which the Christian religion and the churches still have on the national psyche. In many ways it is implicit rather than explicit – the survival of something that is more of a folk religion than a clearly thought out matter of credal affirmations and specific ecclesiastical adherence. They may not go to church very often, but the British still think of themselves as a Christian people and most of them still identify with a particular church. The detailed MORI survey mentioned earlier found that only 4 per cent of the population regard themselves as atheists and a further 4 per cent as agnostics, while a massive 88 per cent claim to belong to one Christian denomination or another – the great majority to one

of the two national established churches. Most of these may not
be regular church-goers but they often still maintain some kind of
relationship, however tenuous, with a local church. Recent research
has established that less than 10 per cent of the British population
never attend a church service. For most the visits may be few and
far between – family occasions like weddings, christenings and
funerals, and perhaps the odd Christmas or Easter service. But the
fact remains that at times of particular celebration and particular
sadness, the great majority of people still turn to the church to
stage-manage the most important milestones in their lives. This
search for ritual, for religious sanction and blessing, for spiritual
meaning, or simply for a nice setting and a bit of a ceremony,
shows no sign of diminishing. More than two-thirds of those aged
between 18 and 34 expect to get married in church.

Talk of church, particularly in the context of a wedding, and
most people automatically think in terms of an old and beautiful
building with pews and stained-glass windows and surmounted by
a spire or tower. Of course there are still many churches like this,
but an increasing number of the buildings that look like real
churches and which were once real churches now turn out on closer
inspection to be warehouses, theatres, visitors' centres, nightclubs,
luxury flats or even, in one case in Newcastle-on-Tyne, a brothel.
Others are simply boarded up and gradually falling into a worse
and worse state of dilapidation. Those which are still open and
fulfilling the function for which they were built often have only a
handful of worshippers at their services, most of them elderly. Yet
just a few hundred yards away drab halls and concrete huts which
seem to make no theological statement and which could easily be
mistaken for second-hand furniture depots or light industrial units
are packed to overflowing with enthusiastic worshippers clapping
and shouting. The contrast between what is happening in these two
very different kinds of church building epitomizes the profound
and fascinating revolution that is currently taking place in the
Christian life of Britain.

Christians are familiar with the terms 'visible' and 'invisible'
being applied to the church. They are usually employed to distinguish the Christian body on earth, the Church militant, from
the great company of Saints in heaven, the Church triumphant. I
want to use the words in a rather different way in this book
because I think they describe very well the ecclesiastical state of
contemporary Britain. What we have is a 'visible' church which is

becoming increasingly invisible, and an 'invisible' church which is becoming more and more visible.

The traditional institutional church, the church of ancient buildings, stained-glass windows, hymns and ordained clergy in dog-collars, is in serious decline. Some would say that it is in terminal decline. The Church of Scotland has extrapolated from present trends that by the year 2047 there will be no members left. The position for the Church of England is probably rather worse. These institutions, which still have the status of being the established churches of the land, are also increasingly marginal to the life of individuals and of the nation. The research for *Britain under the MORIscope* found that they had virtually no role in shaping people's attitudes, even to moral questions. Their protected position and privileges are being eroded. In what could be an important indication of things to come, a Lancashire health authority recently refused to fund a full-time chaplain in one of the biggest hospitals in north-west England on the grounds that it had higher priorities than paying for a clergyman of the established church to minister to the spiritual needs of the patients.

But there is another type of church in Britain today which is in a very different state. It has been, and to some extent remains, largely invisible, because its buildings are not fine historic monuments with great spires pointing heavenwards. Indeed, many of its congregations meet for worship in one another's homes. This other church does not have clergy or the traditional trappings of organized religion; its members are predominantly young (mostly under 35) and prefer choruses and speaking in tongues to traditional hymns and prayers. Nor do they expect or want any state or public patronage. While the Church of England is worried by the thought of its small army of hospital chaplains being thrown off the National Health Service payroll, the independent evangelical and charismatic fellowships are already in the hospitals, running radio stations, producing cassettes, arranging Bible reading and prayer groups among staff and funding their activities by tithing.

The biggest and most obvious contrast between the visible and the invisible church is that the one is in seemingly irreversible decline while the other is enjoying spectacular growth. The MARC census showed an unrelieved picture of falling attendances among all the main traditional denominations in England – and the situation is the same in Scotland and Wales. Between 1979 and 1989 Church of England worshippers fell by 9 per cent, Roman Catholics by 14 per cent, United Reformed Church by 18 per cent and Methodists by 11 per cent. Over the same period attendance at the so-called 'house churches' grew by 114 per cent, at Pentecostal churches by 38 per cent and at other independent evangelical churches and fellowships by 42 per cent.

The next two chapters will briefly explore the current state of these two very different types of church. The distinction and the tensions between them will be a main theme of the book as a whole. In many ways they represent diametrically opposed views of what the church should be. They reflect, too, profound differences about what Christian faith is and what being a Christian means – whether it is a matter of dramatic conversion and being born again, or of a more gradual journey and pilgrimage through life. To some extent their positions are incompatible. Yet, as I hope to show, each has something important to offer the other and they must surely be able to work together for Christ.

– 1 –

The visible church

Through the night of doubt and sorrow
Onward goes the pilgrim band

It is impossible to imagine beginning a survey of the visible church in Britain anywhere else than with the Church of England. I am tempted to say the dear old Church of England because that is how it seems to present itself – as venerable, harmless, muddled and lovable, with all the quirks, the foibles and the occasional frostiness of a favourite maiden aunt. Like Radio 4 and the railways, the Church of England seems woven into the fabric of our national life – we may ignore it, take it for granted, complain about it, and yet it is impossible to imagine England without it. Yet like the BBC and British Rail it is in fact a highly vulnerable institution, facing a massive identity crisis and a very uncertain future. Dr George Carey, the 103rd Archbishop of Canterbury and Primate of All England, has described the church which he leads as 'an elderly lady who sits in a corner muttering ancient platitudes through toothless gums, ignored most of the time.'

Certainly, to judge from statistics of membership and attendance, it is doubtful if the Church of England any longer deserves its title, let alone its privileged position as the legally established church of the nation. There are now more than three times as many Roman Catholics as Anglicans in England. In terms of church-going the Church of England comes only third in the denominational league table with around 1.1 million worshippers on an average Sunday morning, compared with 1.3 million Roman Catholics and 1.2 million at Free Church services. Less than 2 per cent of the English population regularly attend their parish church. The figure is slightly higher in rural areas – the MARC census in October 1989 found the best attendance (around 5 per cent) in rural Somerset,

Gloucestershire and Cumbria – but in inner city parishes it drops
to less than one in a hundred. The extensive survey undertaken
across the country for the Church of England's own *Faith in the
City* report in the mid 1980s revealed that in an average-sized parish
with a population of 8,410 only 119 people regularly worshipped in
the parish church.

Yet the Church of England remains easily the most visible
denomination in the land. It has by far the most numerous premises
and the biggest work-force, with more than 16,000 churches and
over 12,000 ordained ministers. The Church Commissioners who
run its financial affairs administer assets worth over £2.5 billion
and have an annual income and expenditure of over £230 million.
Although the recent recession has significantly eroded these assets
and led to appeals for a much higher level of congregational giving,
the Church of England remains incomparably the wealthiest church
in Britain. As the established church it plays a central part in the
pomp and pageantry that attend so much of our public life and
which television brings to every living room. Coronations, royal
weddings and funerals and other major state occasions take place
in its cathedrals and are conducted by its clergy. It has considerable
media exposure, quite out of proportion to its size and probably
rather more than it would wish, and its bishops are still regarded
as public figures with something significant to say, and as natural
guests for radio and television discussion programmes. The Archbishop of Canterbury enjoys a prominence throughout the United
Kingdom which is accorded to no other church leader. He has
ready and frequent access to the Queen and the Prime Minister,
and even in staunchly Presbyterian Scotland where he has no
standing at all his major sermons and speeches are given considerable coverage in quality newspapers.

It is almost impossible to encapsulate the present state of the
Church of England in a few pages. Attend evensong in a country
parish church which still uses the Book of Common Prayer and
you are struck by a sense of antiquity, peacefulness and unchanging
calm. Go to morning worship in an inner-city parish like Tulse
Hill, where the vicar is a Ugandan, and you are plunged into the
noise, liveliness and rhythms of African worship. Meet a group of
parish clergy on a rural deanery retreat and there is an atmosphere
of quiet spirituality and deep pastoral concern. Yet delve into the
realm of church politics and talk to representatives of the various
factions who do battle in the General Synod and you encounter a

virulent partisan spirit which makes the goings-on in that other debating chamber just across Parliament Square seem positively gentlemanly. Depending on where you go and who you talk to, the Church of England can look like a model of tolerant broad-mindedness or a hotbed of back-biting and petty jealousies, a haven for gentle souls and saintly eccentrics or a paradise for bureaucrats and careerists, a vulnerable and humble part of the body of Christ seeking to minister to his children or a rather over-fat cat that occasionally scratches itself.

What is clear is that it lacks sharp focus and homogeneity. Judged by the prevailing values of the advertising and public relations industries, it is a disaster. It doesn't have a clear brand image or style, nor is it targeted to a particular market. Before he became Primate, Dr Carey talked about running the Church more like a business and bringing in public relations consultants and management strategists to improve its image. So far, thank goodness, nothing too much has happened. The Church of England remains one of our few national institutions which has not fallen victim to the tyranny of image and style, submerged its true identity under a bland corporate logo and become more concerned with what it looks like than what it is. It remains muddled, anguished, vulnerable and complex – just like the human beings which it exists to serve.

The breadth and comprehensiveness of the Church of England have always been two of its great strengths as well as its greatest potential weaknesses. It has always seemed to me that if ever a Biblical text were to be inscribed above the doors of Church House it should be from John 14.2: 'In my father's house are many mansions'. The inhabitants of those mansions are forever quarrelling with each other and threatening to split off on their own, but somehow so far they have always managed to stay under one roof. To get a measure of their diversity, one need do no more than visit three churches which stand within a quarter of a mile of each other in the very centre of London. Just up from Oxford Circus and right next to Broadcasting House stands All Souls, Langham Place, in many ways the cathedral of Evangelicalism, bursting at the seams with young people singing lively hymns and choruses accompanied by a full-scale orchestra. Its vicar, Richard Bewes, comes from a staunchly evangelical family and believes in strong Bible-based preaching. Just down the road in Margaret Street is All Saints Church, a bastion of Anglo-Catholicism where the incumbent is known as Father, the main Sunday services are Low and High Mass, and the vestments, candles, incense and bells are far 'higher' and more elaborate than in most Roman Catholic churches. Further down the road again is St James's Piccadilly, where the vicar, Donald Reeves, is the high priest of liberal Anglicanism. His pulpit is as likely to be occupied by an atheist or guru from one of the New Age religions as by an Anglican divine. The church is full of inter-faith happenings and artistic events and the social gospel is heavily stressed with special ministries to down-and-outs and Aids sufferers.

The three traditions that these churches represent – the Evangelical, the Catholic and the Liberal – have coexisted more or less amicably within the Church of England for at least 150 years. They reflect the three main sources of authority within the Christian church – Scripture, tradition and reason. Most other denominations tend to favour one of the three more definitely and regard the others as subordinate. In trying to hold on to all three sources of authority in roughly equal proportions Anglicans attempt a juggling act which I have heard Richard Holloway, the Episcopal Bishop of Edinburgh, describe as 'the realized impossibility'.

There are now many Anglicans who openly question how long this coalition can be kept together. There have been times in the past when the Church of England looked in danger of breaking up, but the threat is more serious now than at any time since John Wesley led the last great secession movement more than 250 years ago. In the face of a number of highly contentious issues of policy and organization party feeling is particularly strong and relations between the three main groupings within the Church are under unprecedented strain. Prominent clergymen are talking frankly, and in some cases enthusiastically, about a split between liberals and conservatives to form two separate churches. In September 1991 George Austin, Archdeacon of York, and a leading traditionalist, attracted considerable media attention and earned a rebuke from the Archbishop of Canterbury when he suggested in a sermon that divisions within the Church of England should be formally recognized. The idea of a split has also been enthusiastically canvassed by *The Times*' influential religious affairs editor and columnist, Clifford Longley.

It is difficult to establish precisely the present balance of parties within the Church of England. A representative survey of clergy carried out in 1987 put the number of Evangelicals at 40 per cent,

Catholics at 35 per cent and liberals at 25 per cent. This almost certainly overstates the extent of definite party positions. There are still many clergy who would not want to label themselves as belonging to any particular party and who cling to the central churchmanship that in the past helped to keep the Anglican boat from listing too far to either side. In a nationwide survey of 400 Anglican clergy carried out in 1985 as part of the research for the Church's *Faith in the City* report, 21 per cent identified themselves as Evangelical, 23 per cent as High Church and 51 per cent as middle of the road. Within the ranks of the laity, too, middle of the road or broad church sympathies almost certainly predominate. As always, those on the extreme wings tend to make a good deal more noise than those in the middle. None the less, it is clear that more people are aligning themselves in parties. One indication of this is the emergence within the Church of a number of pressure groups, each seemingly bent on attacking other groups in the name of preserving the Church that they love.

Of the three historic parties within the Church of England, there is general agreement that the Evangelicals are on the increase. The majority of young clergy and of the ordinands training in theological colleges fall into this camp. The appointment of an avowed Evangelical, George Carey, to the leadership of the Church also indicates the strength of this group. Certainly it is in evangelical parishes that most of the growth and vigour in contemporary Anglicanism is to be found. Their mix of Biblical preaching, unequivocal doctrine and joyful, spontaneous worship which sometimes borders on the charismatic, seems to appeal particularly to the young. Many Anglican Evangelicals are involved in church planting and in other activities more characteristic of the invisible church. Some are involved in the Evangelical Alliance and in the Anglican Evangelical Assembly. The more party-minded are also likely to be active in the Church Society, whose director, Dr David Samuel, makes periodic outbursts against the ecumenical movement and the increasing flirtation with Rome, and reminds the Church of England of its essentially Protestant character.

Among the clergy, at least, Anglo-Catholics are probably as large a grouping as Evangelicals, but their influence and voice are declining. They are the most worried of the three traditional parties about what is happening to the contemporary Church of England, and the most likely to leave it. From their origins in the Oxford Movement and beyond as the group which stressed above all the catholicity and universality of the Church they have, largely in reaction to the prospect of women's ordination, assumed the characteristics of a rather narrow and sometimes slightly bitter sect. The old High Church spirit, which encompassed a broad spirituality and a strong sense of the importance of national establishment and Church–state links, has been replaced by an increasingly aggressive and negative stance against the rest of the Anglican body. A number of leading Anglo-Catholics have already departed into the Roman Catholic Church, notably the Vicar of the University Church in Oxford, the Principal of Mirfield Theological College and the former church correspondent of the *Daily Telegraph*. If and when women's ordination to the priesthood comes to the Church of England, and it is much more likely to be when than if, this trickle might turn into a torrent or, more probably, a breakaway Anglo-Catholic church might be formed with tenuous and uneasy links to the main Anglican body. Many Anglo-Catholics have already signed up with the Cost of Conscience movement, which claims the support of 4,000 priests, a third of the Church of England strength, and which openly talks of forming a new church-within-a-church in the event of ordination of women to the priesthood and their consecration to the episcopate. But not all Anglo-Catholics are opposed to women's ordination. In an attempt to rally the older and broader High Church spirit Richard Holloway, Bishop of Edinburgh in the Scottish Episcopal Church, has set up a group known as Affirming Catholicism which stresses the importance of remaining within the Anglican fold.

Liberals are perhaps the hardest group to assess in terms of both their present strength and their future. In many ways one would expect them to be in eclipse, squeezed between the more doctrinaire and dogmatic protagonists in the Evangelical and the Catholic camps. But perhaps what is rather in eclipse is old-style moderate or central churchmanship – the broad, tolerant, open-minded spirit that used to be the predominant mood of Anglicanism (and, one might add, of Scottish Presbyterianism) and which perhaps more than any other factor held the Church of England together for so long. In its place there has arisen a more partisan liberalism, in its way as narrow and intolerant as extreme Evangelicalism and Anglo-Catholicism. This new liberalism may not have a very wide grip on the church as a whole – it is scarcely found among the laity – but it is to be found in certain key areas of influence: among academics in university theology departments, among writers and broadcasters, within the ranks of General Synod activists (where it finds focus in the Open Synod group) and, perhaps disproportionately, on the bench of bishops. As a result it has become the dominant tone of the public utterances of the Church of England. It is, of course, most clearly represented by those two stars of Anglican academia so often seized on by the media for their articulate and provocative style, David Jenkins and Don Cupitt, but it also finds expression throughout that whole group of media clerics and theologians who are asked to appear on television discussion programmes and contribute to 'Thought for the Day'.

It is the influence of the liberals that is most often blamed for the decline and present plight of the Church of England. The infamous preface to the 1987–88 *Crockford's* clerical directory, written by the late Gareth Bennett, chaplain of New College, Oxford, was a devastating attack on the liberal leadership of the Church of England. In particular it singled out the then Archbishop of Canterbury, Robert Runcie, quoting the words of Frank Field, Labour MP for Birkenhead and prominent lay Anglo-Catholic, that 'he is usually to be found nailing his colours to the fence' and going on to say that 'it would be good to be assured that he actually knew what he was doing and had a clear basis for his policies other than taking the line of least resistance on each issue'.

These rather personal comments dominated the whole sad episode of the *Crockford's* preface and deflected attention from the main thrust of its argument – that there had been a conspiracy between liberal bishops and academics to destroy the historic traditions of the Church of England (chief among them the Book of Common Prayer), to replace certainty with relativism and equivocation in the realm of doctrine, and to steamroller through innovations like the ordination of women to the priesthood irrespective of opposition. The gist of the criticism was articulated at Dr Bennett's memorial service by his friend and executor Dr Geoffrey Rowell, chaplain of Keble College, Oxford, when he said that the Church of England was in danger of being ruled by trend rather than tradition. It was also put to me strongly in Dr Rowell's rooms in Keble by Michael Brewin, Vicar of Headington and a leading figure in the Cost of Conscience movement: 'For the last twenty years or more, the Church of England has been carried powerlessly along in a liberal stream and we have been watching helplessly as forces have been at work in the name of democracy which have seriously weakened the Church.'

In the aftermath of the *Crockford's* affair a pressure group of traditionalists was formed in 1988 with the title 'Church in Danger' under the leadership of the Earl of Lauderdale and the Conservative MP John Selwyn Gummer. They listed a devastating catalogue of ills afflicting the established church of the land: divisions over the ordination of women as priests, loss of a common reference point for belief and order once provided by the Book of Common Prayer; continuing decline in church attendance and numbers of communicants; loss of pride and confidence in Church tradition; vague and equivocal public statements about Church faith and morals, heavily influenced by passing secular concerns; amendment of Bible teachings to fit current cultural demands; excessive growth and bureaucratization of synodical government; growth in divorce, illegitimacy and abortion unchecked by clear Church guidance; growth of sectarianism – a Church reserved for the wholly committed and intolerant exclusivists; failure to recruit and educate the young and a rising proportion of elderly members; falling academic standards of ordinands; and insensitive closure of church buildings and amalgamation of many parishes.

In a letter to the *Church Times* in September 1990 the trustees of Church in Danger put their point even more strongly, although perhaps a shade less personally than it had been made in the *Crockford's* preface. 'The Church of England,' they wrote, 'the Church of the English people, is being hijacked by a group intent on reforms at any cost which mock at revealed truth, the faith for which our ancestors fought and died, and which even deny scripture. It is hardly surprising that such a Church is failing to inspire and lead people and that a decline in its own standards is leading to a spread of godlessness in society.'

It is easy to dismiss such alarmist remarks as coming from an unrepresentative group who dislike any change and are out of touch with the whole spirit of the age. Yet I suspect that much of what they say strikes a chord with many Christians in many denominations. Several of the issues which they raise – the impact of liberal theology and new trends in worship, the failure of the churches to recruit and educate the young, the development of a more sectarian and exclusivist spirit in the national churches – will be examined in greater depth in later chapters. Here we will concentrate on the specific situation of the Church of England.

There is no doubt that a sense of betrayal by the leadership and of the damage done by liberalism is felt more acutely here than in any other church. Perhaps this is because of the particular authority structure and class composition that distinguishes English Anglicanism. A certain kind of liberalism does seem to have taken a very firm hold among the bishops and academics who exert most influence and authority in the Church of England. In many ways it is very much a 1960s style of liberalism of a kind that most other institutions have now discarded. It also has a rather distinctively public-school and Oxbridge flavour, combining a certain sense of guilt with a rather high-minded idealism and a detachment from the circumstances and lifestyles of the majority of the population. One recalls John Betjeman's caricature of the Wykehamist as 'Broad of Church and broad of mind, broad before and broad behind' – in many ways a very attractive, urbane and companionable figure but perhaps rather too comfortable and cultivated for our more troubled and rough-hewn society.

We have probably witnessed the high point of the liberal ascendancy in the Church of England and the flowering of public-school Oxbridge Christianity that it represented. The totally unexpected appointment of George Carey, the first non-public-school and non-Oxbridge Archbishop of Canterbury in recent times, signifies a very important change of emphasis in the Anglican hierarchy. As an anonymous colleague put it in the *Observer* newspaper: 'Under the last three primates the Church has been like a large Oxbridge college, with the Archbishop of Canterbury as the Master, the bishops as the dons, clergy as undergraduates and the laity as college servants. George doesn't think like that. He has no experience of the senior common room and his arrival has already disrupted that atmosphere.'

The appointment of George Carey may well spell the end of the reign of liberalism in the Church of England in other respects as well. Certainly news of the impending arrival in Canterbury of a committed Evangelical with an unequivocal commitment to the truth of such doctrines as the Resurrection and the Virgin Birth filled the founders of the Church in Danger movement with new hope. John Selwyn Gummer wrote in the *Church of England Newspaper*: 'It bodes well for the Church of England that we shall be led by a man whose view of the Christian faith has not been diminished by the theological minimalists nor distorted by fashion-conscious liberals.' In remarks that he made before his consecration

Carey echoed many of the movement's criticisms of the Church, which he described as 'lukewarm, disobedient, sinful and faithless'. Traditionalists may be worried by his enthusiasm for women priests, modern music and charismatic worship, and by his suggestion that the church might better be renamed 'the Jesus Movement', but they can hardly argue that Anglicanism is still in the grip of an ultra-liberal leadership.

It is too early to assess the full impact of George Carey's appointment. Even at this stage, however, it seems safe to predict that the Evangelical wing within the Church of England will grow in strength and confidence and that there will be much more informality both in worship and in overall style and approach. Whether these changes will be enough to arrest the decline in its membership and influence and to solve its acute crisis of identity and morale is another matter. Quite apart from the tensions which arise from its attempt to hold together three different parties, it also faces a trio of wider problems which are not encountered by any of the other major denominations. It may be appropriate for a body that believes in the Trinity that all its problems should come in threes, but it can be little consolation to the Church of England that it has to act in three wholly different roles simultaneously – as a national established church, as part of a world-wide communion, and as a unique bridge between Roman Catholicism and Protestantism. Working out what the priorities should be between these various roles is one of the Church's biggest current dilemmas.

It is in its role as the legally established church of the land that the Church of England is most public and visible. It is part of the national heritage and part, too, of the burgeoning national heritage industry, with a uniquely important collection of historic buildings in its care and a superb ability to stage-manage great state occasions. It is also the church of the great unchurched majority in England, many of whom still describe themselves as C of E, even though they may seldom if ever darken the doors of their local parish church. There remains a strong sense among the English that the Church of England is their church, a national institution that does not simply belong to its members. It is noticeable that when major changes are made, like the replacement of the Book of Common Prayer by the Alternative Service Book, the greatest outcry comes not on theological grounds from committed believers, but from agnostics and even atheists disturbed by the destruction of a vital part of the nation's cultural heritage.

The question of the continued establishment of the Church of England is likely to be raised increasingly during the 1990s. The Liberal Party has taken up the cause of disestablishment, as has Michael Alison, MP, the Second Church Estates Commissioner who speaks for the Church in the House of Commons. On the face of it, a church which commands the active support of only 2.5 per cent of the English population hardly seems to justify the privileged status brought by establishment, and there are many within the Church who would be happier if it were dropped. I will discuss later my own belief that continued establishment, though on a different basis from the present arrangements, is important in terms of the wider role of a national church and its ability to reach out to the unchurched majority.

The main price that the Church of England pays for the privilege of being the established church is to endure a measure of political control over its own affairs. This is much less extensive than it used to be. Since 1974 the Church has had full control over its worship and doctrine – it is no longer possible for Parliament to veto a new prayer book as it did in 1928. However, Parliament still retains the power to reject measures which affect the government and constitution of the Church – it could, for example, block the ordination of women to the priesthood after it had been approved by the Church's own synod. If this happened, pressure from within the Church for disestablishment would undoubtedly increase. The setting up in 1977 of a Crown Appointments Commission, made up of bishops, clergy and laity, has given the Church more say in choosing bishops and archbishops. However, the final say on episcopal appointments rests with the Prime Minister. In every other province of the Anglican communion, including the Scottish Episcopal Church and the Church in Wales, bishops are directly elected by the clergy.

Another significant step towards giving the Church of England more control over its own affairs was the setting up in 1970 of the General Synod with power to pass legislation on many aspects of the Church's organization. It is a large and complex body modelled in many ways on Parliament. Its total membership of 574 is divided into three houses: bishops, clergy and laity. Any new measure has to gain approval from all three houses with a two-thirds majority, and also to pass through three stages, like a Parliamentary bill. As a further check, contentious matters can be passed down to dioceses for further consideration. The General Synod meets three times a year, twice in London and once in York. In addition, there are diocesan synods which meet twice a year.

The establishment of synodical government has undoubtedly helped to foster party conflict in the Church of England. Elections to Synod, which are held every five years, have come to seem like mini General Elections, with rival groupings issuing manifestos and running slates of candidates. After each election careful calculations are made in the church press of the number of Evangelicals, Catholics and liberals elected and, in the present Synod elected in 1990, about the relative strength of the forces supporting and opposed to the ordination of women to the priesthood.

The Synod has come in for a lot of criticism for being unrepresentative, time-wasting, ineffective and expensive. It certainly seems unnecessarily large, with nearly as many members as the House of Commons to represent an electorate less than a thirtieth of the size. In some ways it is more representative of the nation than the House of Commons: it has far more women, for example, and also more members of ethnic minorities – there are 14 black members in the present Synod. But it is doubtful how far it accurately reflects opinion in the Church of England. It naturally attracts activists and those of strong party views and probably under-represents the middle ground. Its way of working encourages debate and division. It has also led to a proliferation of paperwork, committees and bureaucracy. Like the assemblies of other churches it has succumbed to the temptation to become deliberative as well as legislative, spending much time pontificating on the problems of the world, to no great purpose or effect. It is hard to point to any constructive achievement – unless one counts the introduction of the Alternative Service Book in the 1970s. More often, and perhaps not surprisingly given its cumbersome system of checks and balances, it has been a block to progress, vetoing such proposals as union with the Methodists in 1972 and the Covenanting Scheme with other churches in 1982 which were strongly backed by the bishops.

A Synodical Government Review Commission is currently examining the whole system, and there may be changes in the way the Church of England runs itself in the later 1990s. The only thing that can be said in favour of the synodical system is that it is at least an attempt to introduce democracy into the government of the Church. The most obvious alternative would be to hand power back to the bishops. Some feel that this would actually be more democratic and lead to less divisiveness and party spirit. It would almost certainly make for quicker and less painful decision-making. Others feel that synodical government represents only a façade of democracy, and that real power continues to reside with the diocesan bishops. In his *Crockford's* preface Garry Bennett wrote: 'The reality is that beside the system of synods, with their elections, debates and votes, there exists another system of episcopal executive authority, the characteristics of which are deference, patronage and self-recruitment. It is the influence of the House of Bishops, which over the last five years has increased and is now increasing.'

The whole question of authority is one that preoccupies Anglicans. They are constantly talking and worrying about it. Significantly, the only book on a specific topic which Robert Runcie found time to write during his ten years as Archbishop of Canterbury was entitled *Authority in Crisis? An Anglican Response.* In many ways the crisis is common to all churches and comes from the revolution in thinking about authority which has taken place in the secular world over the last 25 years. How does a church which believes in the given authority of revelation and the Bible come to terms with a society which increasingly says authority must be located in the self and can have no external sources or sanctions? But the Church of England also has particular difficulties in formulating a clear view of where authority should lie because of its historic position as a half-way house between Catholicism and Protestantism. Traditionally Roman Catholicism has stressed the *magisterium* of the Church, and particularly of the episcopacy under the supreme authority of the Pope. Catholics are used to a habit of obedience, although many are now coming to question it. Protestants have been much more inclined to see authority residing in the conscience of the individual believer and to structure their churches on democratic lines, risking an element of anarchy.

Anglicanism has tried to steer a middle course between these two approaches by developing its own unique system of dispersed authority based on bishops acting collegially and on a federation of autonomous provinces linked in communion. The trouble is that increasingly bishops on both the traditional and the liberal wings of the Church are refusing to accept collegial authority, and at the same time individual provinces are more and more inclined to go their own way without much thought to the communion as a whole. The question of women's ordination to the priesthood has put a particular strain on the Anglican principle of dispersed authority.

This is the issue on which bishops are prepared to break ranks and also the issue which has split the Anglican communion down the middle. Several provinces, like the United States, Canada, Australia, New Zealand and Hong Kong, happily accept women not just as priests but as bishops. Others, including most of Africa and Asia, are implacably opposed to the whole idea. The poor Church of England is as ever caught in the middle, agonizing painfully about the whole business.

The Church of England's relationship with the Anglican communion as a whole is rather like that of Britain with the Commonwealth. Historically, it is the mother church of the whole communion, extending to some seventy million members. Until comparatively recently it could reasonably claim to be its leader. Now the Church of England is one of the smallest and least vigorous churches in the world-wide Anglican family. The change can be seen in the Lambeth Conferences which bring the bishops of the Anglican communion together every ten years. Until 1958 the great majority of those present were British expatriates, and those who were not had almost all been educated at university or theological college here. In 1988 the overwhelming majority of delegates were native-born, the largest contingent coming from Africa, and virtually all had been educated in their own country. The primacy that the Church of England exercises over the world-wide Anglican communion is now largely nominal, and it is probably fair to say that the influence we are now feeling in Britain from new styles of worship and music in Africa and the Pacific is much greater than anything we are contributing to the church life of those and other countries.

There is another powerful Anglican influence from abroad which traditionalists here particularly fear. The Episcopal Church in the United States is very vocal and extremely liberal. It was one of the first churches in the Anglican communion to have women priests and the first to have a woman bishop, Barbara Harris, elected in Massachusetts in 1989. It also allows the remarriage of divorced people in church (and indeed has a substantial proportion of divorced people among its clergy), sanctions the marriage of homosexual couples, and takes a very relaxed line on matters of doctrine and belief. It is the example of the American Episcopal Church that Anglican traditionalists have in mind when they say that the Church of England is in danger. This is what they fear it will become unless the drift to liberalism is arrested.

Probably a more important factor forcing the Church of England to re-examine its identity is the changing character of the other major denominations at home. For a long time Anglicans have been able to define themselves as occupying a middle position between Catholicism and Protestantism, combining the best of both traditions while avoiding their excesses. Until recently it was comparatively easy for Anglicans to find unattractive features in the other churches and to feel that their own middle way was somehow better. Roman Catholicism stood for Papal infallibility, Latin services and ultramontane authoritarianism, and had a slightly foreign feel to it. Protestantism in England meant Non-conformity – gathered congregations meeting for rather dull and wordy worship without the benefit of set liturgies, and identifying more with political and social causes than with real spirituality. In the last few decades all this has changed. The Roman Catholic Church has reformed itself, given much more autonomy to its individual hierarchies, substituted the vernacular for Latin as the language of worship, emphasized lay involvement in services, and even introduced hymns and choruses. The result is that the Roman Catholic Mass is now often almost indistinguishable from the Anglican Eucharist. At the same time, there has been a move within the Free Churches towards much greater spirituality and sacramentalism and more use of set prayers and orders of service, with the result that here too there is now a much greater similarity to Anglican practice and procedure.

Where does this leave the Church of England, with its fewer worshippers than either the Roman Catholics or the combined Free Churches? As one might expect the answer is split down the middle. A substantial part of the Church of England would dearly like reunion with Rome, which at times over the last 20 years has looked a distinct possibility. Following the visit of Archbishop Michael Ramsey to Rome to meet Pope Paul VI in 1966 in the aftermath of the Second Vatican Council, an Anglican–Roman Catholic International Commission (ARCIC) was set up. Its deliberations have proceeded to the stage where there are now relatively few disputed points of doctrine. The main problem comes over ministry, and this is why the ordination of women is such a contentious issue. Several Anglican experts believe it was only the possibility of women's ordination that prevented the Roman Catholic Church at the last ARCIC session from moving towards a recognition of the validity of Anglican orders. Others feel that

Rome's acceptance of Anglican orders and any prospect of a reunion of the two churches is still very far off, irrespective of the issue of women priests. They argue that the Church of England could more fruitfully and constructively turn its attention to the Free Churches and seek to bring some of them, particularly the Methodists, back into the Anglican fold. Already, they point out, at parish level Anglicans are co-operating extremely closely with members of other Protestant churches and there are a growing number of ecumenical team ministries and shared church buildings.

There are also those who want to keep the Church of England as it is, occupying its unique position as both catholic and yet reformed; they are the people who tend to talk a lot about the identity of Anglicanism. Actually establishing the nature of this special identity is rather more difficult. Historically, Anglicanism is the result of a rather sharp piece of *realpolitik* by Henry VIII and his advisers. But it has always had its more saintly side, and over the centuries it has matured into something very distinctive, very difficult to define and very English. It may well be that in its very muddle, its tensions, its compromise, its fudging, its attempts to find a place for so many mansions under its roof, it is truer to the heart of Christianity than some other churches which trumpet their faith with more certainty and confidence. For all its critics – and the sad thing is that the fiercest and bitterest of them come from within its own ranks – we should not forget those, mostly from outside, for whom Anglicanism in general and the Church of England in particular offers something uniquely valuable and attractive. I think of Geoffrey Taylor, the *Guardian's* agnostic and acerbic columnist, who recently proposed the formation of a Society of Friends of the Church of England for those like himself who while they could never join felt an enormous affection and respect for it and a great distress over its capacity to tear itself apart. I think, too, of Victoria Knollys, who joined the Church of England in the early 1980s after what she describes as 'an exceedingly painful and unhappy journey from Rome' and who wrote in the *Church Times* of her new home: 'I am saddened that it is decried for its lack of authority, its wishy-washiness and indecision. Many of its adherents seem to see it as a pigpen of a church: messy, untidy and disorganised. To me it is like the publican, standing at the gate, beating his breast: "Lord, have mercy on me, a sinner". It is not suffocated by self-righteousness built up by generations of rule-making; it is humble, uncertain, stumbling. It reminds me of St

Peter, a man who made endless mistakes but who, above all, had a warm heart. To me, the very indecisiveness of the Anglican church leaves room for love to seep through.'

For me the fundamental decency, the endearing charm and the sheer quirky loveliness of the Church of England is epitomized by the atmosphere of the building which serves as its headquarters. Church House is an oasis of old-fashioned bureaucratic courtesy in the very heart of London, tucked away behind Westminster Abbey and just across the road from the Houses of Parliament. Its long corridors and panelled rooms have the kind of furniture you might have found in a country solicitor's office in the 1950s – lots of heavy mahogany bookcases and sensible old-fashioned bureaux. I may say that the Church of Scotland's headquarters in George Street in Edinburgh have exactly the same atmosphere. When I went to visit Eric Shegog, the Church of England's head of communications, there wasn't a word-processor or fax machine in sight. I had to wait while he answered a phone inquiry from *The Archers* production team as to what a bishop would wear for a wedding. He consulted the Bishop of London's secretary just down the road for the answer. Two minutes later she was back on the phone. An avid *Archers* fan, she had realized that the wedding in question (that of Peggy Archer and Jack Woolley) involved a divorced party would a bishop actually take such a service? Eric Shegog felt bound to put this point to the producer, but with true Anglican diffidence and courtesy he didn't like to make too much of it. The radio wedding went ahead, bishop and all, with a press 'photo opportunity' on the steps of All Souls, Langham Place, complete with an actor in cope, mitre and white stole.

A similar old-fashioned charm and whimsy pervades the pages of the Church of England's excellent weekly newspaper, the *Church Times*, which is a great deal more elegantly written than its secular namesake. It recently ran a cookery feature under the title 'Sunday lunch and the sermon', and offered a choice of last-minute Christmas presents which began with the *Oxford Book of English Detective Stories*, continued with a collection of short stories called *The Seven Deadly Sins* and then recommended the World's Classics edition of Jane Austen's *Pride and Prejudice* as 'a pointed gift for a couple planning an elopement or a clergyman bent on social climbing'. Where else would you find the headline over the leading letter on the correspondence page 'The ethics of riding to hounds'?

It is terribly tempting to dismiss the Church of England as an endearing but ineffective anachronism. For every parson who rides to hounds there are hundreds more trying to get to grips with transactional analysis and non-directive counselling and working away quietly but devotedly in the most deprived urban and rural areas in the land. People have been writing off the Church of England for a very long time. In 1747 Bishop Butler refused the See of Canterbury on the grounds that it was 'too late to try to support a falling church', while in the early years of this century Lord Halifax remarked that 'Nothing but the martyrdom of an Archbishop can save the Church of England'. Yet it has a remarkable capacity for keeping on going, and it has its own vivacity and strength. I conclude this survey as I began it, with a snapshot of two very different types of Anglican church which illustrate, I think, the variety and vitality of the contemporary Church of England with all its realized impossibilities and inherent contradictions. Go to evensong at Christ Church Cathedral, Oxford, and you can feast on a banquet of Anglican choral music sung by a choir in candlelight. You can be transported by the timeless and transcendent beauty of seventeenth-century prayers read by canons who in their other incarnation as professors of theology are writing books debunking much of received Christian doctrine. 'Howells in G' and Wiles on *The Myth of God Incarnate* seem to me a fair encapsulation of one aspect of the Anglican tradition – cerebral, civilized and challenging. Go across the road to St Aldate's Church and you can join a packed congregation of young people in singing powerful, emotional hymns and choruses and hear sermons which castigate radical theologians and proclaim the eternal truth of the Gospel. It may be that there will be more of the latter than the former in future, but each has its value, and it is not the least glory of Anglicanism that it has been able to provide both kinds of spiritual fare for so long.

The Church of England has occupied a disproportionate amount of space in this chapter because of the particular complexities of its situation. The other parts of the visible church are more straightforward and can be treated at rather less length. Turning to the other established church in Britain, the Church of Scotland, we find a body which is more homogeneous, more united and generally in rather better shape than its sister south of the border, with nearly 20 per cent of the population on its rolls and 8 per cent regularly worshipping on Sunday mornings. Overall, the Scots are a good deal keener on organized religion than the English, with three times as many church members and twice as many regularly attending services. This doesn't necessarily mean, of course, that they are more Christian. There is still a good deal of social church-going in Scotland, and Presbyterianism is much more ingrained in the Scottish national psyche than Anglicanism is in the English. The old story about the Scottish free-thinker who on being described as an atheist corrected it to 'a Presbyterian atheist' still rings true. There is an extent to which Scotland remains a land of Presbyterian agnostics. The Kirk is an important symbol of national identity and pride. There is also a strong Scottish tradition of interest and debate in theology, and something of this remains today. Religious books sell much better than in England and the two main Scottish ITV companies carry a two-minute mini-sermon after the *News at Ten*, years after their English equivalents abolished the late night Epilogue. Many Scots still enjoy good preaching, and it is the sermon rather than the eucharist which is at the heart of Pres-byterian worship. Clergy in the Church of Scotland are ordained into the ministry of word and sacrament, in that order, and local newspapers always advertise church services with the name of the preacher prominently displayed.

How much longer this greater interest in religion will persist is doubtful. Most observers believe that by the early part of next century Scotland will have sunk to the same level of secularity as England. Although the Church of Scotland has given an even higher priority than the Church of England to remaining the church of the whole nation and maintaining a presence in every parish, falling numbers and financial difficulties have meant that 1,500 charges have been lost over the last 60 years. Both membership and attendance are declining steadily and every year the Church loses almost twice as many people through death and default as it gains through the admission of new communicants. As was pointed out in the introduction, it has been forecast that if present trends continue there will be no one at all left in the Kirk by the year 2047.

For the time being, however, the Church of Scotland is a much stronger force in the land than is its big sister south of the border. On the whole its ministers enjoy more respect, higher status and better pay than Anglican vicars and rectors. This is despite the fact that the Kirk has far fewer assets and endowments and is much less enmeshed in the apparatus of state power. As a Presbyterian church it also lacks bishops and archbishops, and so tends to produce fewer nationally-known figures than the Church of England or the Roman Catholic Church. Although legally established, like the Church of England, the Church of Scotland has since 1921 had total freedom to organize its own affairs and is not subject to the authority of Parliament. Indeed, far from being beholden to politicians, it is MPs who come to the Kirk's annual General Assembly, traditionally regarded as the nearest Scotland gets to its own Parliament, to listen to its debates on the social and political questions of the day. The Assembly, which is made up of roughly equal numbers of ministers and lay elders, is both legislative and deliberative. Like the General Synod, although with perhaps slightly more justification in the absence of any other national forum for debate, it increasingly enjoys the latter role, and commissions lengthy reports and statements on both domestic and international matters which might seem to have little directly to do with the Church.

The General Assembly, held annually for a week in May in Edinburgh, shows the Church of Scotland at its best and worst. Presided over by the Moderator, who still wears eighteenth-century court dress, its proceedings are exceedingly formal, with much bowing and use of arcane legal language. The same is true to a lesser extent at meetings of presbyteries, the main administrative units of the Church. These correspond roughly to Anglican dioceses in terms of their size and jurisdiction but exercise their authority collectively rather than episcopally, being made up of parish ministers and elected elders from each congregation. Instead of motions there are overtures and deliverances. Even at ordinary Sunday services ministers do not give out notices, they deliver intimations. There is a tendency to excessive legalism and formality but there is also a genuine attempt at real democracy. The Moderator of the General Assembly, like the moderator of each presbytery, is elected from the ranks of the clergy and returns to his or her parish or academic post when the year of office is completed. There is no hierarchy in the Kirk; all ministers are on an equal footing and, perhaps as a result, there is comparatively little faction fighting or politics. There is also a substantial amount of lay involvement in decision making. Every local church is governed by a Kirk Session which is made up of the elders, who are ordained for life.

The Church of Scotland may not be quite as lovable as the Church of England, but nor is it as muddled or as divided. There is some tension between those who would emphasize its national and Scottish character and those who see it first and foremost as a Reformed Church, but this is nothing like as acute as the differences of emphasis within Anglicanism. The Kirk's magazine, *Life and Work*, is at once more folksy and more serious than the *Church Times* and carries far fewer news stories about factions and debates within the Church. Increasingly, Anglican newspapers now include pull-out supplements put together by some pressure group or other to promote its cause. The only supplement which comes with *Life and Work* is in Gaelic. If the *Church Times* resembles its secular counterpart in the good old days, *Life and Work* is more like a mixture of the *Expository Times* and the *People's Friend*. It is the journal of a church which is basically at peace with itself and not bent on tearing itself apart. Unlike Anglicans, Presbyterians have never made a great virtue of comprehensiveness, and the tendency in Scotland has always been that when a serious division on faith or order arises, a breakaway group splits off to form a new church. Ecclesiastical histories of Scotland normally have to include a chart resembling an extended family tree to show the many breakaways and reunions that have taken place over the last 400 years. The present Church of Scotland dates from a reunion in 1929 which brought together groups which had parted company nearly a century earlier over the issues of state control and lay patronage. Several smaller Presbyterian churches which chose not to come back into the embrace of the national church remain strong, especially in the Highlands and Islands. They include the Free Church of Scotland and the Free Presbyterians, or 'Wee Frees' who themselves recently split over the issue of whether their best-known member, the Lord Chancellor Lord McKay of Clashfern, should have attended a Roman Catholic Requiem Mass.

Anti-Catholicism is still a force to be reckoned with in Scotland, particularly in the greater Glasgow area. It is not altogether absent from the Church of Scotland, where there is an element associated with the Orange Order, but on the whole its influence is waning. To some extent there are evangelicals, catholics and liberals within the Kirk but they are much less sharply defined groups than in the Church of England. Evangelical clergy are certainly on the increase and there are signs that they are beginning to adopt a more partisan stance on certain issues, notably the ordination of women to the ministry and eldership. High Church Presbyterians, or Scoto-Catholics as they are sometimes known, are a small minority but have some influence through the Church's Panel on Worship and through the Iona Community, founded in 1938 as a focus for a new social gospel and a renewal of Celtic spirituality. There is something of a move to make worship in the Kirk more sacramental – not difficult in a church where it is still the norm to celebrate communion only four times a year.

Traditionally liberalism has had an honoured place in the Church of Scotland in the form of the moderate party who opposed the narrow zeal of the Evangelicals in the nineteenth century. But as in Anglicanism the breadth and tolerance of the old-style moderate ministers seem to have been replaced by a narrower and more partisan left-wing outlook, especially among those who dominate the Assembly's key Church and Nation committee which pronounces on social and political matters. This perhaps causes less unease than it does in England; Scottish Presbyterianism has a long tradition of political radicalism and a commitment to economic and social justice. Also, public opinion in Scotland as a whole is considerably further to the left than it is in England and a national church which speaks out with a socialist voice is more in tune with majority feeling. That said, there is a clear gap between the politics of many ministers and of their congregations. The kind of social church-going that accompanies belonging to the Rotary Club and being a respectable member of society lingers on in Scotland to a much greater extent than in England. In small towns and suburbs the Kirk Session can be a fairly conservative force with lawyers, accountants and small businessmen predominating much more than they do in the average Anglican parochial church council. To some extent, indeed, the predominance of these professions gives a certain tone to the Church. It is generally extremely efficiently run and strong on finance, organization and propriety. It is significant that while the Church of England has a Book of Common Prayer, the Church of Scotland has a Book of Common Order – not that it is much used by ministers, who tend to make up their own prayers. A strong degree of formality and dignity attends the worship, which is arguably more minister-dominated than that of any other major denomination, and there is generally very little responsive prayer or lay participation. It can seem a trifle austere, but it has a dignity which is lacking in Anglican services using the flat words of the Alternative Service Book.

It seems to me that you can tell a lot about a church from the style of architecture it favours for its places of worship. Whereas Anglican churches tend to be Gothic, muddled, mysterious and sometimes rather spiky, the Church of Scotland prefers a somewhat severe classicism, ordered, symmetrical and a touch unimaginative. There is a great sense of earnestness in the Kirk. Indeed, it exhibits more clearly than any other church I know the doctrine of reserve associated with John Henry Newman, maintaining a proper reticence and seriousness of purpose in the face of the Almighty and not descending into the familiarity or trivialization that sometimes characterizes the worship of Anglican and other churches. You won't find many choruses or charismatic congregations in the Kirk. Critics would say you won't find much spirituality or joy there, either, and it is true that the stress on formality and order can militate against contemplative silence and spontaneity. However, thanks to the influence of the Iona Community and a rediscovery of the traditions of the Celtic Church there is a growing interest in spirituality. Allied to the underlying unity and seriousness of purpose in the Kirk and its relatively stronger position in terms of membership and attendance, the overall impression is of a national church in better heart than its big sister south of the border.

In both Scotland and England the national established churches are no longer the largest single denominations, being outnumbered by the Roman Catholics in terms of both membership and attendance. In Wales the position is different. The Church in Wales, which is Anglican but disestablished (like the Episcopal Church in Scotland), is the largest denomination although by only a fairly small margin. The last detailed religious census in the Principality, carried out by the MARC organization in 1982, showed that it had 137,600 members, with the number of Roman Catholics standing at 129,600. Regular Sunday attenders in the two churches were around 100,000 and 85,000 respectively. For long regarded as an alien English influence, the Church in Wales actually seems to have gained support as a result of disestablishment, which took place in 1920 after a long Nonconformist and Liberal campaign led by Lloyd George. Although it is still strongest in English speaking areas like the old counties of Pembrokeshire, Monmouth and Glamorgan a third of its membership is Welsh-speaking. The MARC survey found that, uniquely among Welsh denominations, it was actually registering increasing attendance figures, particularly in respect of the number of children coming to church which was up by 20 per cent over four years. Interestingly, a MARC survey carried out in Scotland in 1984 showed something very similar happening in the much smaller Scottish Episcopal Church, which reported a jump in child attendance of 23 per cent and a rise in adult attendance of 7 per cent since 1980. Both churches are still declining in terms of overall membership (the Scottish Episcopalians are down to 37,000) but they do seem to have a more committed membership than the Church of England, and to have achieved spectacular success in bringing in children.

It may come as something of a surprise to discover that in a land traditionally associated with Nonconformity and the chapel culture of male voice choirs and radical politics, the two largest denominations in terms of membership should be the Anglicans and the Roman Catholics. But in terms of attendance Wales remains strongly Protestant and Free Church. If 20 per cent of those in church on a Sunday morning in the Principality are Roman Catholics and 29 per cent are Anglicans, the majority, 51 per cent, are still in the chapels of the Free Churches. Between them the Presbyterian Church of Wales, the Union of Welsh Independents and Congregationalists, the Baptists and the much smaller Methodist Church have over 200,000 members, about 10 per cent of the population. This is, of course, far fewer than in the heyday of Welsh Nonconformity following the great revival of 1905–6. Devastated by unemployment, the Welsh valleys have become sadly soulless places in the last two or three decades, their Ebenezer and Bethesda chapels for the most part now boarded up or turned into second-hand furniture stores or bingo halls. Christianity has increasingly been pushed back into the Welsh-speaking heartlands of the north-west. Gwynnedd has the highest rate of regular church attendance, 19 per cent – more than double that in Mid-Glamorgan at the other end of the country. Welsh speakers account for two-thirds of the total membership of the biggest free churches, the Presbyterians (or Calvinistic Methodists) and Independents (or Congregationalists).

In England, the Free Churches form the third main denominational block with a total membership of around 1.1 million, significantly lower than that for Anglicans and Roman Catholics. In terms of church attendance, however, they are on more equal terms with the other major denominational groupings: on the Sunday in October 1989 when MARC's census was taken there were 1.2 million adults worshipping in Free Churches, compared with 1.3 million Roman Catholics and only 1.1 million in the Church of England. Free Church members are much more committed in their church-going than Anglicans or Roman Catholics and, as the above figures suggest, their services also attract a number of people who are not actually members. In fact, virtually all the growth in the Free Church sector is to be found in independent evangelical fellowships and other parts of the new, invisible church that will be the subject of the next chapter. The older, visible Free Churches like the Methodists, Congregationalists and Presbyterians which were once the backbone of the strong Nonconformist Conscience that did so much to shape politics and social reform in nineteenth- and early twentieth-century Britain are declining more steeply than any other denomination. It is somehow symbolic that the best-known and most articulate representative of that conscience, Lord Soper, the Methodist minister and life peer, should be a nonagenerian, still vigorous and undiminished in his pacifism and socialism but seeming increasingly like a survivor from another age.

The Methodist Church is now down to about 425,000 members in Britain and expects to drop by another 30 per cent by the end of the decade. It still has a radical cutting edge and practises as well as preaches a strong social gospel. The Urban Theology unit at Sheffield set up by Dr John Vincent, a former President of the Methodist Conference, has been at the forefront of developing a ministry to inner-city areas. The United Reformed Church (URC) has plummeted, from nearly 200,000 members when it was formed in 1972 through a union of Congregational and Presbyterian churches, to not much more than 100,000 today. There has been much talk of a merger between the Methodists and the URC and there are already several local combined congregations which work well. Both churches are also involved in wider ecumenical activities and are moving closer to Anglicanism in their increasing emphasis on sacraments and set liturgies and their greater appreciation of spirituality. There is a small separate Congregationalist Church numbering around 10,000, made up of those who rejected union with Presbyterians.

The Salvation Army, still justly renowned for its work with down-and-outs and in emergencies and still venturing where many other Christians prefer not to go, has also been in steady decline over the last 50 years. There are now more Salvationists in East Africa than in Britain although there are still more than 830 corps in the newly-formed United Kingdom territory, attracting around 60,000 worshippers every week. Over the last few years the Army has divested itself of many of the militaristic terms and images that

once characterized its evangelistic approach. Officers no longer do
'knee drill', but say their prayers, and passing round the collection
plate during services is no longer called 'firing a cartridge'. But the
brass bands remain, thank God, as does a strong commitment to
using new and lively music in worship, including pinching, where
necessary, some of the devil's best tunes. At the other extreme
about 18,000 members of the Society of Friends, or Quakers,
continue to worship without music or song, sitting in silence unless
the Spirit moves them to speak, and to witness, through both
meditation and action, to traditional concerns like peace, justice
and the environment. They also often provide a much-needed
spiritual home for those who find it hard to accept the disciplines
and heartiness of the institutional church. In some ways, perhaps,
the Quakers properly belong to the invisible rather than the visible
church; but their open, tolerant, inclusive, liberal spirit hardly
makes them natural bedfellows of the charismatics and evangelicals
who predominate there.

Most of the members of another historic Free Church are, by
contrast, much more at home in the new invisible church and
should really be counted in its ranks. Uniquely among the traditional Nonconformist denominations, the Baptists have actually
been growing in numbers over the last few decades. According to
the MARC census their membership in England is up from around
160,000 in 1979 to over 170,000 today, with much of the increase
coming from young people in their teens and early twenties. There
are a further 15,000 Baptists in Scotland and nearly 30,000 in
Wales, although here the membership is ageing and predominantly
confined to the remoter Welsh-speaking areas. Like other Nonconformist churches, the Baptists are much involved in trying out
new experimental forms of ministry and worship and are at the
forefront of the hymn explosion that has taken place over recent
years. But on the whole they do not share that enthusiasm of
Methodists, Congregationalists, Quakers and the United Reformed
Church for ecumenical activities which has given the Free Churches
a key place and many of the top positions in the new inter-church
bodies set up in England, Scotland and Wales. In this respect, as
in their strong evangelical faith and their often charismatic style of
worship, they stand much closer to the new invisible church.

There is one other growing denomination in Britain which is
also not much interested in matters ecumenical but which can
hardly be lumped in with the invisible church in terms of its

theology or style of worship. Membership of the Eastern Orthodox churches in this country has grown by 15 per cent over the last 15 years: there are now more than 114 congregations with over 232,000 members. Only a small part of this increase is attributable to immigrants from Greece, Cyprus and Eastern Europe. There has been a steady stream of Anglicans and others 'converting' to Orthodoxy, often because they are attracted by its rich and colourful liturgy, its prayerfulness and sense of mystery, and its holistic 'green' approach to creation. Leading Orthodox figures like Archbishop Anthony Bloom and Bishop Kallistos Ware have also had an important impact on British church life more generally, contributing to the increased interest in spirituality and the greater appreciation of Christian traditions beyond the familiar Western European models of Protestantism and Roman Catholicism which have been among the most encouraging movements of recent years.

In terms of size the Roman Catholic Church should properly come first rather than last in any survey of the Christian scene in Britain today. The total number of Catholics in Britain is around five and a half million, or 10 per cent of the population. It is true that this figure cannot be directly compared with the much smaller membership figures of other denominations since it includes all baptized infants and not, as in the case of Protestant churches, only those who have been confirmed or admitted to full membership. But in terms of regular worshippers, the Roman Catholic Church is now clearly the largest single denomination in Britain with about 1.7 million adults attending Mass every Sunday. Not that it has been immune from the decline in church-going that has afflicted all denominations – the MARC census showed a 14 per cent drop in those attending Mass during the 1980s – but it has held on to its members more successfully than the main Protestant churches.

The continuing authority of traditional Catholic teaching on the importance of bringing up children in the faith and on weekly attendance at Mass has undoubtedly played a part in this. So, perhaps, has authority in more general terms. On the whole the Roman Catholic hierarchy has held much more clearly and rigidly than the leaders of most major Protestant churches to orthodox Christian doctrine and unequivocal moral teaching. This has meant less backsliding and uncertainty about matters of faith among their flocks: opinion polls consistently show that Roman Catholics have a much stronger belief in doctrines like the Resurrection and life beyond death. It has also brought about a significant number of converts seeking to escape from what they see as wishy-washy Protestant liberalism to a more clear-cut and secure faith. This trend has not been confined to Britain. In the USA since 1947 the number of Protestants has declined by 23 per cent and the number of Roman Catholics increased by 40 per cent.

But while strong and clear-cut authority may seem attractive to some outside the Roman Catholic Church, it is also proving increasingly irksome to many within. There is growing concern among many lay Catholics, in Britain as on the Continent, shared also by several priests, about what is seen as the hard and inflexible line taken by the Vatican on issues of sexuality, morality and the freedom to dissent from official teaching. A recent book by Michael Hornsby Smith, *Roman Catholic Beliefs in England: Customary Catholicism and transformations of religious authority* (1991), points to an increasing trend among English Catholics to challenge the teaching of the Pope and bishops especially on the subjects of contraception and inter-communion. There is also growing unease about the rule of celibacy applied to the priesthood.

On the surface at least the Roman Catholic Church appears a good deal more monolithic than the other main denominations in Britain. But it, too, is a house of several mansions. It almost certainly has a greater social diversity and reach than any other church, embracing the upper-class products of Downside and Ampleforth at one end and the inhabitants of some of the poorest parts of inner-city Liverpool and Glasgow at the other. The Catholics are, indeed, the only large denomination who have managed to keep a substantial following among the urban working classes and have not been forced back into small towns and suburbia. They can claim, in a sense that neither of the established churches in Britain can, to be still a church of the people.

There is also remarkable intellectual diversity within contemporary British Catholicism. This is shown by the range of its journals and newspapers. The weekly magazine *The Tablet* is quite the best general survey of current theological issues I know. Other Catholic periodicals like the *Month* and *New Blackfriars* are also highly intellectual and stimulating. At the other end of the spectrum, diocesan newspapers often achieve a level of populism not found in other church publications. For example *Flourish*, the lively tabloid produced by the Archdiocese of Glasgow, has lots of colour photographs of children and animals and a page devoted to racing and football news. It also highlights the strong regional differences to be found within British Catholicism. On the whole Scottish Catholics, particularly in the west, are more working-class and conservative than the English, and display the strong Irish influence found also in north-west England, the other great Catholic stronghold, which sometimes leads to an almost tribal mentality – matched to some extent, it has to be said, on the Protestant side. On the eastern side of the country and in the south, Catholicism wears a much more urbane and British face.

Despite their numerical superiority, Roman Catholics still give the impression of being outside the ecclesiastical mainstream. They certainly receive far less media coverage than the Church of England. This is partly because of long-ingrained prejudices – there is still a latent anti-Romish feeling in the British psyche and a sense that Catholics are somehow aliens, to some extent fuelled by the troubles in Northern Ireland. It may also have something to do with the fact that until very recently the Catholic Church has tended to look inwards rather than outwards and has not been particularly interested in the wider church scene in Britain. There is, of course, a long tradition of Catholic involvement in the social and political life of the nation. Henry Manning, Cardinal Archbishop of Westminster from 1865 to 1892, was actively involved in royal commissions on housing, poverty and education and played a major conciliatory role in settling the bitter strike in the London docks in 1889. Many Catholics have also gone into local government, especially in Glasgow and Liverpool. But there has been a sense in which they have kept themselves in tightly-knit groups. The natural focus for Catholics tends to be more towards either the local or the international than towards the national. They do not share the same sense as the Church of England or the Church of Scotland of being a national church or of the need to build up national structures. Rather, they are strongly influenced by the principle of subsidiarity – now taken over as a buzz-word in the European Commission but first defined by Pope Pius XI in an encyclical in 1931 – which favours decisions being taken and power exercised at the lowest practicable level. This localism is complemented by their strong sense of also belonging to a world-wide church which looks to the Pope as its head and focus.

Another reason for the relatively low profile of the Roman Catholic Church in Britain is that its ordained clergy are thin on the ground compared with those of other denominations. There are just over 4,000 diocesan priests in England and Wales, and even though they are supplemented by another 2,000 in religious orders, several of whom are able to take on parish duties, that is still less than half the ordained manpower available to the Church of England. Catholic priests, on average much older than their Anglican counterparts, tend to be fully occupied in their parish duties and have less time, and less inclination, to become involved in other things. An indication of their greater work-load is the size of an average Sunday morning congregation – 355, compared with just 77 in the Church of England.

But if Catholics still seem in some senses to be outsiders, they are much more integrated into mainstream church life in Britain than they were 30 years ago. In the rather overdramatic words of Michael Hornsby Smith, they have begun to emerge 'from the defensive ghettos of the fortress Church'. The process of integration really began in the aftermath of the Twenty-First Ecumenical Council, held in Rome between 1962 and 1965 and better known as Vatican II. In many ways the effect of the council was to push the Catholic Church in a much more Protestant direction. It transformed worship by ending Latin as the language of the liturgy, bringing the altar down from the east wall so that the priest could face the people, introducing hymns, and making much more of preaching and reading from the Bible. It gave a greater role to the laity and emphasized the collegial and collective authority of bishops while making less of the *magisterium* and infallibility of the Pope. For the first time other Christian churches were officially recognized as being incorporated in Christ and in communion, albeit impaired communion, with the Roman Catholic Church.

Vatican II marked what was in many ways a very Anglican approach. Indeed Clifford Longley, the unfailingly perceptive and stimulating religious affairs editor of *The Times*, has argued that its true begetter was John Henry Newman, the Church of England priest who moved to Rome in 1845. It was his essentially Anglican stress on collegiality, shared authority and broad tolerance which prevailed against the narrower ultramontanism of continental Catholicism. Certainly the open and liberal spirit of Vatican II was taken up with alacrity in Britain and especially in England. It has also been generally adhered to here over subsequent decades, when under more conservative Popes than John XXIII Rome has tended to drift back towards a more authoritarian style. When Pope Paul VI's encyclical *Humanae Vitae* was issued in 1968 condemning all artificial forms of contraception, the English bishops took a fairly relaxed line and made it clear that they did not regard birth control as the acid test of Christianity. In general the Catholic hierarchy in Britain has continued to steer a middle line between the growing conservatism of the Vatican and the radicalism of bishops in some other parts of the world.

In the aftermath of Vatican II there also seemed to be much more involvement by Roman Catholics in public life. Indeed, in the early 1970s the popular press even talked of a Romish takeover of the British establishment, citing the fact that the editor of *The Times*, the Director General of the BBC and the leader of the House of Lords were all strong Catholics. Today Roman Catholics probably form the largest single committed body of Christians in Parliament: the 1991 *Catholic Directory* lists 44 MPs and 80 peers.

Perhaps the key figure in raising the public profile of the Roman Catholic Church in Britain and integrating it more into the ecclesiastical mainstream over the last decade has been Basil Hume, the Cardinal Archbishop of Westminster. A man of transparent saintliness and quiet integrity, he has commended himself as a national spiritual leader to many outside the Catholic fold. His authority rests not just on his personal qualities of holiness and humility, but also on a greater preparedness than other church leaders to be dogmatic and to speak out unequivocally on matters of personal as well as public morality. Certainly he could never be accused of falling prey to the liberalism and relativism that their critics find so prevalent among the bishops of the Church of England.

Derek Worlock, the Archbishop of Liverpool, has also won respect far beyond the confines of the Roman Catholic community. A member of the Second Vatican Council, he has done much to put its reforms into practice in Britain by raising the status of the laity and giving a much greater voice to parish priests. He has also almost certainly done more than anyone to give the Roman Catholic Church in Britain an ecumenical face. His unique relationship with David Sheppard, the Anglican Bishop of Liverpool, and Dr John Newton, the Moderator of the local Free Church Council, has been an inspiration to millions. Together they have helped the inhabitants of one of Britain's most depressed and traumatized cities through a series of disasters, and have shown how unimportant denominational barriers are when it comes to Christian service and witness among the poorest and weakest in our society.

Derek Worlock was one of the chief architects of the Inter-Church process which took place in the mid 1980s and led in 1990 to the creation of new ecumenical bodies – Churches Together in England, Churches Together in Wales and Action for Churches Together in Scotland – which for the first time involved Roman Catholics as full participants. The titles of these new bodies, whose work is loosely co-ordinated by a Council of Churches for Britain and Ireland, show both how far and how little the churches of Britain have come down the long ecumenical road that many of them have trodden for the best part of this century. At many points their journey has looked as though it might lead to the promised land of a single united church. Now that prospect is officially recognized as being off the agenda. But if organic union looks further away than ever, what has been achieved is in some ways more valuable – a real commitment to pilgrimage and sharing together with the involvement of the largest church in the land.

Ecumenism has perhaps been the dominant theme in British church life throughout the twentieth century. It could well be seen as essentially a response to decline. Churches with growing congregations are not on the whole much interested in forging closer links with other denominations, whereas for those who are seeing their numbers and finances drop alarmingly there are obvious attractions in sharing buildings, ministers and other resources. Opponents of the ecumenical movement say it has diverted energies that would have been better spent proclaiming the Gospel or ministering to the needy. It has certainly generated an enormous quantity of commissions, reports and paperwork without much in the way of concrete results. But it has also brought about among Christians more understanding of other traditions, a greater sense of belonging to one church and a new willingness to share and to learn. Perhaps even more importantly ecumenism, albeit slowly and painfully, is tackling that terrible scandal whereby churches have preached the love and unity of Christ and yet spent much of their time tearing apart each other's structures and doctrines.

For a long time the ecumenical movement was fired by a real sense that organic unity was possible, at least among the fractured denominations of Protestantism. This reached its height in Britain in the 1960s. A Faith and Order Conference in Nottingham in 1964 set the target that by Easter 1980 all the Protestant churches in Britain should be reunited. Archbishop Michael Ramsey pushed hard, as a starting point, for the reunion of the Church of England and the Methodists, but failed to carry his own clergy and laity with him and the proposal was defeated in 1972. Ten years later a proposed covenant between the main Protestant churches which would involve acceptance of each other's ministries, inter-communion and closer working relations successfully passed with the necessary two-thirds majorities through both the House of Bishops and the House of Clergy of the General Synod, but was narrowly defeated by the laity.

The failure of the covenant proposals in 1982 marked the end of the attempt to achieve organic unity between the main Protestant churches in England. In Scotland, too, steam was running out of the ecumenical movement as a series of multilateral conversations between the six largest Protestant denominations failed to agree on a shared doctrine of ministry and the recognition of each other's orders. Only in Wales was there any progress, with a more limited covenant being made between the major churches. Soon after the failure of the covenant scheme in England Dr Kenneth Greet, chairman of the Free Church Federal Council, commented: 'The way marked out by a whole generation of ecumenical leaders has proved to be a cul-de-sac.' Union of the Protestant churches in Britain has proved impossible largely because of Anglican refusal to recognize the validity of Free Church orders. The trouble was, of course, that the Church of England looks in two directions – to Rome as well as to other Protestant churches.

But if 1982 was a bad year for ecumenism on the Protestant side, it was singularly fruitful on the Catholic side. The ARCIC I report was published, indicating a wide measure of agreement on fundamental matters of doctrine between Anglicans and Catholics. More significant for those who were not academic theologians was Pope John Paul II's visit to Britain, the first of its kind since the Reformation. English people saw the Pope, the Archbishop of Canterbury and the Moderator of the Free Church Federal Council kneeling together to reaffirm their common baptismal vows before the altar in Canterbury Cathedral. Perhaps even more significantly, Scots saw the Moderator of the Church of Scotland shake hands with the Pope outside the General Assembly building – but out of sight of the glowering statue of John Knox in the quadrangle within. A day later in Glasgow the Pope asked a vast crowd, 'For the future, can we not not make our pilgrimage together, hand in hand?'

The invitation from Rome helped to change the ecumenical agenda from unity to pilgrimage. If it marked a retreat from the heady prospects of the 1960s, it meant too that instead of cobbling together schemes of union and covenant plans, fudging differences and covering them with a bland form of words, Christians could concentrate on working together on practical schemes and finding out about the richness of other traditions and the glorious diversity and variety that is the Body of Christ. It signalled, too, that the Roman Catholics were interested in joining in the pilgrimage. In the aftermath of the Pope's visit lots of things started happening locally – Christians of different persuasions started meeting together to pray, to discuss their faith, to plan joint services and work on areas of special need. In 1985 the leaders of 39 churches in England, Scotland and Wales met to plan a three-year inter-church process of prayer, reflection and debate on the nature and purpose of the church. It was given the inspired title 'Not strangers but pilgrims'. The first major element in the process, a series of local study groups during Lent 1986 which went under the title 'What on earth is the church for?', had a success far beyond the wildest dreams of the organizers. It involved more than a million people, thanks partly to the initiative of BBC local radio stations, every one of which broadcast the course material. More than 500,000 questionnaires were returned by those who had taken part in the study groups, nearly all of them commenting on the great sense of fellowship engendered, rejoicing in the rich diversity of the Christian faith and expressing frustration at the rigidity of denominational structures.

Following the success of the inter-church process more than 300 leading figures from all the main churches in Britain met at Swanwick in Derbyshire in September 1987 and committed themselves to the following declaration: 'It is our conviction that, as a matter of policy at all levels and in all places, our Churches must now move from co-operation to clear commitment to each other, in search of the unity for which Christ prayed, and in common evangelism and service of the world.' Significantly the key words in the declaration, about moving from co-operation to commitment, came from Cardinal Hume, whose speech at the Swanwick gathering, made after careful consultation with all the Catholics present, proved a turning point and signalled the Roman Catholic Church's clear commitment to the ecumenical process.

How far that commitment will go is another matter. There is a good deal of unease among both Protestants and many lay Catholics about the continuing ban on non-Catholics receiving communion at the Mass and Catholics receiving communion in other churches, while most Protestant churches now effectively practise inter-communion. In fact, a growing number of Catholics, particularly those in mixed marriages or involved in local ecumenical groups, are defying the teaching of their bishops and receiving communion from Protestant ministers. It is highly unlikely that the bishops will modify their ban on inter-communion – too many key theological and ecclesiological points are involved in the Roman Catholic doctrine of the Mass. Indeed the latter may be even more important than the former. It is not just the notion of transubstantiation and the doctrine of the Real Presence of Christ in the elements of bread and wine which are at stake, but the particular relationship between communicant, priest, Pope and church which is expressed in participation in the Mass.

While some Protestants feel that the Roman Catholics have not gone far enough in developing closer relations with other denominations, others fear the opposite. They see the new-found Catholic enthusiasm for ecumenism as paving the way for union between the churches on Rome's terms. Robert Runcie ruffled several feathers when he talked in Rome in 1989 of accepting an ecumenical papal primacy over a universal church. Mario Conti, Roman Catholic Bishop of Aberdeen and convenor of Action for Churches Together in Scotland, also seemed to confirm the worst fears of the Wee Frees when he stated in a newspaper interview shortly after the new body was set up that unity must eventually be centred on the See of Rome.

Roman Catholic involvement undoubtedly changes the character of the ecumenical movement in Britain. But what it does is not so much make full inter-communion or organic unity less likely – that was already off the agenda – or pave the way for the recreation of a monolithic Catholic Church; rather, it means that there can be no more fudging and mudging to find the lowest common denominator. The ecumaniacs, those who felt that the passionately held and long fought for differences between the churches could be ended by committees meeting and producing reports couched in sufficiently bland and vague terms, have had their day. In their place are genuine pilgrims who recognize that the journey they are making will involve pain and sacrifice, but who feel it is worth while to tread the road together, sharing, learning and maybe even resting on one another's shoulders for a while, but accepting too that in the end each may diverge to take their own route to the promised land.

– 2 –

The invisible church

Singing songs of expectation,
Marching to the promised land

In his poem 'Dover Beach', which describes so powerfully the loss of religious belief in the modern age, Matthew Arnold writes of the melancholy, long, withdrawing roar of the sea of faith, 're-treating, to the breath of the night wind, down the vast edges drear and naked shingles of the world'.

As the influence of the institutional churches has progressively diminished in twentieth-century Britain, it is perhaps not surprising to find that it has survived most strongly on the very edges of these islands. The sea of faith still washes the shores of the remote and windswept Outer Hebrides. The highest level of church attendance in Britain is to be found on the island of Lewis, where more than two-thirds of the population are church members or adherents and more than half are to be found in church at least once every Sunday. Here, indeed, the church is highly visible, though it could hardly be more different in style and message from the main denominations on the mainland. In the Free Church of Scotland, the largest church on the island, liberalism and ecumenism are dirty words. There is little attempt to make any accommodation to prevailing secular culture; the accent is on preaching an undiluted Gospel of sin, repentance and redemption.

In Stornoway, the chief town of Lewis with a population of around 6,000, the Reverend Murdo Alec Macleod presides over a congregation that in terms of size and commitment must be the envy of virtually every other minister in Britain. His English-language Sunday morning service at the Free Church attracts about 700 with another 400 attending a parallel Gaelic service in a nearby building named, rather surprisingly in this fiercely Protestant

denomination, the seminary. On Sunday evening the church is
packed with up to 1,500 people while between 200 and 300 attend
the seminary. Midweek meetings (English on Tuesday evening,
Gaelic on Wednesday) attract 500 or more. Many of the worshippers are young and a considerable number are, in the evangelical language used by the Free Church, unconverted.

The services which draw such enormous congregations are
among the most austere and forbidding to be found anywhere in
these islands. Entering a Free Church is like stepping back to
Victorian times. The women and girls are all wearing hats and
clutching their Bibles. The men are all dressed in black suits. Silence
prevails and there is none of the chatter that precedes the entrance
of the minister in most churches nowadays. The services often last
for one and a half hours and it is not unusual for the sermon to
go on for 45 minutes. The Gospel preached is that of the law rather
than of love. The prayers, delivered extempore by members of the
congregation called out by the minister, are lengthy and lugubrious
catalogues of the sins and follies of 'the poor, miserable creatures'
that make up the human race. There are neither hymns nor organ –
the only music permitted in the Free Church is the unaccompanied
singing of the psalms, led by a precentor. This can be a moving if
melancholy experience, especially in Gaelic where the practice of
lining out is still followed, the precentor chanting each line of
the psalm and the congregation joining in gradually with
embellishments and harmonies. The congregation sits to sing the
psalms and stands for prayers.

The Free Church exerts a considerable influence on the life of
Lewis. This shows itself most clearly, perhaps, on Sundays when
shops, pubs and other places of entertainment in Stornoway remain
firmly closed. No newspapers are available on the Sabbath and the
television stays switched off in many households. The Free Church
in the Western Isles has recently won a notable victory against
the pressures of commercialism by forcing the ferry operators
Caledonian Macbrayne's to abandon plans to run Sunday services
from the mainland to Lewis and Harris in summer to cater for the
booming tourist trade. At times it can seem that Sabbath observance is taken to excessive lengths by the church. Over tea and cakes
in the manse after a midweek prayer meeting I listened to a lengthy
debate between two elders as to the relative merits of shaving on
Saturday night so as to avoid performing what was not strictly
speaking a work of necessity on the Lord's Day, or performing the

task on Sunday morning on the grounds that it was sinful to enter the Lord's House with a stubbly chin.

The strict demands which the Free Church makes on its members do not seem to be resented. At the same manse fellowship a young man from Skye spoke without any sense of loss about how he had given up both football and singing in a choir after his conversion. A 17-year-old girl told me that counting two services, Bible class and youth fellowship, she spent about six hours every Sunday in church 'but it doesn't seem very much'. An older lady related proudly how, since her conversion as a girl, she had never picked up a novel nor had any desire to read anything other than the Bible or devotional literature. When I asked her why she felt that, unlike so many churches on the mainland, the Free Church had largely held on to its members and was not suffering dwindling congregations, she was in no doubt of the reason: 'It's because we don't leave anything out of the Gospel. We teach the full panoply – predestination, justification, sanctification, glorification.' Murdo Alec Macleod shares the sentiment: 'Christianity is strong in this island because it is Biblical Christianity. The Bible is central to our life, our faith and our witness.'

For much of this century the Free Church of Scotland and other smaller and even stricter denominations, like the Free Presbyterians which still retain a strong following in the outer islands and parts of the Highlands, have felt isolated and out of step with the great majority of Christians on the mainland. They have seen themselves as the last defenders of the true Gospel in a country made up of compromisers, backsliders and unbelievers. But in the last decade or so new allies have been springing up in the most unlikely places: the prosperous new towns of south-east England, the shabbier parts of South London, and the old manufacturing communities of the Midlands. In independent house churches and fellowships and increasingly too in some congregations within the main denominations, more and more people are speaking the language of the Free Church and stressing the themes of conversion and repentance, law and grace, the inerrancy of Scripture, the power of sin and the devil and the importance of a personal relationship with Jesus.

This new movement could hardly be more different in membership, character or outlook from the world of the traditional institutional churches described in the last chapter. Those involved in it, probably around a million people, are mostly under 40, have little or no time for ecumenism, and are largely uninterested in institutional and denominational structures though they are bound together by a series of informal networks and alliances. They are also very committed in terms of both worship and financial support. Surveys suggest that more than 90 per cent of those who belong to these predominantly new churches attend at least one service a week, with many worshipping twice on Sundays and at a midweek meeting. The practice of tithing is common and average giving per member is over £20 a week, compared with just £1 in the Church of England and Church of Scotland. The other major feature that distinguishes this movement from the older established churches is that it is growing rather than declining – and doing so at an impressive rate. House churches, one of the most significant new arrivals on the church scene in the last two or three decades, are increasing in membership by over 50 per cent a year.

I have used the word 'invisible' to describe this growing movement because for the most part we are talking about Christians who meet in houses or halls rather than in traditional and easily identifiable church buildings, and who shun the familiar badges of ministry such as dog-collars and vestments. But in many ways their worship and their witness is anything but invisible – it is confident, noisy, lively and colourful. Certainly they are far from being inaudible. Their choruses are accompanied by amplified synthesizers, rock bands and brass ensembles and often also by clapping and shouting. Increasingly, too, this invisible church is coming out onto the streets, in the annual March for Jesus which takes place every September as well as in rallies, festivals and demonstrations which are part of carefully orchestrated campaigns on such issues as abortion, Sunday trading reforms and tougher pornography laws.

The invisible church is only just beginning to be noticed by the media. It is true that the more sensational aspects of its charismatic wing appeal to the papers, particularly in so far as they are now spreading to the visible church and affecting the Church of England. *Songs of Praise* now features Spring Harvest, Greenbelt and the March for Jesus, the great annual evangelical jamborees which dominate the invisible church calendar and bring its members together in their thousands. But the leaders of the new churches, Gerald Coates, Graham Kendrick and Clive Calver, do not get slots on *Thought for the Day* and are unlikely to become household names like Basil Hume, George Carey and David Sheppard. The official church establishment, and the media establishment, tend to regard them as rather brash and vulgar, over-emotional and subjective, and far too American for British tastes. So in some ways they are, but there can be no denying their appeal to younger people in what is rapidly becoming the British equivalent of the Bible Belt that stretches across the southern states of the USA. It is in the south-east of England, and especially in South London, Surrey and north Hampshire, along the south coast and along the M3 and M4 corridors to Southampton and Bristol that the invisible church is strongest.

Given this concentration in the most prosperous part of the country, it is tempting to label the whole phenomenon yuppified Christianity and to see it as the spiritual legacy of Thatcherism, a privatized religion which sanctions individual success and makes Jesus a kind of personal possession and status symbol rather like the Filofax and the cellular telephone. Certainly the new evangelical house churches and fellowships do appeal to many young successful people, especially those working in the City and in the highly-paid industries of financial services and advertising. But their membership is by no means confined to the well-off and the upwardly mobile. They are to be found in Brixton and Bermondsey as well as Bromley and Beckenham. Many of their followers are, indeed, from the poorer ethnic communities. Black churches, of which there are now around 3,000 with more than 66,000 members, make up a growing and dynamic element within the whole invisible church scene.

Nor is it the case that all the groups making up this movement are of recent origin. The oldest and most indigenous of the 'invisible' churches are the Brethren, who number around 70,000. The Brethren movement originated in Dublin as an attempt to return to the simplicity of apostolic days and break down barriers dividing Christians. The first permanent Brethren congregation was in Plymouth in 1831. A split developed in the late nineteenth century between Open and Exclusive Brethren and today some congregations are noticeably more open and liberal than others. Brethren groups are completely autonomous. They meet weekly for breaking of bread and have no ordained clergy. They remain strong in certain isolated and close-knit communities, such as the fishing villages of north-east Scotland, but also have a following in several cities. Of slightly later vintage are the Pentecostal churches, which have about 80,000 members. They originated in the USA in the early years of this century and stress baptism in the spirit as an experience different from conversion or conventional baptism with water. This spirit baptism evidences itself in such manifestations as healing, exorcisms and speaking in tongues. The Elim Pentecostal Church has 450 churches in the United Kingdom, with its headquarters at Cheltenham. The other main Pentecostalist churches are the Apostolic Church and the Assemblies of God, with headquarters in the USA.

The newest and perhaps the most interesting element within what I have called the invisible church is the house church movement. This began in the mid 1970s and was in part a reaction against both post 1960s liberalism and the dullness and formality of worship in the older churches. It started in South London and spread southwards. One of the first house churches, the Ichthus Fellowship, started by Roger Foster and his wife in their home in Forest Hill, has grown over 20 years from a dozen people to nearly 2,000 who now meet in 25 different groups. The movement spread to Cobham in Surrey where Gerald Coates started the Pioneer Fellowship and then down to the south coast where Roger Ellis began the Revelation Christian Fellowship in Chichester. Both these groups soon mushroomed from a few people sitting at home together reading the Bible to fellowships of several hundred who meet for worship in a hall and sing the songs and choruses of Graham Kendrick, the Charles Wesley of this new evangelical revival and himself a member of the Ichthus Fellowship. Numerous other fellowships have sprung up across southern England and are now increasingly to be found in other parts of the country as well, quite often meeting in the redundant premises of the older established denominations.

The house churches and fellowships (or 'new churches' as they prefer to be known) draw members both from established church backgrounds, often alienated and unmoved by the worship in their local parish church, and from those with no previous Christian belief, including a number of teenage converts who have previously been involved with drink, drugs and Satanic cults. Their growth is partly the result of a carefully planned strategy of 'planting out' new congregations. As soon as a group of worshippers reaches the 100 mark, a number are sent off somewhere else as the nucleus of a new church. In this way there is a constant spawning of new congregations. The level of individual giving is sufficiently high for a group of around a hundred to sustain a full-time paid evangelist.

The house churches and fellowships are completely independent and autonomous. They are, however, linked to each other and to the rest of the invisible church through national campaigns and groups like British Youth for Christ and Campus Crusade for Christ and through magazines like *Christian Family*, *Today* and *Renewal*. These publications make the newspapers of the main denominations look like relics from a past age. They are expensively and glossily produced with full colour throughout, lots of pictures and short, bright articles. There is a good deal of human interest and personal testimony, but virtually no theology.

The organization that comes nearest to providing a focus for the whole invisible church is the Evangelical Alliance. In many ways it fulfils the same function as the ecumenical bodies which link the visible churches. I suppose it could, indeed, be described as providing an umbrella for the anti-ecumaniacs. It is also important in linking the new invisible churches with the growing evangelical and charismatic elements in the old visible ones. The Alliance claims an overall following of around one million, of which the biggest groupings are 400,000 Anglican Evangelicals and 200,000 Baptists. The Salvation Army, the Free Church of Scotland and other old-established evangelical churches are among its members, alongside Pentecostal and black churches and the newer house churches and fellowships. Indeed, the Alliance has helped to integrate the new churches into the long-established evangelical movement in Britain. It was itself founded in 1846, at a time when the activities of Lord Shaftesbury and others were giving evangelicalism both inside and outside the established church a high profile and a radical cutting edge in the field of social reform. To some extent evangelicalism languished for much of the twentieth century as the initiative passed to the liberals and catholics. The revival of the Alliance as a spearhead for the new evangelical movement represented by the rise of black-led churches, house groups and independent fellowships is largely due to the energy of Clive Calver who took over as its director in 1983. He transformed what was largely a moribund and backward-looking organization by replacing traditional evangelicals with younger people from the house church movement, often with charismatic leanings and many drawn from the Mission England Crusade built around Billy Graham's visit in 1984.

The Evangelical Alliance now has a full-time staff of more than 30 housed in an anonymous office block in Kennington Park Road in South London shared with other Christian groups like the Afro-

Caribbean Evangelical Alliance. It co-ordinates the highly effective Christian lobby on such issues as Sunday trading and broadcasting law reform. It has a strong input into Spring Harvest, the annual gathering for teaching and worship which takes over Butlin's holiday camps at Minehead, Skegness, Pwhelli and Ayr for a week in April. This event has grown from involving 2,700 people when it was started in 1979 by Clive Calver and Peter Meadows, the Alliance's communications secretary, to over 80,000 in 1991. The Alliance also takes a leading role in the other major event in the evangelical calendar, the March for Jesus which brings nearly 250,000 people on to the streets every September to witness their faith. As with Spring Harvest, the growth of the numbers involved in the march has been spectacular. It began in 1987 with a march through London organized by the Ichthus Fellowship; three years later there were marches in more than 600 different towns and cities across the country.

The March for Jesus shows up very clearly both the strengths and the weaknesses of the invisible church. There is a joy and confidence in its affirmation of the Good News of the Gospel which is largely lacking in the traditional visible church. Much of its power undoubtedly comes from the music of Graham Kendrick, several of whose hymns were written specially for the march. At one level it is, in the words of its organizers, 'a colourful, carnival-like atmosphere with song, prayer, and celebration of hope in Christ'. It enjoys considerable support across the established denominations, with Roman Catholics as well as Protestants joining in, including in 1990 at least one Catholic bishop, Kevin Rafferty, Auxiliary Bishop of Edinburgh. But there is also considerable unease about the march on the part of many within the traditional visible church. Several Church of England clergymen, including Evangelicals, refused to take part in the 1990 march because they felt there was more to it than just a joyful celebration of hope in Christ. They were extremely uneasy about remarks by the organizers that parts of some cities and certain institutions had become 'demonized' and that the task of the marchers was a kind of corporate exorcism of these forces of evil. Prebendary Michael Saward, vicar of St Mary's, Ealing, and a member of the Church of England Evangelical Council, wrote to the *Church of England Newspaper*, the traditional organ of Anglican Evangelicalism, expressing concern that an extremist view of demonology lay at the heart of the official march theology. The *Church Times* carried similar complaints. One clergyman pointed out that the published programme for the march 'goes on more about Satan than about Jesus', and one of his parishioners objected to the strength of the anti-abortion message which, he said, argued that children in Britain today were equally at risk with those threatened by King Herod and said that 'the most dangerous place for a child to be in this land is in its mother's womb'.

There is no doubt that those behind the March for Jesus do see themselves as fighting the forces of evil. They are not in the least shy of invoking St Paul's language about the principalities and powers of darkness and applying it to our own age. Indeed, they feel that it is liberal embarrassment about facing up to the reality of Satan's power that has caused the decline of the church in Britain throughout the present century. In a letter to the *Church of England Newspaper* Gerald Coates, Director of the Pioneer Trust which organizes the March for Jesus, responded to the worries expressed about it in robust and uncompromising terms: 'It is our prayer that the tide of evil will be stemmed, darkness will be pushed back and the gospel – the ultimate antidote to the works of the devil – will run freely throughout our land in the power of the Holy Spirit. Our prayer for God's kingdom to come, and his will to be done on earth as it is in heaven, does in necessity engage us all in some sort of spiritual warfare as we have declared war on evil and its source.' In a subsequent interview with *The Times* he enlarged on what he had in mind by darkness and evil when he blamed the hold of liberalism both for the decline in church attendance and for leaving inner cities in the grip of Satanic forces like violence, drugs, prostitution and alcohol abuse.

The stress on demonology is only one aspect of the outlook of the new invisible church which worries many of those in the older established denominations. There is also a concern that it is sectarian and exclusivist in spirit, preferring to build up its own agencies rather than work through established inter-church bodies, and generally shunning ecumenism. It has to be said that a similar outlook has until very recently characterized the approach of the Roman Catholic Church which still, for example, prefers to have its own agency for the Third World, CAFOD, rather than work through the inter-denominational Christian Aid. In the same way, Evangelicals have the TEAR Fund. Their attitude is well-expressed by Stephen Abbott, who after a conventional Anglican career first as parish minister and then as chaplain of King's College,

Cambridge, is now head of the leadership team of the non-denominational Fellowship of the King in Bristol. In his book *Join Our Hearts* (Marshall Pickering, 1989), which describes his own passage from the visible to the invisible church, he writes: 'A keen Evangelical church will prefer to support TEAR Fund rather than Christian Aid, the Evangelical Alliance Week of Prayer rather than the Week of Prayer for Christian Unity. I also respect (though I do not agree with) the attitude that causes some churches to stay out of councils of churches because they consider the member churches as not doctrinally pure and hopelessly handicapped by antiquated structures and traditions.'

There is, indeed, an interesting split among members of the Evangelical Alliance on the question of participation in the ecumenical movement and closer co-operation with the older visible churches. Some longer-established groups like the Brethren, the Salvation Army and the Baptist Union of England and Wales have joined the new inter-church bodies set up in 1990. So have the black-led churches, who are noticeably more open and ecumenically-minded than white-dominated charismatic groups. The house churches, the Fellowship of Independent Evangelical Churches and the Pentecostal churches have stayed out, together with some longer-established groups like the Free Church of Scotland and the Baptist Union for Scotland. The Alliance itself sounded a note of considerable caution when the new ecumenical bodies were launched, expressing grave concern about the lack of a proper basis of faith and in particular 'an absence of clear definition regarding both the person and the work of Christ and the inspiration and authority of Scripture'.

The aspect of the invisible church that has attracted most attention in the media is undoubtedly the content and style of its worship. The spread of charismatic Christianity, with its distinctive signs of arms being raised in prayer and during hymn-singing, faces lifted up to heaven, spontaneous cries of 'Praise the Lord' and its more extreme manifestations of healings, exorcisms and speaking in tongues, has been one of the most dramatic and well-documented features of British church life over the last two decades. Like the new-found accent on demonology and the reality of Satan, it has strong Scriptural roots. The account of Pentecost in Acts 2 describes the disciples speaking in tongues when the Holy Spirit descends on them. Charismatics believe that this kind of experience is open to all Christians through baptism in the spirit following their conversion and rebirth. A Spirit-filled faith leads to the exercise of other gifts or charisms mentioned by St Paul, including the gifts of healing and prophecy.

Charismatic Christianity has always been a feature of the Pentecostal churches. It is also widespread among the black-led churches and has been the main theological driving force behind the creation of the new house churches and independent evangelical fellowships. Over the last decade or so it has also penetrated the visible church, making significant headway in the Church of England, among the Roman Catholics and in several Baptist congregations. About the only major denomination it has not really touched is the Church of Scotland. The average Kirk-goer finds the idea of the Anglican kiss of peace embarrassing enough, and certainly would be very unhappy about flinging up his or her hands in the air or dancing in the aisles.

The arrival of charismatic worship in the Church of England has attracted particular notice in the media. An article in the *Daily Telegraph* in December 1990 entitled 'Charisma comes to Kensington' described in somewhat colourful terms the 'temple' of Charismatic Anglicanism in London, Holy Trinity Church, Brompton. It portrayed the vicar, Sandy Millar, as a former barrister who prefers Jermyn Street shirts and jackets to clerical garb and who has no hesitation in proclaiming that 'the age of liberal theology is over', and went on to describe a typical evening service: 'the Sunday night congregation of 700 giggles as the Old Etonian curate, Nicky Gumbell, tells them that "Jesus blows your mind" ... Many of the men are stiff-backed in blazers and brogues and the girls wear pearls and Benetton cardigans. Charismatic Sloane Rangers are a manifestation of a phenomenon that may transform the Church of England over the next ten years.'

Certainly it is the charismatic evangelical congregations in the Church of England which are among the main growth points amid the general atmosphere of decline. In 1985 Holy Trinity, Brompton, became the first Anglican church in London to embark on the technique of 'church planting' pioneered by the house churches. It sent 50 of its 1,000 regular worshippers to nearby St Nicholas, West Kensington, which then had fewer than ten regular attenders and now has more than 600. Two years later another cell was planted in St Mark's, Battersea Rise, which had a regular congregation of just five old ladies. It now has 300 worshippers every week, mostly young professional people working in the City.

Church planting has now spread to other parts of the south and is causing increasing strains within the Church of England. The traditional convention that incumbents do not exercise their ministry outside the boundaries of their own parish is being broken by clergy keen to plant congregations in neighbouring areas.

Many people in the traditional visible churches are uneasy about charismatic Christianity. They feel it is overemotional and potentially dangerous. There is also, I suspect, a strong conviction that it is very un-British. Rooted deep in our national psyche is a suspicion of too much enthusiasm and spontaneity in religion. The Bishop of Bristol's admonition to John Wesley 250 years ago, 'Sir, the pretending to extraordinary revelations and gifts of the Holy Ghost is a horrid thing – a very horrid thing', sums up what many feel about the charismatic movement today. It is certainly true that much of the impulse and many of the leading figures behind it come from the United States. John Wimber, who in many ways has become the high priest of the charismatic revival in Britain, is a Californian preacher whose Vineyard Christian Fellowship now has 300 congregations across the States. A strong proponent of church planting, he is also a millenarian who preaches that we are living in the last days and that a great religious revival is about to sweep over Britain. He believes that the great heresy of the modern church has been to downgrade the supernatural aspects of Christianity, and emphasizes the signs and wonders that come from a true Spirit-filled faith. For him the church should be performing miracles as Jesus did, particularly miracles of healing.

Healing is a subject that the churches as a whole, visible and invisible, have taken up in the last two or three decades. There is an extremely lively Churches Council for Health and Healing, which has its headquarters at St Marylebone Parish Church in Central London and brings together leading figures from all the main denominations. Many churches now have regular healing services involving the laying on of hands and anointing with holy oil. The Roman Catholics, of course, have long believed in the power of faith healing and run pilgrimages to such shrines as Lourdes. Now Protestants too are recognizing the importance of spiritual and emotional factors in both physical and mental health and are realizing how far modern ideas about holistic medicine and stress relief accord with traditional Christian teaching about the cure of souls and the importance of faith to a person's general well-being. But Wimber and his followers go further, claiming to be able to exercise a ministry of prophecy and miraculous healing of the kind practised by Christ. At a rally in the London Docklands attended by more than 8,000 in October 1990 one of the so-called 'Kansas City prophets' associated with Wimber came to the microphone and announced 'There are 27 people here tonight who are going to be healed of cancer. I want them to stand up.'

It is this kind of approach, so reminiscent of the activities of American television evangelists, that many people find off-putting and manipulative. It seems to deal too much in shock tactics and slogans. John Wimber dubs himself 'Mr Signs and Wonders' while members of the Jesus Army, a growing movement which has its headquarters in an independent Baptist church in Northampton, go around in leather jackets and T-shirts emblazoned with the mottoes 'Blood, Fire and Covenant' or 'Love, Power and Sacrifice'. For those used to the gentle world of deanery synods, jumble sales and Lent study groups there is something rather forbidding and frightening about the topics on which the new evangelical churches choose to concentrate and the language they use. The 1991 Spring Harvest included seminars on occultism, homosexuality, addiction, eating disorders and the blasphemy laws. A recent booklet from the Evangelical Alliance entitled *Doorways to Danger* begins with the alarming statement: 'A neighbourhood seance. An astrologer's telephone helpline. Teenagers' fun with ouija boards. These seemingly innocent entertainments could be entrances into a sinister world of evil and destruction.'

This kind of language may sound extremist and alarmist to those who inhabit a world that is generally ordered, civilized and governed by Christian values – the world of the visible churches. In this world Hallowe'en parties at school may seem harmless enough and the philosophies of the New Age an interesting starting point for inter-faith dialogue. But there is another, darker world, equally real and almost certainly expanding, a world which is itself highly sensational, profoundly disturbing and for which adjectives like Satanic and demonic hardly seem too strong – the world of battered wives, abused children, video nasties and child pornography rings. There are also increasing numbers of people, especially young people, addicted to drugs and drink, without meaningful and secure employment and with little purpose or value in their lives except what they are fed by the media. The new evangelical churches have the strength and the courage to operate in this world and to reach out to its victims. It is hardly surprising if that experience gives them a heightened sense of the power of evil and a millenarian conviction that we may be living in the last days. Those of us who inhabit the other more ordered and settled world should pause before dismissing them as extremist.

It seems to me that what I have described as the visible and the invisible churches speak to and cater for two entirely different groups in our society. The first is made up of those whose lives are largely ordered and without major upsets, who have themselves probably been brought up with Christian values and certainly in stable homes. The other consists of those whose lives have been fractured, dislocated and disorderly, who have often come to Christianity from outside, and sometimes after dabbling in the occult, witchcraft or drugs. I suspect there are also significant psychological and theological differences between the followers of the two kinds of church. Following the lines I have taken as headings for these first two chapters, one might call them the pilgrims and the marchers. The visible church tends to attract those who see themselves as going on steadily in their faith, growing gradually in it, sometimes falling back a bit. The invisible church, by contrast, appeals to those who have a much more dramatic sense of conversion and of making the decision to follow Christ, and a rather greater assurance of their salvation.

The pilgrims continue on their quest, welcoming others as companions in a journey that has many twists and deviations. The marchers have a much clearer sense of their destination and a greater certainty that they have already reached it. They also believe that there is only one route and feel an overwhelming compulsion to bring others along it. I find it highly significant that in its statement about the new ecumenical bodies set up in 1990 the Evangelical Alliance expressed some unease about the use of the phrase 'pilgrims together' to describe the relations between churches. 'Before setting out on our journey', it commented, 'we must agree our ultimate destination as well as the map we are following' – a classic statement of the marchers' creed.

These two patterns of Christian discipleship have always existed, of course. Both are found in the Bible. I suppose that in their different ways Peter and Thomas, the steady but sometimes doubting disciples, were both pilgrims while Paul, with all the enthusiasm, the censoriousness and the missionary zeal of the convert, seeing the Christian task as a constant battle against the forces of evil, was the marcher. For him, as for many in the new invisible church today, there were few doubts and no great problem over authority. He would, indeed, feel very much at home with the bold and unequivocal language in which Graham Kendrick's hymns proclaim Jesus' 'meekness and majesty' and tell the world to 'Make way, make way for the king of kings'.

I am very conscious that this chapter has provided just a whistle-stop tour of a very diverse and complex landscape. I am conscious, too, that there is another smaller (and quieter) invisible church which is very different in style and outlook from the one I have been describing – more catholic, more liberal, and centred on spirituality and the social gospel. I am thinking of the prayer groups associated with the Iona Community, the groups set up on the model of basic Christian communities of Latin America like the Columban houses, and the root groups of young people living in run-down urban areas. There are also networks like the Lifestyle movement set up by Alfred Dammers, former Dean of Bristol Cathedral, whose members try to live according to simple rules of prayer, service and sharing, and communal residential projects like the Pilsdon Community in west Dorset which does so much to heal broken minds and spirits and the Community of Christ the Sower that Robert Van de Weyer has established at Little Gidding. These and other similar communities are in the van of the great revival of spirituality that is one of the most exciting signs in the Christian life of contemporary Britain. They are often also deeply involved in living out the social implications of the Gospel and engaged in highly practical projects in the field of social action and therapy.

The mushrooming of these communities in recent years has little if anything to do with the rise of the charismatic movement and the revival of evangelicalism. There may be other reasons, too, why people are preferring to meet in their own homes or in informal groups for worship rather than gathering in a church building. It could be a reflection of the broader social and cultural trend towards more home-based leisure activities which is spelling doom not just for churches but for cinemas, theatres and voluntary organizations. Television, video recorders and personal computers may be responsible for this change in our social habits, but whatever the reason it is certainly the case that people are simply less prepared to come out of their homes than they used to be.

There is no doubt, however, that it is the increasing influence of evangelicalism and the charismatic movement within the Christian life of Britain that has accounted for most of the growth and development in both the visible and the invisible churches over recent years. These are the forces that lie behind the growth of Bible study groups meeting in people's homes from less than 10,000 to more than 100,000 over the last decade. We have already noted that within the established denominations it is the more evangelically and charismatically inclined congregations which have increased in size against the general trend of decline. With their strong links to the growing house church movement these are the groups which have most commitment to the present decade of evangelism and are best placed to carry out the missionary task which it has set. Unlike many in the more liberal and traditional parts of the church, they do not have inhibitions about showing commitment and proselytizing. They have fire in their bellies and they want to get their foot in the door.

Evangelicalism is the most dynamic force in contemporary British Christianity. In the past it may have been easy for liberals and catholics to dismiss it as shallow, emotional and over-subjective, rooted too much in personal experience and without theological depth. Over recent years evangelicalism has matured and come of age. There is less emphasis on personal pietism and privatized belief and much more awareness of the corporate dimension of Christianity and the demands of the social gospel. There is also much more intellectual rigour. The days are gone when the evangelical creed could be summed up by such facile lapel-badge slogans as 'Smile, Jesus loves you'. Serious magazines like *Third Way, Churchman* and *Evangelical Quarterly* and institutions like the London Institute for Contemporary Christianity and Rutherford House in Scotland are hammering out a rigorous and coherent theological position. There is less falling back on simple catch-phrases and the reiteration of quotations from the Bible, and much more emphasis on apologetics and dialogue.

But for all this change, there remains a very clear insistence that there can be no compromising with the fundamentals of Christian belief. This is, of course, one of the traditional hallmarks of evangelicalism and it is arguably the feature which now most clearly distinguishes what I have called the new invisible church (plus the evangelical and charismatic elements within the traditional churches) from the old visible church. Lest there be any doubt about what evangelicals believe, here is Clive Calver's definition, from his book on the recent growth of evangelicalism in Britain, *He Brings Us Together* (Hodder and Stoughton, 1987):

An evangelical is, at root, someone who first of all holds to the traditional credal doctrinal statements of the Church. He or she believes that Jesus is in fact the Son of God, that he did perform miracles, rose from the dead and through his crucifixion offered an atoning sacrifice for the sins of all who would put their faith and trust in him ...

Evangelicals are people of the book. They recognise Scripture as truth ... For evangelicals the fact that the Bible is God's absolute Word to mankind is beyond dispute. ...

But evangelicals are not just distinguished by their adherence to doctrinal or biblical truth. They recognise mankind as 'fallen', polluted by sin, given over to practices which are anti-God, and alienated from God by their own actions. Satan is viewed as a personal opponent ...

It is to Jesus Christ alone that the evangelical looks for salvation. A 'pluralist' philosophy, which claims there are several routes through different faiths to God, is wholeheartedly rejected ... The presupposition of 'universalism' – that one day all will be saved – is wholeheartedly dismissed. The truth of the matter is viewed in this way. For those who reject Christ's offer of salvation is the tragic expectation of eternity without God. For those who begin a new life in relationship with Christ on earth there is the glorious hope that this is only the beginning of a never-ending story.

To many that will seem a clear and unexceptionable statement of orthodox Christian belief – the kind of faith that is still being taught in Sunday School lessons and in the preaching from many pulpits up and down the country. But it runs counter to the whole drift of academic theology over the last half-century or so. The growth of the new invisible church may in part represent a reaction to the dullness and drabness of much conventional church worship but it is also a massive grass-roots revolt against modern theological thinking and its increasing influence in the mainstream churches. It is to an analysis of that thinking, and why it has provoked such a reaction, that we turn next.

– 3 –

Theology and belief

One the object of our journey,
One the faith that never tires

The English have never been much interested in theology, being content to leave the intricacies of dogmatics, systematics and apologetics to the Germans and the Scots, who have much more of an appetite for God-talk. While the Church of England has provided many distinguished historians, hymn writers, liturgists and even a few saints, one would be hard put to name any great English theologians.

In the last decade or so, however, things have changed. Debates about the historicity of the Virgin Birth and the Resurrection have hit the headlines and become front-page news, and academic Anglican theologians like David Jenkins the Bishop of Durham, and Don Cupitt the Dean of Emmanuel College, Cambridge, have become national celebrities. What has caught the attention of the media is the fact that these two priests in particular seem happy to make statements which bring into serious question the fundamental tenets of the Christian religion. They are seen as representing the tip of an iceberg of unbelief within the Church of England. William Oddie, former religious affairs correspondent of the *Daily Telegraph*, had Cupitt particularly in mind when he gave as the reasons for his own resignation from Anglican orders and reception into the Roman Catholic Church, in January 1991, the extreme laxness in matters of belief within the Church of England and the fact that 'at least one Anglican priest openly denies the objective reality of God'.

It is not just within Anglicanism that an apparently new and very liberal theology which seems to deny many of the traditional tenets of Christianity appears to have become ascendant. The same is true, though perhaps to a lesser extent, throughout much of what I have already characterized as the visible church. Indeed, as we have seen, the spread of this new liberal theology has perhaps been the major factor behind the creation of the alternative 'invisible' church over the last two or three decades. In his book *He Brings Us Together* Clive Calver describes David Jenkins as the best recruiting sergeant for the new evangelical movement in Britain and dates its particular take-off to 1984, the year in which he made his much-publicized sceptical remarks about the Virgin Birth and the Resurrection.

Certainly the theological gap between liberals and conservatives, or relativists and fundamentalists as they often prefer to call one another, is by far the deepest divide within the British churches today. It is a much more significant split than that between Catholics and Protestants. Until comparatively recently it would have been taken as axiomatic that the main area of theological controversy still centred around the issues that caused the Reformation. There has, however, been enormous progress in reaching an agreed position on many of the doctrines which have caused division and ill-feeling between Roman Catholics and Protestants over the last 400 years. A key statement produced in 1987 by the Second Anglican Roman Catholic International Commission did much to clear up the long-disputed question as to whether the Christian is justified, or saved, primarily through faith or by works. It proclaimed clearly that salvation is by God's grace alone, received through faith, and leading to a liberation from self-centredness which enables active concern for others. The idea that salvation can be earned by merit, which proved so repellent to Luther and the founding fathers of the Reformation, was firmly repudiated. *The Times*, one of the few newspapers to notice the statement and to recognize its significance, made it front-page news under the headline 'Churches heal their 400 year old rift' and hailed it as 'an historic breakthrough' which would 'solve the basic dispute which led to the Reformation in the sixteenth century'.

Another traditional matter of dispute between Roman Catholics and Protestants, the question of what actually happens in the communion service or Eucharist, has been made much less contentious as a result of changes in the Catholic Mass in the aftermath of Vatican II and an increasing appreciation of sacramentalism and mystery on the Protestant side. It would be wrong to suggest that there are now no differences between Catholics and Protestants in terms of theology and understanding of the sacraments, but much of the fierceness and prejudice of the doctrinal battles of the past has now been defused. One of the most significant and heartening developments of recent years has been the much greater understanding and appreciation of traditional Roman Catholic doctrine on the part of Protestant theologians of an evangelical persuasion. George Carey's book *The Meeting of the Waters* is a good example of this new attitude.

But if the battle lines of the Reformation have at last been largely abandoned, new lines have been drawn in their place which cut across existing denominational boundaries and seem likely to be defended every bit as fiercely. In one camp are the theological liberals who believe that both Scripture and tradition have lost their authority, and want to restate Christianity in terms that make sense to those living in the modern age. In the other are the conservatives who believe that the authority of Scripture is absolute and unique and that the traditional doctrines of the church cannot be updated or tampered with. At the heart of their dispute is the question of whether Christianity is at root a revealed or a natural religion. Those who stress its revealed nature believe in the givenness of certain doctrines which owe their authority to the fact that they have been revealed by God, through the Bible and the traditional teaching and sacraments of the Church. The question of whether they are reasonable, logical or susceptible of proof does not come into it – they are given by God and that is that. Those who stress natural theology, by contrast, believe that Christian doctrine is never contrary to reason or to the principles of natural law, thus it is right and proper that it should be refashioned in the light of prevailing scientific and cultural values. The debate is not a new one although it has acquired much greater force with the advance of science and the general questioning of authority in the later twentieth century. In essence it reflects two fundamentally different views of the nature of the Christian faith. Nearly 150 years ago Bishop Charles Gore observed that the church is divided between those who see Christianity as a revelation from above downward and those who see it as an evolution from below upwards.

By far the most influential theological thinking in the twentieth century has come from the German-speaking world. This is true of Roman Catholicism as well as Protestantism. The two most significant post-war Catholic theologians have probably been Karl

Rahner, a German Jesuit, and Hans Küng, who was born in Switzerland. Almost certainly the single most influential contemporary Protestant theologian is Jürgen Moltmann, for many years Professor of Systematic Theology at the University of Tübingen. The work of three other men who did most of their work in the first half of this century has largely dictated the terms of theological debate in Britain over the last 40 years. Karl Barth (1886–1968) stands in many ways as the father of the modern conservatives. Reacting strongly against the liberalism of German Protestant theology in the post-Enlightenment period, he strongly emphasized the revealed nature of Christianity, stressed the need for absolute faith, and was deeply sceptical of all human attempts at interpretation or modification. Rudolf Bultmann (1884–1976) was strongly influenced by existential philosophy and believed that Christianity was all about authentic existence and being alive to God's constant call to decision and commitment. Once this was grasped, everything else could be stripped away. Bultmann was primarily a New Testament scholar, and much of his life's work was spent casting grave doubts on the historicity and authenticity of large parts of the Bible. The New Testament, he argued, was largely mythology, full of primitive supernatural stories and resting on an outdated view of the universe, and it urgently needed to be demythologized. Paul Tillich (1886–1965) took this process even further. For him it was necessary to get away altogether from personal notions of God and Jesus Christ. Rather, God should be conceived as our 'ultimate concern' or 'the ground of all being' and Christ as 'new being'.

In Britain the influence of Bultmann and Tillich has been considerably greater than that of Barth – except perhaps in Scotland where for a period in the 1960s the main lecture room at New College, the theology faculty at Edinburgh University, became known as the Barthroom. It took some time for their call to demythologize and depersonalize God to be taken up here. Although Tillich's book *Shaking the Foundations* was first published in Britain in 1949 and Bultmann's *The New Testament and Mythology* four years later, it was not until 1963, when John Robinson wrote *Honest to God*, that their ideas received clear popular expression and reached a substantial English readership. The impact of *Honest to God* was enormous, certainly greater than that of any other theological work published in Britain this century. It sold over a million copies within four years and its author became the darling of the new world of Sunday supplements and television discussion programmes. What particularly appealed to the media was the fact that an Anglican bishop – Robinson occupied the Suffragan See of Woolwich – was arguing that use of the word 'God' should be given up for a generation, that much of the Bible was myth and that the whole idea of a personal deity needed to be jettisoned. It didn't matter that what Robinson was saying had been echoing around the corridors of Marburg and Tübingen Universities for several decades. Here was a Church of England bishop, who had promised at his consecration to defend and promote the faith, effectively proclaiming the death of God.

As the new theology filtered through British universities, theological colleges, schools, books and sermons it lost much of its German subtlety and complexity. When Bultmann used the word 'myth' he didn't quite mean it in the sense in which it is popularly understood – as the opposite of truth. He was not saying that the New Testament was full of lies, but rather that the truth it contained needed to be reinterpreted in a way that made sense to modern minds. In fact Tillich and other German theologians strongly believed in the importance of metaphors and symbols in Christianity and stressed the value of myth as a kind of saga or epic story incorporating a reality. These subtleties were lost on those who pounced on the call to demythologize the Bible without pondering the many qualifications in Bultmann's admittedly voluminous and rather tortuous writings. The sense that the whole fabric of Christianity was under attack was powerfully reinforced by the fact that for John Robinson the new theology went hand-in-hand with a new morality. If the old supernatural props like Heaven and Hell and the notion of God as a judge looking down on us were to be knocked away, then so too was the old moral code based on external authority and absolute principles of right and wrong. In its place came situational or existential ethics in which all behaviour was relative and contingent and the only absolute was love. Those preaching from church pulpits might as well take their texts from the Beatles and the proponents of flower power – indeed, many of them did.

Alongside the attack on the authority of the supernatural and of moral absolutes went a potentially almost more devastating attack on the authority of the Bible, traditionally held by Christians to be the revealed word of God and the ultimate source of all doctrine. Once again, Britain was relatively late in picking up the full implications of a movement that had been under way in Germany for over a century – the application to the Bible of the kind of rigorous textual, literary and historical analysis that was applied to other forms of literature. Biblical criticism revealed much that was deeply upsetting to Christians who for generations had been led to believe that the Bible was somehow unlike other books, uniquely inspired and uniquely true. Increasingly scholars who were approaching it as a collection of human documents were pointing to its many inconsistencies, its dubious authenticity and the falsity of its witness on a number of key points.

There are, of course, certain stories in the Scriptures which few Christians regard as being literally true. I do not imagine that there are many church-goers in Britain today who would want to deny the theory of evolution and hold fast to the account in the opening chapter of Genesis which suggests that all living things appeared on the earth within seven days of its creation. In the United States, by contrast, there is a substantial and growing creationist lobby which insists on the literal truth of the Genesis story and seeks to ban the teaching of evolution in schools. Some of the more evangelical groups in the invisible church here are of the same view, and in a sense they have a point. If we accept the opening chapters of the Bible as being factually inaccurate, what is left as true beyond doubt? The answer is, according to the practitioners of Biblical criticism, not very much. The miracle of the parting of the Red Sea to let Moses and the fleeing Israelites through, for example, no longer looks so miraculous when we learn from Old Testament scholars that there has been a mistranslation of a Hebrew phrase which in fact means a sea of reeds. We may feel able to dispense with some of the supernatural trappings in the New Testament, like the angels and beasts that appear in the Book of Revelation, without losing the essentials of our faith. But it is rather more worrying when we are told, as we are by Bultmann and other scholars, that key parts of St John's Gospel, including the much-loved and much-quoted prologue, represent Gnostic heresy and cannot properly be described as Christian; that most of the Pauline epistles were not written by Paul at all; and that many of the sayings attributed to Jesus in the three Synoptic Gospels of Matthew, Mark and Luke are almost certainly apocryphal.

It is over the life and the nature of Jesus that Biblical criticism has cast most doubts on traditional Christian beliefs. Once again, there is nothing new in this. The first serious attempt to demolish

the view of Jesus as the incarnation of God with unique supernatural powers to work miracles and rise from the dead was made
by the German theologian David Friedrich Strauss in the mid
1830s. His *Life of Jesus Critically Examined* translated into English
in 1846 by Mary Ann Evans (the novelist George Eliot), argued
that most of the stories about Jesus which appear in the Gospels
had been invented by their authors to make his life fulfil the legends
and prophecies of the Old Testament. Over the succeeding century
and a half a small army of Biblical scholars, predominantly German
but increasingly to be found here as well, have used a battery of
academic techniques from the fields of literary criticism, linguistics,
history and sociology to discredit not just the Virgin Birth and the
miracle stories but virtually all the central Christian claims about
Jesus, including his divinity, his atoning or sacrificial death on the
Cross to save sinners, and his resurrection from the dead and
ascension into heaven.

Perhaps traditional believers can derive some comfort from the
fact that these scholars seem unable to agree among themselves on
who or what Jesus actually was. Some see him simply as a prophet,
others as a political and social revolutionary crucified for his insur-
rectionary ideas. Some argue that he was a Jewish zealot opposing
Roman control of Palestine, others that he was a wandering charismatic who attracted followers like a guru today. But what nearly
all are agreed on is that he was most emphatically not what the
creeds of the church affirm, 'the only-begotten Son of God, Begotten of his Father before all worlds, God of God, Light of Light,
Very God of very God, Begotten, not made, Being of one substance
with the Father, By whom all things were made: Who for us men,
and for our salvation, came down from heaven, and was incarnate
by the Holy Ghost of the Virgin Mary, was made man, and was
crucified also for us under Pontius Pilate.'

It is not just the work of Biblical critics on the Continent that
has cast increasing doubt on the veracity of these words, still
said in so many churches every Sunday. British theologians, and
Anglicans in particular, have long had a special interest in patristics,
the study of the early fathers of the Church who framed the great
creeds which express the essentials of Christian doctrine. For a
long time this speciality encouraged orthodoxy. Generations of
Anglican ordinands were sheltered from the more negative and
destructive findings of German theologians and brought up to have
an intimate knowledge of the *filioque* clause, the principle of *homo-*

iousia and other aspects of the early creeds, which they came to see as masterly attempts to express the central Christian mysteries of the Trinity, the Incarnation and the Atonement. However, English patristics scholars started using the new tools of literary critical analysis on the creeds, with the same devastating results that the Germans had already achieved with respect to the Bible.

In 1978 a book appeared with the provocative title *The Myth of God Incarnate*. In it a group of leading patristics scholars, the great majority in Anglican orders and including Maurice Wiles, Professor of Divinity at Oxford, seriously questioned the historical basis of the doctrine of the Incarnation. They argued that the creeds went much further than the Gospels in the claims which they made about Jesus' divinity, and a great deal further than his own very tentative claims. The whole notion of the Incarnation, that God had uniquely taken on flesh to reveal himself through Jesus, they believed to be a myth invented, several hundred years after Jesus died, by Christians who were strongly influenced by Greek ideas of the Logos and who wanted to make Jesus something more than what he actually was, a simple human being like themselves.

The book provoked a fierce debate among British theologians. Charles Moule, former Professor of Divinity at Cambridge, rallied the traditionalists, arguing that the Gospels clearly depicted Jesus as existing in a dimension which transcended the normal and temporal, and that there was no question of evolution from a purely human view of him to a divine one. The idea that the Incarnation was a myth was also strongly attacked in the pages of *New Blackfriars* by Herbert McCabe, a leading Dominican theologian, who rested his case on the inerrant authority of the Church and the early Councils which formulated the creeds. But the argument was less about authority and more about the tension between revelation and reason. On the whole, people had accepted the creeds and what they said about Jesus because they regarded them as given. To have started unravelling and questioning them would have been to probe their essential mystery and subject it to rational analysis in a way that was almost blasphemous. Archbishop William Temple had seen the great glory of the Chalcedonian Creed, which expressed the idea of Jesus having two natures and being both fully human and fully divine, as being its refusal to define. It left scope for wonder and imagination and preserved a sense of mystery. But Maurice Wiles felt this was no good for late twentieth-century minds, which demanded something more definite and logical: 'When one is asked to believe something which one cannot even spell out at all in intelligible terms, it is right to stop and push the questioning one stage further back. Are we sure that the concept of an incarnate being, one who is both fully God and fully man, is after all an intelligible concept?'

Many church-goers will doubtless go on saying the creed without too much thought as to its intelligibility or logicality. But opinion polls and more detailed surveys suggest that the major stumbling blocks for non-believers to accepting the Christian faith are the supernatural elements such as miracles, the Virgin Birth, and the Resurrection. It was partly in an effort to help these people into belief that David Jenkins made his much-publicized remarks on these matters in the mid 1980s. What he was trying to do was to show that Christian faith does not depend on acceptance of these supernatural events. Biblical scholarship, he pointed out, had found the evidence for the historicity of these events to be dubious to say the least and strongly suggested that they had been inserted into the Gospels to conform with Jewish expectations and pagan legends. For Jenkins, as for Bultmann, reliance on the supernatural actually gets in the way of the essential message of Christianity which is about faith, commitment and suffering love, and not a kind of fairy tale about an old man in the sky who can perform conjuring tricks with bones and interfere with the laws of nature on a whim, like some divine Batman or Superman. He did not deny that the Resurrection of Jesus was a reality in the minds of the disciples, but for him it was essentially a spiritual reality, a matter of faith in the living presence of their Lord. Their faith did not depend on whether his body disappeared from the tomb in which it had lain and somehow came to life again – nor should the faith of Christians today.

What David Jenkins said was actually considerably less radical than either *Honest to God* or *The Myth of God Incarnate* had been. He did not proclaim the death of God, deny the divinity of Jesus or fundamentally question the doctrine of the Incarnation. But because he spoke in direct and colourful language and because he repeated his doubts about the historicity of the Virgin Birth and the empty tomb in a television interview shortly before his con-secration in York Minster to the Bishopric of Durham, one of the senior appointments in the Church of England, the media seized on his remarks as yet another example of unbelief in the leadership of the national church. The fact that shortly after his consecration the Minster was struck by lightning and severely damaged was taken by some of his opponents as a sign that the God of miracles and supernatural interventions in whom they believed was very much alive and kicking, and had made his displeasure known in a pretty clear way.

The arguments David Jenkins and other contemporary theologians are seeking to put across in an attempt to make Christianity more intelligible to modern minds are difficult and complex. Unfortunately, the media trivialize and distort them, and what gets through to most people is a generally negative message which seems to be much more about what you can't believe in than what you can. For this the theologians themselves cannot be held completely blameless. There has been a negativity about much theological writing over the last generation or so, typified by the title of a book produced by John Robinson in 1967: *But that I can't believe*. Following Bultmann, scholars have found it much easier to debunk favourite Bible passages and knock down long-held doctrines than to build up new metaphors and symbols in their place. It does not help that much of their work has been written in a dry, jargon-ridden academic style which seems at every point to avoid actually making any positive and definite assertions about anything, least of all about God. The *Guardian* columnist Geoffrey Taylor surely struck a chord with many people when he wrote: 'One can't live entirely on a diet of ambiguity, and it would be pleasant to think that as time goes by the odd affirmation (tentative, of course) might emerge. It is all very well to say that God is love, or that God is under and in and through and by and beyond and out the other side of. It sometimes seems that theology can be written entirely in prepositions. But such an assertion does not get us very far.' (*Guardian*, 5 September 1989.)

The march of liberal theology within the main churches has not gone unchallenged among academics. One of the most vigorous attacks on it so far has come from Michael Dummet, Wykeham Professor of Logic at Oxford University and one of the leading Roman Catholic intellectuals in contemporary Britain. In a series of articles in *New Blackfriars* in 1987 he said that those who denied the Virgin Birth, Jesus' own sense that he was the Son of God, and the physical fact of the Resurrection, and who remained within the Roman Catholic Church, were frauds whose presence should be tolerated no longer. He was immediately rebuked by another leading Catholic intellectual, Professor Nicholas Lash, Professor of Divinity at Cambridge, for his 'flat-footed and anachronistic literalism'. When Channel 4 ran a television series entitled *Jesus – the Evidence* which presented many of the sceptical findings of Biblical scholars about the historicity of the Gospels, the Evangelical Alliance mustered 41 theologians to protest about its bias.

There is no doubt at all that at a popular level the work of the demythologizers and the debunkers, as they have been portrayed not entirely unjustly in the media, has helped the fundamentalists and conservative evangelicals more than anyone else. It has left many people confused, and much clearer on what Christian belief is not about than on what it is. By contrast, the evangelicals' unequivocal belief in the authority of the Scriptures and therefore in the divinity of Jesus and the physical reality of his Resurrection is appealing in its certainty and clarity. What I have described as the invisible church would almost certainly not have grown as it has in the last two decades if it had not offered such a clear contrast to the apparent lack of belief in the mainstream Protestant churches. Within both the visible and the invisible churches, the rise of the charismatic movement with its stress on the supernatural and the workings of the Spirit in the physical world can be seen as a reaction to the extreme rationalism of modern liberal theology with its constant underplaying of miracles and other evidence of divine interference in the natural order.

The high-water mark of liberal theology in Britain was almost certainly reached in the mid-1980s. Since then there has been a steady retreat from it on the part of the leadership of the main churches. In 1985 a debate in the General Synod of the Church of England showed that a clear majority of both the House of Clergy and the House of Laity supported the traditional teachings of the Church on issues such as the Virgin Birth and the Resurrection. The following year the House of Bishops of the Church of England published a statement which clearly reasserted the traditional view that both these doctrines rested on objective historical facts. On the Virgin Birth it said: 'All of us accept, first, that the belief that Our Lord was conceived in the womb of Mary by the creative power of God the Holy Spirit without the intervention of a human father can be held with full intellectual integrity; secondly, that only this belief, enshrined in the Creeds, can claim to be the teaching of the universal Church; and thirdly, that this House acknowledges and upholds this belief as expressing the faith of the Church of

England.' On the other major issue which the Bishop of Durham raised, it was equally clear: 'Yes, we believe that Jesus's Resurrection was something that happened, regardless of observers, narrators or believers. Jesus truly died and was buried, and as truly rose again to eternal life.' It also acknowledged that the faith of the Church of England was expressed in the fact of the empty tomb, while accepting that scholarship can offer no conclusive demonstration of it.

The bishops' statement marks a clear shift on the part of the Church of England hierarchy towards a more positive statement of what Christians do believe in. It also signals an important move back towards a more traditional position on key doctrines which have been under fire from scholars, and a clear assertion of the importance of the supernatural and the mysterious in Christianity. Significantly, the statement clearly reaffirmed the doctrine of the Incarnation, describing it as 'the central miracle, the heart of the Christian understanding of God'. Under George Carey's leadership the Church is likely to distance itself yet further from the extremes of liberal theology and put greater stress on positive beliefs and traditional doctrines. He himself had made no secret of his own strong belief in the objective reality of the Virgin Birth, the empty tomb and the last judgement. Other churches also show signs of moving into a new post liberal age. In 1990 the Church of Scotland produced a new statement of faith, designed to replace the traditional creeds in their archaic language. It clearly testifies to a faith in Jesus as God, the Son, who became one of us by the power of the Holy Spirit, was raised from death by the power of God, and will come again in power and glory to judge the world and make all things new.

Liberal theology, however, is certainly not dead. It is still very much alive in the divinity faculties of the universities and is to be found in such places as the constantly stimulating 'Face to Faith' column in the *Guardian* which continues to give a welcome platform to unabashed demythologizers and debunkers of orthodoxy and tradition. But we will, I suspect, hear less of it from bishops and church leaders. In many ways it is proper, and not just because we are in a decade of evangelism, that they should be more concerned with promoting, defending and spreading the faith than with constantly subjecting it to negative critical examination. But it will be a great pity if, as part of an understandable and right reaction to the excessive negativism of much twentieth-century theology, the churches as a whole now close their minds to all the new thinking that is going on among intellectuals and scholars. There are several current movements in theology which are a good deal more positive and which have something very valuable to offer British churches as they seek to witness to Christianity in a rapidly changing society struggling to come to terms with the dawning of the twenty-first century.

Most of these new movements have their roots in America. Liberation theology stands apart from the others in coming out of the developing South rather than from the developed North. It began in Brazil but has spread to many parts of Latin America and has also been taken up by churches in Africa and Asia. Resting strongly on Biblical foundations, especially on the Exodus story, the writings of the prophets and the Beatitudes, it finds in Christianity a definite and distinct bias towards the poor and oppressed. The good news of the Gospel is expressed as liberation, not just in a spiritual sense but also in economic, political and social terms as well. In Latin America particularly the espousal of liberation theology has gone hand in hand with radical political action by the churches, raising consciousness and building up alternative power structures among the weak and marginalized. It has also led to the establishment of thousands of basic Christian communities, simple cells with lay leadership which are in some ways comparable to the new house churches over here, but which preach and practise a much more radical social and political gospel.

Liberation theology, which takes much of its social and economic analysis from Marxism, has had most impact in the world-wide Roman Catholic Church. Its influence in Britain has so far been fairly small, but is growing. Those struggling to find a role for the churches in depressed inner-city areas are increasingly turning to it as providing both a critique and a way out of social deprivation and economic inequality. David Sheppard's important book *Bias to the Poor*, which called on the church in Britain to show a clear commitment to the weakest and most deprived members of society, drew much of its argument from liberation theology. It was also mentioned approvingly in the Church of England's 1985 report *Faith in the City*, which perhaps made it easier for some Conservative MPs to denounce this as a Marxist document. The conception of the Christian Gospel as a liberating force is gaining ground, although recent events in Eastern Europe have tended to shift the political direction somewhat. Many of those at the forefront of reform movements in Poland, Rumania and Czecho-slovakia have used the same Biblical texts and the same notion of Christ the liberator as the proponents of liberation theology in Latin America, but for them Marxism has been the enemy rather than a friend. The 1990s are likely to see a broadening of the whole liberation theology movement to take account of this new dimension and to give more weight to political, cultural, intellectual and spiritual factors as well as economic and social ones.

It is also a fairly safe bet that the 1990s will see feminist theology increase its influence in Britain. This movement, strong in the United States where it dominates several university divinity facul-ties, is about something more fundamental than the ordination of women to the priesthood or the purging of sexist language from hymns and prayers. These are, of course, the aspects which capture the attention of the media and which are easy to mock, as the Principal of St Stephen's House, Oxford, recently did in a rallying cry to Anglo-Catholics to resist women's ordination and inclusive language in the liturgy when he predicted that the day is not far off when the British will have to steel themselves to the Trinity being invoked as 'God the Parent, God the Offspring and God the Holy Spirit, three non-gender-specific persons in one God'. Behind the movement for women's ordination and the concern with the sexist language of church services is a point which deserves to be heard and to be taken seriously by all Christians.

What concerns feminist theologians is the whole male-dominated mould in which Christianity is cast. It is not just that the three persons of the Godhead are traditionally seen as male, that God became flesh in male form and that his commonest titles of king, emperor, conqueror suggest aggressively male and macho images. Their unease is about something wider than this – the fact that from the Bible onwards the male has been taken to represent the whole of humanity and women have been portrayed as derivative from and wholly subordinate to men, characterized by passivity and receptivity. Built deep into Christianity, they feel, is the oppression and subordination of women. For some, this patri-archal element is so integral and fundamental to the Christian religion that they have felt bound to reject it. In 1971 Mary Daly, a leading American feminist, preached a sermon in Harvard Uni-versity Chapel in which she invited women to join her in a new exodus, out of the oppression of the Church. In Britain Daphne Hampson, lecturer in systematic theology at St Andrews Univer-

sity, describes herself as a post-Christian feminist, having come to
the view that any real commitment to the idea of equality between
men and women is wholly incompatible with Christianity.

Dr Hampson has put forward her views with admirable clarity
in a powerful book, *Feminism and Theology*, published in 1990.
She argues that Christianity stands or falls as a historical religion
since it holds that God was supremely made known in one period
and one person. It cannot lose this historical relevance without
undoing itself, and herein lies the problem. For the unique figure
of Jesus Christ, who is the revelation of God in history and through
whom all humanity is taken up into God, is unquestionably male.
For her, this is no accident but part of a clear pattern of male
domination which pervades the whole of Scripture and the Christian tradition. Throughout the Bible she can find virtually no
references to women other than in submissive, subordinate roles.
Christianity, she concludes, is a patriarchal myth that has hurt
women and has been, indeed, to a considerable extent responsible
for their exploitation and subordination by men. Feminism, for
her, represents the death-knell of Christianity as a viable religion.

Very few other feminist theologians, on this side of the Atlantic
at least, go as far as this in their critique of Christianity. They do,
however, suggest that we need to alter radically our image of God,
to include feminine as well as masculine attributes. This means
more than simply referring to God as mother and the Holy Spirit
as she. What they have in mind is developing a much less authoritarian and patriarchal picture of God, and stressing his vulnerability and compassion rather than his immutability and
omnipotence. They also stress the need to recover a sense of the
intuitive and the sensual in Christianity. The rediscovery of that
small but inspired (and inspiring) line of female mystics stretching
from Hildegaard of Bingen and Dame Julian of Norwich to Evelyn
Underhill and Ruth Pitter is already providing an important cor-
rective to the often over-rational and excessively analytical nature
of much Christian thought in the West.

Some theologians feel that far from sounding the death-knell for
orthodox Christianity, feminism will actually strengthen it. Janet
Soskice, for example, has argued persuasively that feminist theology will lead to a deepened understanding of the fullness of
the doctrine of the Trinity and so bring a renewed orthodoxy to
contemporary Western Christianity, which is so often sub-
Trinitarian in concentrating almost exclusively on the Father and

the Son and virtually neglecting the Holy Spirit. There is already evidence that new feminist perspectives are helping to correct distortions which have arisen in the teachings of the churches over centuries of operating in male-dominated societies, particularly in the whole area of creation theology and attitudes towards the natural world.

Another American movement already influential in academic circles here is likely to have a growing impact on worship and thinking in British churches during the coming decade. Process theologians make many of the same points as feminists about the distortions caused by seeing God in terms of a series of absolutes, and about the need to redefine him in much more vulnerable and relativist terms. The father of process theology is generally taken to be Alfred North Whitehead (1861–1947), a British-born mathematician who became Professor of Philosophy at Harvard. He felt that the picture most Christians have of God is seriously distorted by a number of wholly extraneous and indeed deeply un-Christian influences which crept into the early church, reflecting the prevailing intellectual and cultural environment in which it grew up. The idea of a ruthless moralist and judge is an import from Hebrew religion, the concept of an unmoved, static deity who cannot be influenced or changed in any way belongs to Greek philosophy, while the image of God as king or emperor comes from the world of Imperial Rome. The one model of God we are actually given in the Christian New Testament is a very different one – that of the wandering Galilean who heals, serves and suffers.

Deeply influenced by the scientific theories of evolution and relativity, Whitehead and his American disciples think of creation as an ongoing process in which all is changing, dynamic and relative. God ceases to be the unchanging, omnipotent being of so many traditional hymns and prayers and is seen rather as a continuously evolving and creative figure, the 'self-surpassing surpasser' who is constantly moving ahead of himself, just as he is always ahead of us, luring us on through his love to ever new opportunities and possibilities. The language of process theology is often rather forbidding but it can be expressed in relatively simple terms, as in Whitehead's description of God as 'the poet of the world, leading it by his vision of truth, beauty and goodness'. Its implications are considerable and exciting. If God is not simply impassive but can be moved and influenced by his creatures, then prayer takes on a much greater significance. He also becomes a much less remote figure. Following lines suggested by process thought, several contemporary theologians have developed the idea of God's vulnerability and portray him as the one who suffers and feels pain with us, rather than the old man in the sky who looks down impassively on our trials and tribulations. The greater emphasis on God's vulnerability and sensitivity is already being reflected in church worship, particularly in the area of pastoral care and counselling.

Another fascinating development which is likely to gain ground in the 1990s is the growing convergence between theology and science. Traditionally practitioners of these two disciplines have been on opposing sides in the ongoing debate between faith and reason. At times, indeed, they have seemed like sworn enemies – one thinks of Galileo's treatment at the hands of the Inquisition for advocating the Copernican system, or Bishop Wilberforce's ridiculing of Thomas Huxley's exposition of the theory of evolution. In the last decade or so, however, scientists and theologians have begun to enter into a fruitful dialogue and to recognize that they have much to learn from each other. To a large extent this new convergence is the result of recent developments in the fields of physics and biology. On the one hand, scientists are increasingly coming to a point in their research about the basic constituents of matter and the origins of life where they feel that equations and formulae are no longer appropriate. They are being driven to use the language of religion and poetry in an effort to sum up the beauty and mystery that they are encountering at the very frontiers of their disciplines. On the other hand, theologians are finding much in the theories of quantum physics and relativity which helps to make sense of traditional Christian assertions about God – for example, the fact that it is possible for him to stand outside time and yet intervene in it.

While most of the running in process theology is still being made by Americans, Britain is very much at the forefront of new thinking about the relationship between theology and science. Predictably, the most rigorous and thorough work in this area has been done in Scotland, notably by Ian Barbour and Thomas Torrance. Torrance in particular has argued that both relativity and quantum theory have produced a new convergence between scientific and theological thinking, on the basis of the principle of contingent order. Modern science has found that the universe is both contingent, in the sense that it might have been different from what it is, and orderly, in the sense that it has an open-structured order. This fits in with the view of theologians 'that on the one hand, the universe depends entirely upon the beneficent free will and act of the Creator for its being and form ... and on the other that it is given an independent reality of its own completely differentiated from the self-sufficient eternal reality of God'. In other words, modern science has considerably illuminated the age-old Christian conundrum of how there can be both free will and determinism in the world. The concept of contingent order allows a relationship between the creative freedom of God and the created freedom of the universe.

Two English scientists turned Anglican priests have also made an important contribution in this field. Dr Arthur Peacocke is a biochemist who has written books on the subject of creation and science and, more generally, on the relationship of science and theology in the twentieth century. Dr John Polkinghorne, President of Queen's College, Cambridge, is a physicist who has also written widely and very stimulatingly on the growing convergence between religion and science. Both men are struck by the extent to which the post-Enlightenment idea of God as a Divine watchmaker in the sky, standing back and watching his creation tick away, is no longer tenable as a result of the total discrediting of the fixed, self-contained mechanistic universe of Newtonian physics. In its place quantum physics has revealed a much more dynamic and open-ended system which is in a constant state of becoming. This, they argue, allows for a much more continuous and reciprocal relationship between God and his creation. Peacocke finds very helpful the medieval idea of the dance of creation, and sees God as the composer 'who beginning with an arrangement of notes in an apparently simple tune, elaborates and expands it into a fugue by a variety of devices of fragmentation and reassociation' (*Creation and the World of Science*). Polkinghorne is equally excited by the picture of the universe as an open and continuing process presented by quantum physics. 'The death of mere mechanism', he has written, 'begins to open up the description of a world endowed, not only with elements of static being, but also with genuine becoming ... I believe that the whole physical world has an openness to novelty, by which it explores the fruitful potentiality with which it has been endowed. Theologically, I would describe this as the gift of freedom by the Creator to his creation.' (*The Times*, 9 July 1988.)

What is beginning to emerge in the writings of these and other theologians with scientific knowledge and understanding is a new natural theology. The idea that the existence of God can be proved from the rational and orderly nature of the universe and the exquisite design of the world of nature is one that used to hold much currency, particularly in Roman Catholic circles, but which has largely fallen out of fashion in modern times. It is now undergoing a considerable revival, largely because of recent developments in science. The new science of chaology has fascinating implications for Christian theology, not least in supporting the Biblical view of God as the one who fashions order out of chaos in the manner that the potter moulds his lump of clay to create beautiful objects. The anthropic principle, described as the most intriguing new scientific idea of the last decade, appears to offer even more support for those seeking a new natural theology which proves the existence of God from the design of the universe. Scientists have now established that the emergence of human life on this earth was the result of a remarkably precise distribution of energy and matter in the first micro-seconds of creation. Even the slightest variations in the speed of light, Planck's constant, the mass of protons compared with neutrons or the total quantities of hydrogen and helium, would have made the development of the universe as we know it impossible. The conditions which have controlled every detail of the universe's development seem to have been exactly programmed at or just before the first moment of time so that, against odds of billions and billions to one, human life would emerge.

The astonishing fact that Professor Stephen Hawking's book *A Brief History of Time* has been longer on the best-seller lists than any other volume except *The Diary of an Edwardian Country Lady* indicates the level of general interest in fundamental questions about the nature and meaning of our universe. It was, indeed, Hawking's book which first introduced the anthropic principle to the non-scientific world. I predict that we are going to see many more books which tackle this and other subjects at the interface of science and religion, and that within the churches there will be increasing interest in natural theology.

One very important aspect of this rediscovery of natural theology already percolating into the life and thinking of the churches is a 'greener' attitude towards the environment. There is much ground to be made up here. Christianity has, for understandable reasons, had a bad press among those concerned with conservation and ecology. The churches are blamed for encouraging the exploitation and domination of the natural world by preaching that it exists solely for human use and pleasure, on the basis of God's commission to Adam in Genesis 1.26 to have dominion over the birds of the air, the fish of the sea, the cattle and over all the earth. Those involved in the green movement also complain that Christians seem to worship a wholly transcendent God who has no real concern for his non-human creation, and to encourage a view that all things physical and material, including the world of nature, are somehow fallen and corrupt and that only the spiritual is pure.

In response to these criticisms and to the current environmental crisis the churches are rediscovering the essentially green message of the Bible, which speaks so clearly of God's concern for all creation. The distortion caused by centuries of concentrating on human sin and salvation is at last being corrected as theologians embrace a wider cosmic view of Christ's redemptive purposes. This move away from the narrow anthropocentrism that has bedevilled Western Christianity since the time of St Augustine is being greatly helped by the new perspectives brought by feminist and process theology, and by the rediscovery of the 'green' spirituality of the Celtic and Eastern Orthodox churches and of medieval mystics like Hildegaard of Bingen, with their sense of the unity of all creation and the goodness of the natural world. Among contemporary theologians there is much more stress on creation and less on sin and salvation. One of the most radical proponents of this new creation-centred theology is Matthew Fox, an American Dominican, whose book *Original Blessing* argues that the whole emphasis of Christianity should be shifted away from original sin and towards a celebration of God's good creation. A centre for creation-centred spirituality has been established at St James's Church in Piccadilly, and there is a lively and growing Christian Ecology Group which is spreading the holistic gospel through the land.

The 'greening' of the churches will, I suspect, be one of the most significant trends of the 1990s. It is also likely to go hand-in-hand with another development only just in its infancy – dialogue with other faiths. In many ways the environmental crisis has helped the inter-faith movement. On the face of it, religions like Buddhism and Hinduism are a good deal more environment-friendly than Christianity. Realizing how much their own tradition has neglected the natural world, a growing number of Christians are coming to see the value of the more holistic approach of Eastern religions. It was because of concern about the environment that Pope John Paul II brought together representatives of all the major world faiths for a meeting in Assisi. Here in Britain churches have been involved in a number of festivals of creation which have included elements of worship from several different faiths. At a service in 1989 in Canterbury Cathedral, for example, Yanomani Indians from Brazil took part with a chant about the power of trees.

The move towards much greater dialogue and sharing with other faiths is not, of course, simply the result of common concern about the environment. It is also the natural outcome of the whole trend in religious education over the last 20 or 30 years, which has been towards understanding other faiths. This is a natural response to the fact that we live in a pluralistic culture in which Christianity is no longer the only expression of religious faith. Among academics there is now a significant school of comparative religionists who tend to preach a kind of religious relativism. Christianity is the way, the truth and the life for Christians, but not for those brought up within a non-Christian culture. Exclusive claims made by Christians are regarded as imperialistic and arrogant. The gurus of this movement, Professor John Hick, formerly of Birmingham University, and Professor Ninian Smart, formerly of Lancaster, both of whom now hold academic posts in California, have done much work identifying common themes which run through all the world's religions. There is a growing tendency among those schooled in such an approach and involved in the inter-faith move-ment towards syncretism, stressing the oneness of all religions and building a personal faith which combines elements from each of them. As well as encouraging relativism, the belief that no one religion can make exclusive and absolute claims also promotes universalism – the feeling that no one is beyond the pale of sal-vation.

The growth of dialogue and sharing between different faiths raises profound questions for the churches. How far can Christians be syncretists and relativists? Does there not come a point in talking to those of other faiths when they have to draw a line and say, You are wrong? Must they not respect Jesus' statement that no man comes to the Father but by him, and his call to convert all nations and make disciples of all men? The growing espousal of univ-ersalism has equally problematic implications. There are increas-ingly few Christians within the main visible churches who believe that those who are not Christians will end up in Hell. Indeed, the whole concept of Hell has largely been abandoned by the mainstream denominations – the novelist David Lodge has dated its disappearance from the Roman Catholic Church, where it perhaps lingered longest, to some point in the 1960s. But if you are saying that people can come to God through other religions and that no one is doomed to eternal damnation by staying outside the Christian pale, then what is the point of having churches, and what on earth is the point of a decade of evangelism?

The growing number of evangelical Christians within both the visible and the invisible churches have no doubts about what the proper response to these questions should be. They view with horror the involvement of nature-worshipping Indians in a service at the national shrine of English Christianity, and are profoundly unhappy about the growth of the inter-faith movement. A prominent group of Anglican Evangelicals, supported by a number of Anglo-Catholics, launched a campaign in November 1991 to put an end to involvement by the Church of England in prayer and worship with those of other faiths. The Open Letter Group, as it is known, insists that Jesus Christ is 'the only saviour and hope of mankind' and that the churches should actively be seeking to convert those of other faiths to Christianity. This approach has been strongly condemned by a number of liberal bishops who are prominent in inter-faith dialogue and who are already very concerned about increasing Christian evangelistic activity among Jews. The whole issue of relationships with other faiths seems certain to become increasingly divisive.

The differences in attitude can already be seen very clearly in terms of the range of Christian responses to the emergence of the so-called New Age religion. The protagonists of this new movement claim that the Age of Pisces, a sign traditionally associated with Christianity, is giving way to the Age of Aquarius, a 2,000-year period where a more holistic and intuitive faith will predominate. The manifestations of New Age spirituality are extremely diverse and disparate – everything from feminist tarots to meditation, via acupuncture and aromatherapy. Some Christians feel that the churches should enthusiastically embrace much of the New Age philosophy and welcome the chance it brings to rediscover aspects of their own tradition that have been lost in the West, like faith-healing and meditation. Perhaps the leading exponent of this view is Adrian Smith, a Roman Catholic missionary priest who spent

15 years in Zambia. He has practised transcendental meditation since 1976 and studied under the Maharishi Mahesh Yogi. In a book published in 1983, *TM: An Aid to Christian Growth*, he argued that far from being suspicious about the meditation techniques associated with Eastern religions, Christians should study and practise them as a way into a life of deeper prayer and contemplation. A subsequent book, *God and the Aquarian Age* (1991), describes the dawning Age of Aquarius as part of God's unfolding plan for his creation and predicts an exciting new era for Christianity, characterized by much less intellectual detachment and a great outpouring of the Spirit.

At the other extreme is the response of the Evangelical Alliance which in 1990 issued a pamphlet with the title *New Age Promise – Age Old Promise?* This describes the so-called New Age religion as firmly rooted in pagan rites, occult practices and Eastern spirituality which are, in fact, centuries old, and with which Christians should have nothing to do. It provides a clear summary of the differences between Christian teaching and the philosophy of the New Age. Christianity holds that we are creatures of God, made by him but not part of him. He is personal and can only be approached through Jesus. We can do things that are wrong and we need to be forgiven. Human transformation is only possible through each person turning away from what they know to be wrong and receiving the gift of God's forgiveness, made available through the death of Jesus on the Cross. According to the pamphlet, New Age philosophy is wholly incompatible with Christianity on all these points. It sees God not as a person but as a force that runs right through creation. Physical matter can be worshipped, and objects like crystals have special powers. The earth can be worshipped as a mother. If all is God, then so are we. Each person can decide his or her own lifestyle – there is no absolute morality, no such thing as doing wrong and no need for forgiveness. The universe is in a state of evolution or becoming and humanity, as part of this process, is becoming more conscious of itself and will eventually fuse with the infinite. Individuals can achieve enlightenment by tapping their inner resources, realizing their own divine nature and getting in touch with their higher consciousness. There is no need for the salvific act worked by Jesus – for the New Agers he is simply one divine person among many. The pamphlet goes on to advise Christians to 'pray for the discernment of the Holy Spirit so that you're able to recognise New Age influence in training courses, advertising, fashion items etc.', and to 'teach young people the truths about crystals, rainbows and other pieces of God's creation hi-jacked by New Agers.'

We are back, here, to the fundamental dilemma as to how far Christians should stand out against the culture of the age in which they live and how far they should rather accommodate themselves to it. There are many who would agree with the Evangelical Alliance that the New Age has nothing in common with Christianity and that it should be rejected as a woolly and potentially dangerous mix of pagan, occult and oriental religions. There are others who would rather counsel an open-minded approach and who are prepared to recognize that it may contain insights of value to Christians. They could point out that the celebration of Christmas is the result of a subtle synthesis of Christianity and paganism. Indeed, if one stripped away from the church calendar all those festivals which have their origins in pagan rites and nature worship, there would not be very much left. This, of course, is precisely why evangelical churches like the Free Church of Scotland do not celebrate Christmas or have harvest festivals.

To some extent the adversarial atmosphere which seems to permeate so much of church life, and seems particularly prevalent in the realm of theology and belief, is a reflection of the impact of the media. As Geoffrey Rowell, chaplain of Keble College, Oxford, put it to me: 'The media need to magnify adversarial positions. Stereotypes and caricatures are not usually helpful in theological debate. The point that the Tractarians were making by their doctrine of reserve, the inescapable linking of theological discussion to reverence before the mystery of God, does not consort well with the confrontation of television debate or the appetite of the tabloids for scandal.' But, that said, there always has been and there always will be disagreement between theological liberals and conservative evangelicals. It reflects a fundamental difference in human personalities. As John Cole, an Anglican priest who is also a psychologist, put it in an article in *The Times* (7 November 1987): 'The fundamental difference between the absolutist and the relativist theologian is one of innate temperament, the absolutists having many of the characteristics of William James's tough-minded individual, while the relativist is more like his tender-minded type. Both are sincere and devout men seeking, as best they know how, to serve God and their fellow men. God in his wisdom appears to have created not only absolutist and relativistic theologians, but also endowed the rest of humanity with one or other of their temperaments.'

If it is inevitable that there will continue to be deep divisions within the Christian community over questions of faith and belief, what seems sad, but is surely not inevitable, is that these arguments are increasingly carried on in the abstract and do not arise in the worshipping and pastoral life of the church. Over the last 20 or 30 years there has been a progressive divorce between theology and the churches. In his *Crockford's* preface Garry Bennett rightly diagnosed this trend as one of the major ills besetting the contemporary Church of England. Traditionally, he pointed out, 'the context of theological study was the corporate life of the Church and the end was to deepen its spirituality and forward its mission'. During the 1960s and 1970s, however, theology became increasingly an academic specialization rooted in the universities. At the same time the administrative burden on bishops and clergy made the once-common figure of the churchman–theologian increasingly rare. Indeed, Dr Bennett identified Archbishop Michael Ramsey as the last of the breed. That, perhaps, was being a little unfair; in many ways David Jenkins stands in that tradition. His attempts to grapple with questions which are causing real difficulty both to church-goers and to people outside the church can be seen as reflecting his pastoral concerns as a bishop as much as his academic interests as a theologian. But there is no doubt that there are fewer and fewer people within the churches (and this is true of all denominations and not just the Church of England) with the time, the energy, or perhaps the inclination and the capacity, to pursue serious theological study and reflection.

At the same time theology has suffered, like so many other disciplines, from the trend towards academic specialization. It has become a victim of the compartmentalization of British university life. No longer the queen of the sciences, it has become downgraded and thoroughly secularized in its new status as just another subject area in higher education. For students the attraction of reading divinity is often that it is one of the easiest subjects in terms of entry requirements and does not make the demands of a language or science. Those who teach it are less and less likely to be priests or ministers with pastoral experience. Indeed, they are not even necessarily believing Christians. Ordinands who are training for the ministry or priesthood in universities and theological colleges receive a massive dose of Biblical criticism and scepticism and a good deal of secular sociology, but very little spirituality, prayer or pastoral care. They are then expected to go into a parish and cope with the doubts and demands of people perplexed and crushed by modern living. It is small wonder that a recent survey of the Roman Catholic diocese of Middlesbrough revealed that nearly half the priests confessed to having occasional doubts about the existence of God; or that 95 per cent of those at a conference of probationer ministers in the Church of Scotland said they did not expect to be able to go through their ministries with theological integrity. They felt that it would be too disturbing to expose their congregations to what they knew to be the real theological questions. Nor did they even feel that they could share such questions with fellow ministers, as that would be seen as a mark of failure. The great majority expected that within a year or two parish activity would have taken over and virtually irreversible theological brain-death would have set in.

It is very important that we close the increasing divide between the challenging but exciting theology being taught and talked about in universities and the actual exercise of the church's pastoral care and worship. It is wrong to accept it as an inevitable and unbridgeable gap between the rarefied atmosphere of academia and the simple faith of the people in the pews. The fact is that over-specialization and narrow academic attitudes have made theology a great deal more inaccessible than it should be. This process of obfuscation has been greatly abetted by the replacement of history by sociology as the natural handmaiden of theological study, with a consequent proliferation of jargon and the loss of a humane perspective. It is also patently the case that so-called ordinary church-goers are not just credulous souls looking for simple comfort and cosy certainties. Hundreds of thousands of people take part in Bible study groups and discussion evenings. There is an enormous market for books on theological issues and for serious religious programmes on television and radio. In an interesting and commendable move to deal with what she calls 'the alarming level of theological under-nourishment among ordinary thoughtful Christians', the Scottish theologian Elizabeth Templeton has proposed setting up a theological resource centre in Edinburgh located in a café or shop where people could drop in, browse through books and articles, find out what was going on in terms of courses and classes and 'put their own theological questions on the map and have them tackled'.

Maybe we will see such informal places for 'God-talk' develop over the coming decade. Maybe, too, we will learn from those parts of the Christian communion which have avoided our separation of thinking about the big issues from the day-to-day life of the churches. In Latin America theology is part of the basic Christian communities: thoughts about God and Christ and all the deep and fundamental questions which theology tackles arise from the experience of living, working and praying together. Within the Eastern Orthodox churches theology remains very closely tied to spirituality: you think about God when you pray to him and you pray that your faith may be deepened by understanding. It would be good if we could develop a similar kind of integration between theology and worship in Britain.

– 4 –

Worship and buildings

One the strain that lips of thousands
Lift as from the heart of one

The selection schools at which the Church of Scotland chooses its candidates for ordination include a series of exercises which involve dealing with situations that might arise in a parish ministry. The one I was faced with was the case of the clapped-out organ and whether or not it should be replaced. The older members of the congregation, led by the organist and choir, insisted that a new organ was essential to maintain musical standards and offer up the best to God, even though the cost would be upwards of £50,000. The younger members felt that it was immoral for the church to spend this amount of money for such a purpose when millions were starving in Africa, and that a cheap piano or a couple of guitars would actually lead to livelier singing.

This kind of debate is going to be heard in more and more churches during the coming decade, not only because many organs installed around a century ago are reaching the end of their useful lives. It reflects widespread disagreement, not just about music, but about language, style, architecture, the whole meaning and purpose of worship today and, indeed, whether we need special church buildings at all. To a considerable extent the argument is between what I have characterized as the visible and the invisible churches, although it is also being carried on within the main established denominations.

At its extreme, one side accuses the other of seeing the church as a museum, devoted to preserving at enormous cost, and for an ever-dwindling clientele, ancient buildings, archaic language and highbrow music with little meaning for many people today. Those on the other side shudder at what they take to be the cheap banality and shallowness of singalong choruses and modern prayers, and ask if this really is the best we can offer up to God.

At the root of this debate are important questions about the nature of worship – is it primarily something that is directed at God or is its purpose to involve and enthuse those taking part? Should it let our hearts and minds soar heavenwards, or equip us for social action and work in the world? Even more fundamentally, what is the church? Is it, as most ordinary church-goers probably see it, and certainly as the proverbial man or woman in the street does, primarily a special building to which people go every Sunday morning to sing hymns, say prayers and listen to a sermon? Or, as theologians do, should we think much more in terms of the church being the body of Christ or the people of God? Does the fact that we equate the church predominantly with bricks and mortar get in the way of a proper understanding of what the Christian community is? Certainly many congregations are more preoccupied with leaking roofs and raising money for fabric repairs than they are with evangelism or social action. Would it not be better for the church to get rid of its old buildings and meet in simple and unpretentious surroundings which conform better to Our Lord's remarks about the Son of Man having nowhere to lay his head? Yet do not ancient and beautiful church buildings often speak eloquent sermons in stone and stand as powerful symbols of the eternal in a world of ugliness and change?

The fact is, of course, that all these points of view have some validity. They reflect the tensions that the church must always live with as it stands in its uneasy and difficult role, in this world but not wholly of it, seeking to witness to a faith that is at once incarnational and material and also numinous and mysterious. To some extent the church is only a provisional, temporary, *ad hoc* affair whose whole *raison d'être* is not to become too settled or established but rather to point the way to what is to come. At the same time it can speak through the beauty of its buildings, the richness of its music and the power of its liturgy to the heights and depths of the Christian mystery. There is no reason, of course, why simplicity and beauty, social action and meaningful worship cannot go together. One of the best contemporary examples I know of a successful conjunction of all these elements is the Iona Community which combines practical work for justice and peace with innovative and creative worship. Its founder, George MacLeod, saw a narrow dividing line between 'Glory to God in the Highest' and

'Glory to God in the High Street'. For him that meant not just writing the kinds of prayers that sound right in the shopping precinct or the supermarket, but also restoring a medieval abbey and rediscovering the riches and colour of Celtic spirituality.

The Iona Community perhaps provides a model as to how some of the arguments about worship in the contemporary church can be resolved. Its prayers and hymns combine a dignity and depth of language with an up-to-date approach and a strong social message in a way that gives them a great appeal to both young and old. But there is no easy formula for resolving the debate on the subject of worship that is currently raising passions in so many churches. As well as reflecting a continuing tension that can never be fully resolved, it is also a consequence of changing cultural values which have wide ramifications far beyond the world of the churches. Thanks mainly to television ours is increasingly a visual rather than a literary culture. Young people in particular think largely in terms of images and are unused either at school or at home to digesting long chunks of the written or spoken word. They are also for the most part immersed in a particular musical culture – that of commercial pop music – and find classical music, and particularly the traditional music of the church, very alien.

The worship of the main established churches is still firmly rooted in a pre-television and pre-pop music culture. It is very cerebral, very wordy, and does not offer much in the way of visual distraction or contemporary musical sounds. In the words of George Carey: 'Much of our worship is boring, tedious, long and mind-numbing. The miracle of Christianity, I sometimes think cynically, is that people still come in great numbers – so something must be going on. Of course, something is going on, but we could do much better. Worship is the shop window of the Church and obviously is not attracting as many "buyers" as it should.' This, of course, is language calculated to disturb the traditionalists, who would shudder at the idea that the church can be compared to a supermarket trying to attract customers, and would point out that the object of worship is to please God and not titillate the congregation. None the less, Carey is right in identifying the poor quality of much worship as a major factor in the decline in church-going. He has already signalled that he regards the injection of more enthusiasm and vigour into Church of England services as a major priority of his period as Archbishop of Canterbury. This is likely to involve more use of visual media such as liturgical dance and mime and

perhaps also more of the uninhibited body language and spontaneous expressions of joy associated with the charismatic movement. In its rather more sober Presbyterian way the Church of
Scotland's Panel on Worship is also examining radical new depar-
tures in the structuring of services, such as breaking up the sermon
into short bites interspersed with songs and prayer.

If recent experience is anything to go by, these changes are likely
to meet with fierce resistance from many both inside and outside
the churches. The traditional forms of service in the two main
established churches are jealously guarded as part of the national
heritage, not just by their members but by many who hardly ever
darken their doors. Abandoning the traditional Sunday morning
service in the Church of Scotland, affectionately known as 'the
hymn sandwich', in favour of a more sacramental or participatory
approach would cause ripples of discontent far beyond the eldership of the Kirk. The English Free Churches, by contrast, have
managed quietly to shift their services in a much more sacramental
direction, introducing more frequent communion and more set
liturgies, without very much protest. The Roman Catholics have
also achieved the almost wholesale transformation of the Mass in
the wake of Vatican II with remarkably little dislocation and
opposition. It is true that there is a small (and possibly growing)
minority who deplore the loss of Latin, the moving of the altar
into the centre of the church and the increased lay participation as
robbing the service of its mystery and universality. There is perhaps
a larger and mostly silent majority who regret, as a lady confided
to me in the Catholic stronghold of South Uist, that there is much
less time for quiet prayer and meditation now that the congregation
is constantly being urged to respond or sing hymns. But it is a
tribute to the hegemony of Roman Catholicism, and perhaps also
to the authority of its hierarchy, that a total revolution in its
worship should have been accomplished in a generation with comparatively little upset.

The Church of England, on the other hand, is still smarting from
the outcry provoked by the liturgical changes which it has made
over the last two decades. The opprobrium that has been heaped
on them by members of the literary establishment, supported by
the Prince of Wales, indicates how far Anglican worship is regarded
as a national cultural possession. What has caused particular
offence, as much outside the Church as within it, has been the
virtual disappearance from use of the 1662 Book of Common

Prayer. Although much of the debate about the merits of the book and the services which have replaced it has centred on purely literary considerations, it has also raised important theological and ecclesiological questions. The demise of what is generally acknowledged to be a masterpiece both of English prose and of devotional writing after a 300-year reign as the prayer book of the nation has certainly been swift and ignominious. Its death-knell was sounded by an innocuous-seeming Act of Parliament called the Prayer Book (Alternative and Other Services) Measure, passed in 1965. The trouble was that the new services this authorized, which appeared fast and furiously through the 1970s in little red, green and blue booklets looking and reading more like instruction manuals than prayer books, seemed to take on the status of replacements rather than alternatives to the old prayer book. They were gathered together in 1980 into the Alternative Service Book (ASB). Initially authorized to be used until 1990, this has recently had its life extended until 2000 and is now the only prayer book being used in many parishes. It remains only a provisional liturgy, and it is quite likely that it will in time be replaced by another book incorporating some of the new services which are now being drawn up by the Church of England's Liturgical Commission. Nobody seriously expects the return of the old prayer book when, if ever, all the experimenting is over and there is general agreement that it will have disappeared entirely from everyday use by the end of the century.

It is hard to exaggerate the sense of bereavement and anger that many people feel about the loss of the Book of Common Prayer and the manner of its going. Several see it as the most destructive act of a liberal conspiracy which threatens the whole fabric of Anglicanism. Gareth Bennett devoted a substantial section of his 1987 *Crockford's* preface to what he called 'the case of the disappearing book'. For him the common liturgical language which the 1662 book provided was one of the key factors which kept the Church of England and the wider Anglican communion together. Its elimination in the space of one generation meant, he felt, that 'any attempt to define Anglicanism by reference to its tradition of worship is now on very insecure ground'. His close friend William Oddie was even more outspoken. In an article in the *Daily Telegraph* (21 January 1991) explaining why he had quit the Church of England and become a Roman Catholic, he wrote: 'Contempt for the opinions of the men and women in the pews has been the hallmark of the higher clergy of this generation: how, otherwise, could they have uprooted, with little pastoral sense, with an insensitivity amounting to actual cruelty, the liturgical tradition at the heart of it all?' He went on to quote a leading article in *The Times* which suggested that 'The removal of the one central pillar, the Book of Common Prayer, imposed throughout the Church by an act of uniformity, has left the Anglican credal and liturgical edifice standing with no visible means of support, liable to collapse under its own weight.' For Oddie, that collapse is already under way and nothing will stop it – 'Only the Prayer Book guaranteed the Church against (in its own words) being "like children, carried away by every blast of vain doctrine".' Other Anglican clergy have told me that the disappearance of the Book of Common Prayer has turned the Church of England into a dissenting sect and opened the floodgates to extempore prayer and the undisciplined excesses of charismatic worship.

There is, surely, a hysterical note in these reactions. The conspiracy theory hardly stands up. It is important to remember that the 1662 Prayer Book has not been banned – the alternative services are what they say they are, and have not been forced on a reluctant clergy by a group of trendy bishops. Where they are used, and that is now in the great majority of parishes, it is because the clergy find them more meaningful both pastorally and liturgically than the Book of Common Prayer. There is also a good deal of evidence that many congregations also like the ASB, even if some of the language is a bit flat and some of the services, as they are printed, are rather difficult to follow. It seems to be making rather a lot of the Book of Common Prayer to see it as a bulwark against everything from extreme liberalism to charismatics. It is also ironic, to say the least, that its staunchest defenders like Dr Bennett and Dr Oddie should be drawn from the Anglo-Catholic wing of the Church of England. The theology expressed in its pages is, like that of the Thirty-nine Articles, very Protestant and evangelical. It belongs to the period of the Reformation, and long before its supersession by the ASB many thoughtful people must have found that they had to suspend belief as they mouthed its beautiful and euphonious words.

It is, of course, the beauty and euphony of its language that has led the loss of the Prayer Book to be mourned so much outside the Church as well as within it. The Prayer Book Society, which campaigns vigorously for its continued use, has many avowed agnostics and even atheists on its committee. In a powerful piece in the *Sunday Telegraph* (14 February 1988) entitled 'Bad Language in Church', one of them, the novelist P. D. James, wrote of the ASB wedding service that 'it could have been written by the DHSS'. The Prince of Wales voiced similar criticisms in a speech presenting the Thomas Cranmer Schools prize in December 1989. The language of the Book of Common Prayer and the Authorized Version of the Bible, he suggested, was the language of beauty and holiness. The language of the ASB and the New English Bible, by contrast, was 'mean, trite and ordinary', producing phrases 'too banal to be remembered ... How can we be lifted up by a sentence which itself needs lifting – on a stretcher?' He went on to speculate that 'If English is spoken in Heaven God undoubtedly employs Cranmer as his speech-writer. The angels of lesser ministries probably use the language of the New English Bible and the Alternative Service Book for internal memos.'

I have to admit to agreeing wholeheartedly with those who are unhappy about the language of many of the modern versions of the Bible. My own particular *bête noire*, the Good News Bible first published in 1976 and now the second most commonly used Bible in British churches, has a banality and flatness which I find totally inappropriate for reading in public. But there are modern translations of the Bible which retain a dignity and resonance in their language – notably the recently published Revised English Bible, which has been specifically produced for reading in church. It is also legitimate to ask how far high literary merit should be a valid criterion for judging the worth of material whose purpose is primarily evangelistic. George Carey is fond of quoting William Temple's dictum that the Church of England is dying of good taste, and one can understand his point: often it seems as though it is the guardians of highbrow literary and musical culture who are stifling the new prayers and songs in the church which speak directly to modern worshippers.

But the debate over the disappearance of the Prayer Book and the Authorized Version of the Bible also raises profounder theological points. To many in the churches today, Prince Charles's remarks strike a disconcerting note. Even though it is made half in jest, the very suggestion that English might be the language of heaven and that there is a hierarchy of lesser ministries presided over by God jars on ears attuned to liberation or process theology. Is not one of the main reasons for dispensing with the Prayer Book and the

Authorized Version the fact that they speak of God in terms that are now largely discredited, as a remote authoritarian figure up in the sky? In his book *The Old Country* Alan Bennett reflects: 'I imagine that when it comes to the next prayer book they won't write He, meaning Him with a capital h. God will be written in the lower case to banish any lurking feeling of inferiority his worshippers might feel.' Prince Charles quoted this in his speech and went on to give an instance of such levelling-down language in the New English Bible – the replacement of the Authorized Version's 'Hearken to my words' with 'Give me a hearing'. To him the first phrase is poetic, memorable and arresting, the second flat, patronizing and unmemorable. But for many modern theologians the phrase in the Authorized Version is too dictatorial and smacks of the myth of Jesus, the God–Man moulded in the image of Roman Imperialism rather than the humble, vulnerable Galilean.

We are back here to the relationship between worship and theology which we touched on at the end of the last chapter. If theology should always be anchored in prayer, then the reverse is also true and liturgy should be in step with belief. Aspects of the Prayer Book service, much loved and deeply embedded in the English national consciousness as they may be, simply do not fit with modern thinking. For example, the 1662 marriage service suggests that procreation is the primary purpose of marriage. In a debate in the General Synod in July 1990 Michael Saward, Vicar of Ealing, remarked that when couples came to him asking for the 'old service' he always pointed out that since what it said was incompatible with the use of contraception, if they intended to practise family planning they should really have one of the new services. In the same debate Sir John Stokes, a Conservative MP, defended the 1662 marriage service for its 'strong and robust words which tell people this is not just some civil ceremony but something aweful and fundamental'. The trouble is that awefulness and fundamentalism is exactly what many in the church are trying to escape from.

There are, I think, other more serious theological objections to the multiplicity of modern services and versions of the Bible which have appeared over the last 20 or 30 years. By their very proliferation, and by their tendency to spell everything out, they have robbed church worship of much of its sense of mystery and transcendence. It is in search of this lost element in most Western worship that an increasing number of people are being attracted to the Eastern Orthodox churches. What has also been lost is that great sense of universality which came from the fact that you could wander into any church in the land and always be sure of reciting the same prayers and hearing the Bible read in the same version. This was almost as true in Scotland as it was in England – the Church of Scotland's Book of Common Order followed the language of the Book of Common Prayer very closely right up to the new edition of 1979. The same prayers and Bible readings were also used in school assemblies. This universality in the language of worship gave a great sense of the church as the one body of Christ, and it also led to a great familiarity with prayers and Scripture passages.

I count myself immensely privileged to be a member of perhaps the last generation that was brought up on the Book of Common Prayer and the Authorized Version of the Bible. Both because of the memorable poetic language they contain, and more particularly because of the universality of their use in schools and churches, substantial passages from both have sunk deep into my subconscious and remain a marvellous storehouse of spiritual resources which I can draw on at any time. Children growing up today do not have any chance of memorizing and storing away prayers and phrases from the Bible. More than ten different versions of the Bible are in regular use in schools and churches, and there is very little repetition of well-known prayers or passages. Rather, the tendency is to be constantly changing services. Most of the current material being produced by the Church of England's Liturgical Commission is designed to be used for an experimental period of anything between one and seven years. Other churches adopt a similarly provisional approach, often putting their prayers and orders of service in loose-leaf folders and ring binders so they can easily be changed and new material substituted. We have lost that great stock of common prayers and Biblical passages which were passed on almost orally from generation to generation and which could be drawn on in times of trouble or of great joy.

Another kind of universality has been lost as well. The great prayers from the Book of Common Prayer may have been archaic, but partly because of this they had a timeless quality. They dealt in generalities and seemed to speak to all sorts and conditions of men (and women) in all sorts of different situations. The modern trend is for prayers to be extremely specific, indeed highly topical. In intercessory prayer, instead of simply reciting a general collect for peace, we present God with a shopping list of all the world's trouble spots. The *Daily Telegraph* journalist Margot Lawrence rightly deplores this trend as 'bandwagon religion' which 'marks a headlines-and-heartstrings event like a football disaster or railway crash with emotional prayers' and 'ignores the hundred or so families bereaved every week through death on the roads'. She sees the obsession with topicality in prayer as 'wholly inimical to that steadiness, rationality and dignity which was one of the best aspects of English churchmanship' and asks 'When will religious leaders find the courage to ignore media values and lead us back to the timeless and enduring aspects of the faith?' A similar criticism has recently been made about Church of Scotland sermons by a former moderator, Thomas Torrance. In the Kirk's magazine *Life and Work* he asked, 'Is it any wonder that people cease attending the church on Sundays when what they hear from the pulpit is what they have already read in their daily and weekly newspapers or can hear at home through radio and television?'

It is, of course, important for worship to be anchored in the experience of this world and not to become etherealized and other-worldly. But it does often seem in contemporary services as though the pendulum has swung too far away from transcendence and towards topicality. Making liturgical language very specific and directed can also make it very threatening and exclusive. Some, of course, would argue that this is not a bad thing, and that the purpose of prayer and worship is not just to comfort and console but to challenge and force people to make a decision. But there is no doubt that the substitution for the timeless and generalized prose of the Prayer Book of much more explicit and direct language has made many people feel threatened by and excluded from church services.

In the Church of England more than a change in liturgical language has been involved in producing this feeling of exclusion. The whole pattern of Sunday worship has changed in a way that has left those on the fringes of the national church feeling more isolated than before. Thirty years ago the main services in most Anglican parish churches were mattins and evensong. Communion was perhaps celebrated early on a Sunday morning with only a small congregation present, and on major festivals and feast days. Now communion is the main service every week, often in the context of a family eucharist. Mattins and evensong have largely disappeared. This has had two unfortunate consequences.

The establishment of the family service as the main focal point of the week's worship has tended to encourage clergy to reduce things to a lowest common denominator and provide an easily digestible package which will appeal to children. The language is simplified, the sermon cut down to a short address, and bright and cheerful choruses substituted for longer and more difficult hymns. At the same time the concentration on communion has greatly sharpened the sense of commitment required by adults attending church, and has made it more difficult for those who are not sure enough of their faith to be confirmed.

It is ironic, indeed, that a service which was designed to bring everyone together and celebrate the oneness of the Christian family has in some ways had the reverse effect and encouraged a sense of exclusiveness. Family eucharists can often make the single, the bereaved, the childless, the victims of broken homes and the lonely feel even more isolated and unhappy. For them the enforced jollity and the accent on children and family life can be profoundly alienating, as the emphasis on the centrality of the eucharist can be for those who are not confirmed – a category which in the words of Margot Thompson, honorary secretary of the Prayer Book Society, 'includes many devout or inquiring souls who for one reason or another have not felt ready to undertake the full commitment of seeking confirmation'. Their dilemma was well brought out in an article in the *Guardian* by Geoffrey Taylor: 'It is undeniable that the adoption of the Alternative Service Book as the standard for Anglican services has forced a choice on people which they feel unable to accept. They are obliged to make either a total commitment or none at all. ... Under the former dispensation a person could go to morning or evening service, sing a few hymns, recollect well-known and invigorating sentences, and come away feeling spiritually refreshed. That, unfortunately, is no longer possible. Virtually every service is now a Holy Communion service. I guess there are many thousands of people who feel they would be making an act of betrayal (of themselves, that is) as well as "dissembling before the face of Almighty God", as the Prayer Book used to say, if they profaned this sacrament by pretending to be what they are not.'

Other churches are not facing this particular problem to the same extent. For Roman Catholics, of course, the Mass has always been central and all attenders have expected to participate in it, while in the Free Churches and the Church of Scotland communion services are still the exception rather than the norm and most Sunday morning worship conforms much more closely to the old-style Anglican mattins. There is, in fact, increasing pressure within the Church of Scotland for more frequent communion services. There is also a growing body of opinion within the Kirk that children should be admitted to communion before they are formally confirmed or admitted as members. Such a move, which is also receiving increasing support in the Church of England, would serve to make communion services less exclusive and demand less of a commitment from those taking part, but opponents fear that it would diminish the significance of the sacrament.

In several areas, indeed, all the major churches are under pressure from within their own ranks to be more rather than less demanding in the kind of commitment they ask their members to make. This is in large part a result of the rising influence of evangelicals, although it is perhaps also a consequence of numerical decline, which makes the main denominations less like broad national churches and more like gathered congregations. The idea of the church as a 'holy huddle', a community of the faithful or the elect, is gathering ground – and as a result it is becoming harder for the outsider and the honest doubter to feel comfortable in its midst.

The debate currently raging in both the Church of England and the Church of Scotland on the subject of baptism is perhaps the clearest indication of the spread of this new attitude. A growing number of clergy in both denominations are now questioning the wisdom of infant baptism, particularly when the parents involved are not members of the church. They point out that baptism is a solemn sacrament which involves serious promises and commitments which should not be entered into lightly. Some feel that a new service to give thanks for the birth of a baby should be instituted to satisfy the social demand for christening services, with baptism being left until a decision can be made by the person concerned. Others are prepared to accept the continuation of infant baptism but only if greater demands are made of parents.

At present the liberal majorities in both the national churches are resisting moves to restrict infant baptism on the grounds that they would close doors to people seeking to enter the church. They respond to the evangelicals' calls for clearer demands of parental commitment by quoting Jesus' words 'Suffer the little children to come unto me' and pointing out that baptism is a sacrament of God's grace, which should be freely available to all and not made conditional by the church. The 1991 General Assembly of the Church of Scotland voted to ease restrictions imposed in 1963 which effectively allowed baptism only to children whose parents were either members or adherents of the Church or willing to signify their intention of joining. Ministers may now in certain circumstances baptize children whose parents are not church members. The Assembly stopped short, however, of sanctioning baptism in all cases where parents simply professed the Christian faith. The Church of England's more liberal policy of effectively allowing baptism on demand was reaffirmed at the July 1991 session of the General Synod when an attempt by evangelicals to restrict it to children of active church-goers was defeated after a heated debate.

A similar debate is also taking place over marriage, with a growing number of clergy refusing to conduct church weddings for couples who are not church members and do not have any clear Christian faith. At issue here, of course, is how far the churches, and the national established churches in particular, are simply gathered communities of the faithful, and how far they exist for the whole community. There is no doubt that the former view is gaining ground but this is not to say that it is unchallenged. A substantial number of clergy, especially in the Church of England and the Church of Scotland, still see their pastoral responsibilities as extending to the whole population of the parish, unchurched as well as churched. Indeed, many regard the occasional offices of baptism, marriage and burial as providing unique pastoral and evangelistic opportunities. They view with some concern what they see as the more exclusivist and sectarian spirit which is gaining ground among some of their colleagues.

There is yet another kind of exclusivism which has come into church worship and ironically, like the family eucharist, it is actually the result of trying to involve people more. One of the most spectacular changes in the style of services across nearly all the denominations over the last generation has been the increase in lay involvement. In many ways this has been an excellent development. It has liberated worship from being in the hands solely of priests and ministers, giving many other people the chance to use their talents, and has introduced much more variety and interest into services. It has made an important theological statement about the value of the whole people of God. But it has also brought elements that can be embarrassing, distracting and inappropriate. The sign of peace exchanged in most Anglican communion services is one example of this. The British are not naturally a tactile people and many are uneasy about embracing or shaking hands in the middle of a church service. Charismatic practices, like lifting up hands during prayer and clapping to hymns and choruses, also cause a good deal of embarrassment when they are introduced to congregations who have been used to something more orderly and staid.

The tilting of the whole balance of worship in favour of much greater congregational participation has had another unfortunate effect. It has left much less opportunity for quiet reflection and meditation. In the olden days there may not have been very much pure silence in church – the churches have never been very good at being silent – but there were at least plenty of opportunities to sit quietly and reflect as the choir sung an anthem, the organist played a voluntary or the priest intoned a prayer which was so well known that it wasn't necessary to concentrate on the words. Now virtually every moment of every service is filled with responsive prayers, singing hymns or choruses, or some other activity. The one main exception to this trend among the major denominations has been the Church of Scotland, whose services remain strongly minister-dominated and involve very little lay participation beyond the singing of hymns. It is interesting that the Kirk's panel on worship, responding to calls for greater congregational participation in services, has issued a warning against simply adopting responsive prayers, easy choruses and joke-laden sermons as a way of achieving this.

I suspect that it is the trend towards greater lay participation and to lower artistic standards which lies at the root of the current turmoil in the world of church music. There is, perhaps, no area of church life over the last decade or so that has aroused quite such strong passions. An indication of how high feelings are running on the musicians' side can be found from a brief glance through the letters columns of their specialist journals. Once these were largely filled with learned debates about the relative merits of 'Stanford in B flat' and 'Howells in G', but now they contain fierce attacks on the clergy and church authorities. A recent correspondent to the *Organists' Review*, for example, suggested that the use of modern secular tunes in the New English Hymnal was tantamount to crucifying Christ all over again. Organists complain about the chatter that goes on during the voluntary before a service and the stampede to get out of church during the recessional after it. They also feel that these are encouraged by the clergy. A letter in *Church Music Quarterly* deplores the tendency of clergy 'to fidget during the singing as if they can't wait for their turn to come' and to count the congregation during the anthem. It concludes, 'Evensong minus clergy is an excellent idea. Perhaps in the not too distant future, clergy will be dispensed with altogether, and choir and congregation can combine to provide an inspirational service.'

Among the clergy there is equal unease about the attitudes of church musicians. Vicars complain that organists and choir members see themselves as performers, not worshippers, and switch off during the sermon, even to the extent of reading books or writing letters. One vicar wrote to his organist about 'the tyranny of excellence' and another prayed in church for the music to be less formal and accurate and more of a heart-felt response with rough and ready edges. A South London incumbent even took his complaint into the heart of enemy territory, writing in the *Organists' Review* that 'the church needs to rid itself of money-orientated organists, difficult to displace and with no regard for the total fellowship of the church. Small wonder that some churches give up the organ – finding that local volunteer talent on other instruments can be an equally acceptable lead and accompaniment for worship.'

Behind these boldly stated opinions lies a growing divergence of views about the role of music in church services. Organists tend to be traditionalists by temperament and perfectionists by training. They look to the pure and distinctive sound of highly trained English cathedral choirs as their model and inspiration. An increasing number of clergy, by contrast, have little or no training in or feeling for classical music and are by temperament modernists who believe that it is important to make church music much more accessible and less 'churchy', even if this means aiming for a less pure and perfect sound.

In the Church of England in particular the tradition of sung services has come under a triple assault in the last 20 years or so from the widespread abandonment of mattins and evensong in favour of informal family services, the introduction of the Alternative Service Book with its modern language prayers which have proved difficult to set to music, and the rising influence of the evangelical and charismatic movements with their easy singalong hymns and catchy choruses. Increasingly churches have given up anthems, chanted psalms, Merbecke's much-loved setting of the 1662 communion service and complex choral settings of the Magnificat and Nunc Dimittis, in favour of *Mission Praise* choruses, modern versions of the psalms and easy congregational settings of the ASB communion services. As a result organists and choirs feel themselves progressively devalued and redundant.

One of the most outspoken critics of these developments has been Simon Preston, who resigned in 1987 from his position as organist at Westminster Abbey because he felt he could no longer work there without compromising his standards as a professional musician. 'There are now two kinds of musician in Britain,' he told me in an interview shortly afterwards, 'ordinary musicians who aim for the highest standards they can, and church musicians who are forced to cut corners and actually aim for the second-rate. The clergy can't come to terms with the fact that musicians are very dedicated people. They see choirs as just being there to encourage and sing along with the congregation and that is something I just can't accept.'

This raises the difficult question of how far music in church should be a performance and how far an act of worship. Simon Preston sees no necessary conflict between the two. He says that when people go to a church like Westminster Abbey they expect to hear beautiful music sung superbly and professionally by a highly trained choir and that this is worshipful, offering the highest standards of performance to God rather than adopting a populist approach and compromising musical standards. But many clergy would argue that this is to turn an act of worship into a concert performance, and that high artistic standards should not be the governing criteria when it comes to judging what is worshipful. The conflict is compounded by the fact that the traditional role of churches, especially the Church of England, as major patrons and employers of musicians is declining, largely for economic reasons. One of the biggest complaints of church musicians today has nothing to do with declining musical standards but rather with their terms and conditions of service. As a distinguished organist told me, these have been progressively eroded over the last two or three decades: 'In the old days the parish would provide a house and the organist would probably have a substantial teaching practice. Now churches are more likely to advertise for someone who can play the guitar and who is regarded as being on the same level as the verger and other lay helpers.' There is also concern at the fact that organists have no security of tenure. In the graphic words of Gavin Barrett, editor of the *Organists' Review*: 'A vicar who gets out of bed one morning and decides that he wants to rock around the font instead of listening to Palestrina can fire his organist on the spot.'

Money is also a major bone of contention. The annual stipend for an organist in a busy urban parish church is still often only around £1,000 a year, with perhaps £10 or so for turning out to play at a wedding or funeral. Many organists consider this grossly inadequate pay for giving up one evening a week for choir practice and much of Sunday for services, particularly when they are increasingly unhappy about what they are being asked to do. To quote Gavin Barrett again, 'The tradition in this country is that musicians have given their service to the church out of love rather than for money. That is fine so long as they are getting some job satisfaction. But if they have no independent liturgical role and all they are doing is playing the odd hymn and voluntaries at either end of the service that no one bothers to listen to, it is hardly surprising that fewer and fewer accomplished young musicians want anything to do with the Church.' In other countries, both the status and the remuneration of church musicians is much higher. In Scandinavia and western Germany most organists in the Lutheran Church are paid by the state and earn up to £25,000 a year, with further opportunities to supplement their earnings through teaching. There is a considerable demand in Norway for trained British organists, and a steady trickle are taking up posts there. Many church musicians here also cast longing eyes across the Atlantic. Most American churches employ full-time ministers of music who have sole charge of this side of worship and earn salaries two or three times as high as English cathedral organists.

On the other side, however, it is often pointed out by clergy that organists are only one of a number of dedicated and talented volunteer helpers who give their services to the church, and that it seems unfair they should be singled out for payment while others get nothing. There is also a feeling that organs and choirs may have had their day, outside cathedrals and certain very large parish churches. There is a serious dearth of organists in many areas and young people, including musical young people, do not seem to have the enthusiasm and affection for the instrument of their elders. It is perhaps worth remembering that organs have only had a comparatively brief reign as the main instrumental accompaniment to hymns and psalms. When they were introduced into churches 150 or so years ago in the aftermath of the Oxford Movement they were often resisted as an unwelcome and un-British innovation. The instrumental praise bands that are now replacing organs in many churches are really taking us back to a longer and older tradition of church music-making in Britain, epitomized by the groups of string and woodwind players who used to stand in the west galleries of churches, and who feature so prominently in the novels of Thomas Hardy.

Old-style pipe organs are not going to disappear from our churches. But they are going to get fewer – and at a cost of up to £500,000 each this is hardly surprising. When their Victorian organ finally wears out, many congregations are now opting for an electronic console which for less than £20,000 can reproduce all the sounds and stops of a cathedral organ. The purists shudder but it is hard for most people to tell the difference. The trend towards other kinds of accompaniment for psalms, hymns and songs is likely to increase. A growing number of churches now have instrumental ensembles which bring a welcome variety of sounds and musical styles into worship and often involve young people. Some of the bigger evangelical churches have full-scale orchestras, although few can emulate the All Souls Orchestra under Noel Treddinick which has many professional players. More and more churches are now tending to appoint directors of music, with a wider and perhaps less élitist brief than organists. The accent is on encouraging singing and music-making among the whole congregation and not just concentrating on a small and highly trained choir. Smaller congregations are relying increasingly on a piano or a guitar to lead the singing. There is even something of a move back to unaccompanied singing – and this is surely preferable to what I found in one small rural church in Scotland, where for each hymn the minister slotted in a pre-recorded cassette to which the congregation could sing along if they wished.

It is, of course, not just the new instruments being used in church that are causing concern to many musicians, but also what is being played on them. A letter to *Life and Work* signed by 22 Church of Scotland organists in 1987 complained of 'doggerel verse, trivial tunes, inept harmonisation and psalms and canticles set to music which may be apt for places of entertainment but not apt for the sanctuary.' It cited as a particularly ghastly example of this a hymn for Palm Sunday set to the tune of 'What shall we do with the

drunken sailor?' The introduction into the services of the main
denominations of simple repetitive choruses of a kind previously
confined largely to Sunday Schools and mission halls has also
raised many hackles. A Surrey organist wrote to the Bishop of
Guildford complaining that one vicar had demanded the Moody
and Sankey chorus, 'I am H-A-P-P-Y' as a fitting musical contribution to a service, and asked 'Are the artistic standards of Radio
One and the TV commercial appropriate for the House of God?'

Here, of course, we are back to the arguments over the language
of modern versions of the Bible and prayer books and onto the
very difficult ground of taste. I have to confess a personal bias here.
I have a particular affection for the great corpus of hymns built up
over the last 300 or more years and widely reckoned to be the
outstanding contribution of the English-speaking world to the
universal Christian Church. I am also fearful that it could be lost
to future generations. With the demise of school assemblies, phrases
such as 'abide with me', 'fight the good fight' and 'all things bright
and beautiful' may disappear from the national folk consciousness
in which they have been embedded for so long. Those schools
which do still maintain acts of worship and communal singing
increasingly use modern songs and choruses. A more direct assault
comes from those who seek to alter the words of hymns to remove
what they regard as archaic or sexist language. This can be done
with great sensitivity as, for example, in the new Baptist Hymn
Book published in 1991, but it can also lead to great impov-
erishment. One recent hymn book has reduced the dignity of 'The
day thou gavest, Lord, is ended, the darkness falls at thy behest'
to the banal 'The day you gave us, Lord, is ended, the sun is sinking
in the west'. The drive to purge hymns of any language that could
possibly be construed as sexist has also robbed some classic texts
of their power and dignity. The second verse of the fine pilgrim
hymn I have used as the motif for this book, 'Through the night
of doubt and sorrow', loses much of its force when the phrase
'brother clasps the hand of brother' is rendered 'person clasps the
hands of person'.

The treasury of British hymnody contains verses by such spiritual
and literary giants as Bunyan, Milton and Tennyson and melodies
by Handel, Sullivan and Vaughan Williams. It is not just a reposi-
tory of the cosy and the comfortably bland. There was much soul-
searching and wrestling with doubt among the great hymn-writers
of the past, which gives their work a profundity and depth not

always found among their successors today. At a time of rapid
cultural change and creeping materialism we surely need the order,
the harmony and the spirituality of hymns that have been passed
down from generation to generation in what has been as much an
oral as a literary tradition. In the great church of the unchurched
that so many now inhabit, I suspect that lines from vaguely familiar
hymns mean much more than Bible passages. It would be sad if
this last lingering part of the folk religion that still keeps Christianity deeply embedded in our national culture were to disappear.

But this is not to say that there is no place for modern hymns
and songs in church. It is true that both the words and the music
of some are shallow, trite and repetitive. They can be oversentimental and over-subjective – but then, so were many Victorian
hymns. On the other hand there is a host of modern hymns which
are deep and challenging in their theological message and which
are supported by good, memorable tunes. Several of them have
already established themselves as being of enduring value and will
surely continue to be sung in a hundred years' time – one thinks
of Sydney Carter's 'Lord of the Dance' and 'One more step along
the world I go', Timothy Dudley Smith's 'Tell out my soul, the
greatness of the Lord' and some of the work of Brian Wren and
Patrick Appleford. In Scotland John Bell's strongly incarnational
songs like 'Will you come and follow me', 'A touching place' and
'Come with me, come wander' continue the tradition of setting
religious lyrics to traditional folk tunes. The worship of many
churches in Britain today is being considerably enlivened by music
from other countries like the haunting chants from Taizé and
vigorous marching songs from Africa. Much that comes from
across the Atlantic is trite and commercial but there are some fine
modern American worship songs like Leonard Smith's 'Our God
reigns' and Sebastian Temple's setting of the great prayer traditionally attributed to St Francis, 'Make me a channel of your
peace'. Here at home the house church movement has produced in
Graham Kendrick arguably the most talented hymn writer and
composer of today. His songs like 'Shine, Jesus, shine', 'Meekness and majesty' and 'Make way, make way for Christ the King'
have rightly been taken up throughout the visible and invisible
churches as powerful contemporary expressions of the Christian
message.

The so-called hymn explosion that began in the 1960s shows no
sign of abating. The 1990s are likely to see a further flood of new

song books and worship material. Much of it will be ephemeral
and will soon be forgotten – but that was also the fate of hundreds
of the hymns written by Charles Wesley. There will be some gems
which will stand alongside the best hymns of the past. The fact is,
of course, that there is no reason at all why in music as in other
aspects of the life of the church the new cannot coexist happily
with the old. This was seen at George Carey's enthronement as
Archbishop of Canterbury in April 1991 which, despite dark fore-
bodings and prophecies of impending disaster from the traditionalists, successfully combined traditional hymns and anthems
with contemporary choral settings and modern songs like 'Sing of
the Lord's Goodness' and 'We are marching in the Light of God'.
What is sad about the debate over church music is that it has
become so polarized, and that the protagonists on either side seem
to see no half-way house between Cathedral Choral Evensong and
a non-stop sequence of clap-happy choruses. Christian worship is
a constantly evolving tradition which should continue to make use
of the best of the past while seeking new contemporary ways of
expression.

There is certainly an urgent need for better musical training on
the part of the clergy and others who lead worship. At present they
are given virtually none. A recent survey by the Church of Scotland
found that 78 per cent of ministers regarded the training they had
received in music and worship at theological college as totally
inadequate. The situation in other churches is little better. Ordinands come out of their training filled with sociology and psy-
chology but knowing virtually nothing of hymnody or psalmody.
The sad result is that all too often very little thought is given to
the choice of music for services and a note of the hymns for the
day is scribbled down at the last minute and left on the organist's
stool. At the same time organists and church musicians need to be
given more instruction on current theological and liturgical trends
so that they can appreciate the thinking that lies behind a service
and find appropriate musical expression for it. Music can be one
of the most direct pathways to heaven, perhaps more powerful
even than words, and it deserves very much more serious attention,
and much more collaboration, than it is receiving from clergy and
church musicians at the moment.

Maintaining high standards of church music is, of course, an
expensive business. It has been calculated that the average annual
cost of worship in each of the 42 Anglican cathedrals is £250,000,

with the choir being by far the biggest item of expenditure. Many of the choir schools which train and supply the boys who give the Anglican choral tradition its distinctive sound are in financial difficulties, finding it harder to recruit suitable pupils and worried about loss of charitable status in the event of the election of a government hostile to independent education. Commercial sponsorship is increasingly sought as a way of meeting some of the cost of cathedral music. Bristol Cathedral Choir has signed an agreement with a local nuclear power company which provides it with £25,000 a year over a ten-year period. In return the company has its logo featured on song books, records and cathedral literature. Ely Cathedral is looking for a similar arrangement, and one idea that has been floated is for the sponsor's name to appear on the medallions worn by choristers.

It is not just choirs that are looking for sponsors. Faced with soaring maintenance and repair bills, cathedrals are seeking financial aid wherever they can find it. As the result of a sponsorship deal, the windows in the Lady Chapel at Ely bear the logos of such companies as TSB, Tesco and Lloyds Bank, prompting the observation from one newspaper columnist that the cathedral has become the site of 'the only advertising hoardings in Britain which are destined to last, perhaps, 500 years'.

Purists may well squirm at the thought of the forces of Mammon invading the temples of God in so blatant a way. But as Stanley Kiaer, director of the Christian Association of Business Executives, has pointed out, 'Powerful patrons in the Middle Ages and before built cathedrals. It is very appropriate that their equivalents should keep them going today.' The fact is that unless they do receive substantial financial aid from either private or public sources over the next decade, many of Britain's finest cathedrals and parish churches are in very serious danger of falling into decay. Winchester Cathedral is currently appealing for £7 million and Salisbury for £6.5 million for urgent structural repairs. Between them, the 21 oldest and biggest Anglican cathedrals are expected to swallow up more than £70 million in essential repairs to their fabric during the 1990s. That is quite apart from normal running costs, averaging around £600,000 a year for each cathedral. The other 21 smaller and more modern cathedrals will require further expenditure totalling around £40 million. There is no way that the Church itself can meet anything like that amount from its own resources.

The congregations of historic parish churches across the country are also faced with heavy bills for roof repairs, new electrical wiring and dry rot treatment. A considerable amount of time and effort on the part of both clergy and laity is now taken up with problems over the fabric of their churches, a situation prevalent in both urban and rural areas. More than 60 per cent of the urban clergy interviewed for the Church of England's *Faith in the City* report said they faced problems with their buildings, and more than half reported serious problems. A Commission on Rural Church Buildings chaired by the Bishop of Norwich has recently urged parochial church councils to keep country churches open wherever possible, and called for more state aid to help preserve the great legacy of medieval church buildings in the English countryside. One of Robert Runcie's last actions as Archbishop of Canterbury was to write to Mrs Thatcher asking for substantial Government help to ensure the preservation of historic church buildings and particularly to safeguard the future of the great English cathedrals.

The Government does recognize that historic church buildings are an important part of the nation's architectural heritage, and contributes towards their maintenance and repair. The Department of the Environment initiated a scheme in 1977 for grant-aiding churches carrying out repairs to their fabric. It is now administered by English Heritage, which disburses grants totalling nearly £10 million a year to churches, the great majority of which are Anglican parish churches. The 1990 White Paper on the Environment for the first time indicated agreement to the principle of state aid for cathedrals, followed by an £11.5 million Government grant to English Heritage to distribute to the 42 Anglican and 19 Roman Catholic cathedrals in England over the next three years. This sum, however, will meet only a tenth of the cost of essential repairs required over this period, and is small compared with what is given by governments in other European countries. In France and Germany cathedrals are owned and maintained by the state, while the Italian Government has an agreement with the Vatican to meet 60–70 per cent of cathedral maintenance costs.

Sadly, not just old buildings are a drain on the resources of the main denominations. Many comparatively modern church buildings are proving equally or even more expensive to maintain. A recent feature in the *Church Times* entitled 'The churches that are too old at 50 – or even 30' pointed to the alarming number of churches built in the last 50 years which are now in a worse state of decay than those which have stood for centuries. Often the problems are connected with flat roofs, poor-quality construction or materials that have proved to have a very short life. Holy Cross Church in Inns Cross, Bristol, is being pulled down after just 30 years because pieces of concrete are falling from the tower and water is cascading down through the porch. St Oswald's Church in Netherton, built in 1961, lasted just 20 years before it had to be demolished because cement had eroded the steel girders.

It is hardly surprising that a growing number of clergy in the traditional visible church are casting an envious and approving eye at those who lead the house groups and fellowships that make up the new invisible church. They are almost entirely free of worries about fabric and repairs. Where house churches become too big to meet in people's homes, they find cheap and simple accommodation by renting or buying a hall. If and when they do decide to build their own meeting place, it is usually a relatively simple affair, involving a minimum of capital outlay and a minimum ongoing commitment to repairs. Unencumbered by ancient buildings and all the problems they bring, the invisible churches are able to get on with the business of worship and evangelism. Many in the visible churches, by contrast, feel that their role as custodians of ancient monuments has become so burdensome as virtually to squeeze out other more spiritual priorities. Should the church really devote so much of its energy and resources to old buildings?

Not surprisingly, this question is asked most frequently in the Church of England, which has over 12,000 listed buildings in its care. When the average congregation huddles in a small corner of a vast medieval or Victorian church, feeling damp and cold, and when 80 per cent of Anglican churches now have house groups, the thought of vacating church buildings and following the example of the new churches, with worship taking place in people's homes, has certain obvious attractions. Could not the redundant church buildings be either sold or used for some socially desirable purpose like flats for the elderly or community centres, those of significant architectural or historic interest being handed over to English Heritage to be looked after like other national monuments? Such a step might serve both to ease the Church's financial worries and also make a powerful theological statement about the relative unimportance of material things. The argument was powerfully put by a correspondent to the *Guardian* in October 1990 who advocated that the Church of England allow its cathedrals to fall into ruins which would offer the opportunity for 'nostalgic indulgence'. He went on: 'These religious dinosaurs have more than outlived their purpose. As awe inspiring symbols of the arbitrary power of the medieval church, they certainly did their job. That job is now over and has been for about 300 years. The current task of all religions should surely be the amelioration of the suffering of people which is so apparent in the world today. I cannot think of any compelling argument which places the maintenance of these monoliths over the maintenance of human lives.'

The Church of Scotland faces a similar dilemma, though on a smaller scale. It owns virtually all the ancient Scottish cathedrals, which are run as ordinary parish churches although the parts not used for worship are generally cared for by Scottish Heritage. Because of the duplication of churches in many Scottish towns and cities resulting from previous ecclesiastical splits, since healed, the Church of Scotland is closing down buildings at a very much faster rate than the Church of England. Indeed, the Royal Fine Art Commission in Scotland calculates that it will have disposed of 400 of its existing 1,600 churches by the end of this decade, which works out at an average of 40 a year or one church being closed every nine days. Already many striking church buildings have found alternative uses. A former parish church in Callander is now the Rob Roy Visitor Centre, churches in Dundee and Glasgow have been turned into nightclubs and dance studios and one in Elgin has even been transformed into a pub – named, appropriately enough, 'High Spirits'.

Many people regard the abandonment of unneeded church buildings as an act of sacrilege. They see them as 'sermons in stones' which testify through their age, their beauty and their very existence to a heritage of Christian worship, and make a silent but eloquent witness to things eternal. A memorandum from the Friends of Friendless Churches asserts that 'an ancient and beautiful church fulfils its primary function merely by existing ... It is only in modern times that the belief has arisen that a church has to be filled regularly with worshippers to justify its existence.' This school of thought would have the church care lovingly, not just for those buildings where there is still a worshipping congregation, however small, but also for those which are clearly redundant and surplus to requirements. Rather than being demolished, sold off or converted to alternative use, they should be preserved so that they still speak of the faith and may become places of pilgrimage and spiritual refreshment. This is the philosophy behind the Redundant

Churches Fund, which receives 40 per cent of its funding from church sources and 60 per cent from the state and has spent more than £12 million in the last 20 years on caring for English churches no longer required for regular worship. Anthony Barnes, the director of the fund, has even been tempted to describe the 270 redundant churches in its care as 'the leading edge of the new Anglicanism – quiet places in a noisy world, often remote and blessedly free from guitar twanging and corybantic ecstasies'.

If the church is going to keep its old buildings open then one obvious way to raise some of the money necessary for their upkeep is to charge an entrance fee to the many people who come to them not as worshippers but as tourists. Until the middle of the nineteenth century most Anglican cathedrals did, in fact, charge for admission – visitors to St Paul's, for example, were charged twopence a head, except at times of divine service. In the summer of 1991 St Paul's reintroduced an experimental charge of £2 for visitors, while allowing free access to a side chapel for private prayer. Ely Cathedral also levies an admission charge, although entrance is free on Sundays and at times of services. There has been considerable controversy over the introduction of these charges, but it seems very likely that other cathedrals will soon be following suit. At present most do not even recoup from donations the extra charges they incur in keeping open and providing facilities for visitors, let alone make anything to help towards running costs and repairs. At Norwich it has been calculated that a 20-minute visit costs the cathedral 20 pence, yet the 600,000 people who visit it every year put an average of only 11 pence each into the collection box. Canterbury Cathedral gets even less – just 9 pence per visitor. Overall, Britain's cathedrals receive just £5 million annually from the voluntary donations of visitors, a tiny fraction of their running costs. For some years most have tried to shame tourists into giving more by putting up large notices above collecting boxes detailing their running costs. But this strategy has not worked – St Paul's suggested visitors give £1 but received donations averaging only 15 pence per head.

At first sight there seems something wrong with charging people to enter the house of God. It seems to smack of bringing money-changers into the temple. But to some extent churches have always been involved in commercial and money-making activities – and charging people to admire carvings and stained-glass windows is surely a good deal less reprehensible than selling them indulgences and pardons. We are used to stalls in the naves of our major cathedrals and churches selling booklets, postcards, slides and souvenir pencils and mugs. Is it any worse to charge for admission and to develop other ways of raising money? This is an issue the Church of England in particular is going to have to grapple with increasingly over the next few years, and the signs are that it is going to cause a lot of pain and distress. Already there have been serious tensions at three cathedrals over how far money-making operations should go and who should have responsibility for them. At Lincoln, a fund-raising trip to Australia based around the cathedral's copy of Magna Carta ended up making a substantial loss and led to an acrimonious and much-publicized row between the Dean and the Chapter. The Cathedral's marketing director was subsequently sacked for being too commercially orientated, although she pointed out that the building had originally been financed by an endless round of masses for the souls of the dead. The Chapter of St Paul's Cathedral, facing a £400,000 deficit and needing to find over £4 million for urgent repairs, dismissed its chief executive, Dr Malcolm Postgate, because of fears that he wanted to turn the cathedral into a shopping arcade or theme park. In fact, he claimed that his aim was simply to make the cathedral 'commercially viable' and to transform St Paul's into an institution that would make enough profit to be able to give money to charity. More recently, the Bishop of Salisbury has expressed concern about the increasing use of the thirteenth-century cathedral at the heart of his diocese as a place of entertainment and profit and warned the Dean and Chapter against over-commercialization. In a report following a 'visitation' of the cathedral he complained that financial considerations seemed to have taken over to such an extent that the overwhelming impact on the visitor was of appeals for money. He was also highly critical of the use of the cathedral nave as a venue for the BBC programme, *The Antiques Roadshow*.

The debate about how far commercial considerations should govern the running of Britain's cathedrals and major churches is likely to continue over the coming years. One point that has clearly emerged from the unhappy experiences at Lincoln and St Paul's is the need to overhaul the ancient structures by which the affairs of cathedrals are administered. There is something very British, very touching and very amateurish in leaving major decisions about running buildings which are among the country's top tourist attractions, often requiring millions of pounds spent on them, to a small

group of clergymen who know little of architecture, finance or the
ways of the world. A working party chaired by the Dean of Bristol
has recommended that lay administrators and accountants should
be appointed to cathedral governing bodies to advise on decisions
which are not taken solely by the Dean and Chapter. Traditionalists
may deplore this as yet another example of market forces prevailing
over more spiritual values, but if the alternative is to see Britain's
cathedrals sink further into debt and fall into disrepair, then
perhaps it is time the clerical amateurs called it a day.

There is a danger of the debate about what should be done with
cathedrals and churches becoming polarized between those who
stress the importance of tourism and those who cling to the centrality of worship. There is no necessary conflict between these two
objectives – indeed, they are to a large extent complementary.
There is a very fine dividing line between the tourist and the pilgrim.
In some ways today's package tourists are the heirs of the pilgrims
who roamed medieval Christendom visiting sacred shrines and
holy relics. If someone comes to a cathedral or church as a sightseer
and ends up listening to the organist playing, staying for part of a
service, pondering on the beauty of a stained-glass window or
simply moved by the atmosphere of stillness and calm, who is to
say that he has not become a worshipper? A recent survey suggests
that more than two-thirds of the population make at least one visit
to a church in the course of a year other than to attend a service.
Of these, more than half said they went out of 'general interest'
while a third said that they had a spiritual motive for their visit.
The extent to which those visiting a church for general interest can
become in some sense worshippers is recognized by a book on
redundant churches entitled *Day Trip or Pilgrimage?* and a manual
for churches called *Helping the Stones to Speak*.

In recognizing and developing the tourist potential of cathedrals
and churches we may well also be helping to make them places of
pilgrimage. This is why efforts on the part of churches to encourage
tourism are to be applauded. In Scotland an annual competition
is now held to find the most welcoming church in the country. The
judges are charged to look not just at the welcome given to those
attending services but also at how far tourists are catered for and
how well the church explains to casual visitors its history and
purpose. In England the Diocese of Lincoln has recently appointed
a Tourism Development Officer. At a time when tourism is the
fastest-growing industry in Britain and when 'heritage' has become

a buzz-word there is no doubt that those churches which have a large number of ancient buildings have a great opportunity not just to attract visitors and raise funds but also to evangelize and turn tourists into pilgrims. In a letter to *The Times* in October 1990 Peter Brett, one of the residentiary canons at Canterbury Cathedral, wrote that 'a building imbued with the worship of centuries, well preserved, lovingly used, bearing the marks of active religious life and presented with an eye to the appraisal of the casual visitor, is one of the most effective tools of mission that the Church has to hand. Witness many an example of an English country church which in evoking respect for its condition leads many to pause to reflect on what it stands for. The scale of opportunity for mission on the part of a well maintained and well ordered cathedral is immense. Our cathedrals are major visitor attractions and of the millions who pass through them each year there are thousands for whom they represent the state of the Christian faith.'

Humbler parish churches can also speak eloquently to those who visit them of a heritage of faith and prayer. Sadly, however, it is becoming increasingly dangerous to keep them permanently open because of rising levels of vandalism and theft. The Ecclesiastical Insurance Group estimates that an attack on a parish church in England takes place every four hours, and that nearly half Britain's 16,000 Anglican churches suffer arson, vandalism or theft during the course of a year. While valuable items like crosses and candlesticks can be locked up during the week safely out of harm's way, thieves are increasingly wrenching collecting boxes from walls and one gang even used a fork-lift truck to remove a set of 120-year-old stained-glass windows from a North London church. The overwhelming instinct of clergy and laity in the Church of England is to keep their church buildings open wherever possible (many Scottish kirks by contrast remain firmly locked up from Monday to Saturday) but this is becoming increasingly difficult, especially in urban areas.

Perhaps one way of helping to beat crime and vandalism, and also to enhance the role and profile of the church in the community, is to use church buildings for non-worship activities during the week. Many exciting schemes have been put into operation in recent years. In the Bride Valley in West Dorset churches are being used as resource centres to explain the community to the many people who have come to live in the area in retirement. Increasingly both urban and rural churches are adapting their buildings to provide space for local activities. Meadowside St Paul's Church in the centre of Dundee has built a new hall complex for the community and established a bookshop and café on the main street. A link block between the church and the halls includes a resource centre for Sunday Schools and shower facilities which are used during the week by lunchtime keep-fit enthusiasts from the local business community. At Flax Bourton in the Diocese of Bath and Wells parishioners solved the problem of dry rot in the church and lack of a community building in the village by creating an open space in the nave with movable seating for use throughout the week. The congregation of Christ Church, Woking, took advantage of the creation of a shopping centre next door to sell off the parish hall and finance the opening up of the interior of their church, creating space for liturgical dance and drama. At the entrance, linked to the shopping centre by a covered walkway, they have established a bookshop and a coffee shop which is used mostly by retired people during the day and functions as a drop-in centre for young people in the evenings. A church which used to be cold, dark and locked for most of the week is now light, open and in use by local people every day.

Of course, not everyone is happy about the modern fashion for opening up church interiors to encourage more flexible and informal use. Trendy clergy are castigated for turning fine old medieval sanctuaries into open-plan areas and ripping out ancient screens and pews in favour of rows of easily stackable tubular seats. It is true that some very insensitive things have been done, like the replacement of stone pillars by steel posts in the nave of one medieval church to create more room. Somehow, a balance has to be struck between meeting contemporary needs and preserving the art and craftsmanship of the past. The church is not a museum. It is concerned with proclaiming the living word of God in terms which will be understandable to each generation. Christians need to avoid sentimental nostalgia and clinging to familiar things from the past simply because they are old and venerable. There are more old church buildings around than are needed for worship today, and if some of them can be diverted to socially useful purposes then it is surely right that they should be. Many imaginative uses are being found for redundant churches. In one diocese alone (Oxford) they have been turned into houses and flats, school buildings, community centres, a photographic studio, a farrier's forge, a jewellery workshop, and places of worship for Polish Roman Catholics and Elim Pentecostalists.

But often the most historic and architecturally important churches cannot find alternative uses. There is a limit to the number for which groups like the Redundant Churches Fund, the Friends of Friendless Churches or indeed public bodies like English Heritage can shoulder responsibility. The churches, and the Church of England in particular, will remain as custodians of a very large number of buildings of great antiquity and beauty, and have a responsibility to look after and preserve these buildings which goes beyond their role as places of worship. It is right that this task of conserving what is an important part of the nation's heritage should be supported out of public funds. Many who are not church members deeply value the existence of ancient church buildings throughout the land. There may be times when clergy and those responsible for church finance find it irksome to be paying for the upkeep of expensive and awkward old properties which attract few worshippers. Perhaps they should ponder on St Paul's words about holding on to whatever is pure, whatever is lovely and whatever is gracious. The church would do no service to the cause of Christianity by divesting itself of all its old buildings on the grounds that they get in the way of its real mission.

The fact is that church buildings are icons, windows on eternity through which we may gaze and glimpse something of the glory and splendour of the Christian mystery. This is true not just of magnificent medieval cathedrals but also of the Victorian and Edwardian churches which stand in many run-down parts of our cities and which, however plain they are in appearance, are often the oldest and noblest buildings in the locality. To try to set the claims of the poor and the needy or the demand for evangelism against the desire to repair a crumbling church, replace a worn-out organ or conserve a stained-glass window is to raise false and forced distinctions in the life and witness of the Christian community. Music, liturgy, art and buildings can be agents of evangelism just as much as sermons, Bible groups or mission rallies. Worship can be as relevant to contemporary needs and as beneficial to the broken, the disadvantaged and the marginalized as political action or economic aid. It can be deeply therapeutic, helping to heal troubled minds and wounded spirits, and profoundly uplifting, giving people a sense of their infinite worth. In this decade of evangelism, the churches would do well to reflect on the centrality of worship in Christian life and to celebrate the rich variety of ways both old and new in which it is being expressed in Britain today.

In many ways, indeed, the different styles of worship practised in the visible and invisible churches are complementary. There is room for both the informal, more charismatic approach of the house churches and evangelical fellowships and for the more traditional and formal services favoured by the older denominations. It would be sad if the visible church responded to the decline in its numbers by jettisoning its distinctive traditions and throwing away the incomparable riches that it possesses in terms of buildings, music and liturgical language. The invisible church is very much better placed to provide for those who want informal and self-consciously contemporary worship. There are still a very large number of people, by no means confined to the ranks of the elderly or to regular church-goers, who find God rather through participation in services of a more traditional nature and through the contemplation of architectural beauty and great music.

There is a very real problem about the continued funding of those churches which maintain ancient buildings and choirs and organists of professional standard. In several other European countries, notably Germany and Scandinavia, the main churches are supported by the state with religious taxes being levied on the majority of inhabitants. Clergy and organists are effectively salaried public officials and the church is relieved of the cost of preserving its ancient buildings. In the United States, by contrast, where there is no direct public funding for religion, churches are generously supported by their members, who provide enough money to maintain professional musicians and to erect fine new buildings of a high architectural standard.

The main British churches lack either of these financial props and it is unlikely that they will enjoy them in the foreseeable future. They are already having to cut back their activities – the diocese of Chelmsford is talking about the need to axe twenty vicars to balance its budget. There is going to be an increasing temptation for churches to divest themselves of expensive old buildings and economise on 'optional extras' like organs and choirs unless substantial public and private help is forthcoming to preserve what is after all as much a national cultural heritage as a specifically Christian concern.

– 5 –

Political and social involvement

One the conflict, one the peril,
One the march in God begun

The most common reason for the churches to hit the headlines in the British press over the last 10 years has not been their declining numbers, radical theology or abandonment of traditional forms of worship, but rather the frequency and vehemence of their attacks on the Government. There was a time in the mid-1980s, indeed, when if they had not been in the throes of abandoning the old 'hot metal' technology for the new, popular papers would have been well advised to keep the headline 'Bishops bash Thatcher' permanently in type, so frequently was it in use over stories of the latest episcopal assault on the Prime Minister's perceived creed of free market economics and unbridled individualism. Nor was the attack all one way. Tory MPs and ideologues retaliated with trenchant criticisms of church leaders for interfering in politics and neglecting their proper task of saving souls and raising the nation's falling moral standards.

The debate as to how far Christians should stick to spiritual matters and how far they should actively involve themselves in social, economic and political questions is, of course, a long-standing one. It reflects two very different interpretations of the New Testament. Broadly speaking the division is between those who espouse the 'kingdom theology' of the Gospels and those who stress rather the more conservative and quietist theology of the Pauline epistles. The former see Jesus as a social and political radical with a definite bias towards the poor and oppressed and a strong commitment to peace, justice and economic equality. They feel that the church is most clearly responding to his call when it engages in active campaigning in these areas, speaks out against war, oppression and inequality of all kinds and so helps to hasten the coming of God's kingdom on earth. The latter tend rather to feel that these matters are better left in God's hands and that the church should concentrate on spiritual priorities, preaching individual repentance and redemption and personal morality, and not get involved in the murky reaches of politics.

There are a number of reasons why this debate has become more public and more polarized in the last decade or so. To a considerable extent it reflects the more general polarization in politics resulting from the breakdown of the post-war consensus characterized as Butskellism and based on the Welfare State and the mixed economy. In many ways that consensus was built on Christian principles and the churches were involved in shaping some of its key institutions – Archbishop William Temple, for example, played a significant role in the creation of the Welfare State. It is hardly surprising, therefore, to find the churches at the forefront of opposition to what they perceive to be the dismantling of those institutions, and of the whole consensus of values that underpinned them, under the aegis of a government motivated by a very different ideology based on competitive individualism and the rule of the market. The personalities of the main protagonists involved have also played a part in heightening the conflict between church and state. More clearly than any other twentieth-century Prime Minister, Margaret Thatcher subscribed to the second of the two views of Christianity outlined in the last paragraph, and believed that the business of the church was to preach personal morality, not to involve itself in more general social and economic issues. She also believed with an almost religious conviction in the rightness of what she was doing. It was ironic that throughout the 1980s she faced a bench of bishops who represented the acme of liberalism in the Church of England, and whose thinking was still very much rooted in 1960s notions of corporatist social democracy of a kind that most of the rest of the establishment had abandoned.

The lack of any effective political opposition to the Conservatives also helped to thrust the churches into the limelight. It is hardly too much to claim that in many ways the churches, and the Church of England in particular, provided the most consistent and spirited opposition to the Tory governments of the 1980s. The experience of that decade scotched once and for all the old notion that the Church of England is just the Tory party at prayer. It is worth sketching briefly the successive clashes that took place between

Mrs Thatcher's administrations and the Church of England under Robert Runcie's leadership, before we go on to consider how far the advent of John Major and George Carey has changed the relations between church and government.

The churches first crossed swords with Mrs Thatcher's Government over the British Nationality Bill in 1981. This did not represent any departure: since the early 1960s every piece of legislation restricting immigration into Britain has been criticized by the churches on the grounds of racial discrimination. Opposition to the 1981 Act was particularly strong because of its introduction of the concept of patriality, which in effect gave access to whites from the Commonwealth but denied it to blacks. The deep unease felt across all the major denominations was summed up by Robert Runcie, who denounced the bill in a succession of powerful speeches in the House of Lords and, in the words of his biographer, 'came near to acting as leader of the opposition'. This was a title he found himself given by the media more and more as the decade wore on. In 1982 his low-key sermon in the thanksgiving service after the Falklands War reportedly annoyed the Prime Minister, and was denounced by several Conservative MPs for being insufficiently patriotic and triumphalist. The following year a report by the General Synod's working group on nuclear warfare entitled *The Church and the Bomb*, which was unequivocally unilateralist in tone, provided the popular press with further evidence of the left-wing stance of the established church. The fact that Dr Runcie argued against its acceptance and that it was actually rejected by the Synod was largely ignored.

The document on which the tabloid newspapers really went to town and which established in the minds of many of their readers that the Church of England was in the grip of Marxism was the *Faith in the City* report published in November 1985. In the aftermath of the inner-city riots which shook England in the early 1980s, the Church set up a high-powered commission, chaired by Sir Richard O'Brien, former chairman of the Manpower Services Commission, to look into the condition of the country's urban priority areas. Its report was certainly strongly critical of Government policy. It laid the blame for the massive urban deprivation existing in affluent Britain on the fundamental structure of the economy, and complained that 'public policy' was 'inadequate and superficial'. The Government was taken to task for lacking the will to devote adequate resources to deprived urban areas, and the whole thrust of its ideology and philosophy was called into serious question. 'To affirm the importance of wealth creation is not enough', the report stated: 'economic policy should be as concerned with the distribution of income and wealth as with its creation. What seems to be lacking at present is an adequate appreciation of the importance of the distributive consequences. ... We believe that at present too much emphasis is being given to individualism and not enough to collective obligation. In the absence of a spirit of collective obligation, or the political will to foster it, there is no guarantee that the pursuit of innumerable individual self-interests will add up to an improvement in the common good.'

Faith in the City received considerable publicity. There was no shortage of Conservative politicians ready to denounce it, including one Cabinet minister whose comment that it was 'a Marxist document' was carefully leaked to newspapers through the Downing Street press office. John Carlisle, Tory MP for Luton North, declared that 'the Church of England seems now to be run by a load of Communist clerics' and Peter Bruinvels, MP for Leicester East and a member of the General Synod, described the report as 'blatant Marxist theory' and accused the Church of 'stabbing its own loyal flock in the back' by publishing it. These and other critics largely overlooked the fact that the report was in many ways just as critical of the Church itself as it was of the Government. Of its recommendations, 38 were specifically directed to the Church as against only 23 to the Government and the nation.

What particularly upset Mrs Thatcher and her colleagues about *Faith in the City* was its strong implication that morality and Christian principle lay exclusively on the side of egalitarianism and interventionism. More than any other political leader since Gladstone, Mrs Thatcher sought religious legitimation for her policies. Like Gladstone, she believed that minimum state intervention, low public spending and encouragement of competition, self-reliance and individual initiative had a clear Christian and moral basis as well as making good economic sense. She genuinely hoped and expected that church leaders, and especially the leaders of the established churches, would share this view. In fact, only one religious leader in Britain shared her values and that was Lord Jakobovits, the Chief Rabbi. This was not really surprising, for in a sense her religion was grounded in the Old Testament rather than the New. The importance of family and nation, the virtues of patriotism and courage, standing up for what you believed in and if necessary being prepared to fight for it – these were the values of the Israelites rather than of the Galilean carpenter who talked about loving your enemy, turning the other cheek, forsaking your family to follow him and selling all you have and giving it to the poor.

Margaret Thatcher had herself, of course, been schooled in the Protestant ethic of hard work, thrift and competitive individualism by her Methodist father. The extent to which she upheld this ethic, at a time when most churches, including the Methodists, had dropped it in favour of a much more social and collectivist interpretation of the Christian Gospel, was apparent from her address to the General Assembly of the Church of Scotland in May 1988. The 'sermon on the Mound', as it came to be known (the General Assembly hall is situated on a hill in the centre of Edinburgh known as the Mound), was an extraordinary event. It showed the importance that a British Prime Minister at the end of the twentieth century could still attach to giving a theological basis to government policy and winning the churches' support. It also showed how far out of touch Mrs Thatcher was with contemporary Christian thought in Britain. Her choice of Biblical quotations was highly significant and heavily Pauline – from Thessalonians the stricture 'If a man will not work, he shall not eat' and from Timothy the warning that anyone who neglects to provide for his own house (meaning his own family) has disowned the faith and 'is worse than an infidel'. From the Gospels she quoted the parable of the talents and the story of the woman with the alabaster jar of ointment. From both of these she drew the moral that we can only respond to calls for help if we have first worked hard and used our talents to create the necessary wealth. She might well have repeated her celebrated exegesis of the parable of the Good Samaritan, in which she pointed out that he would not have been much use to the man who had fallen among thieves if he had not had a full purse of money.

The overall message of the 'sermon on the Mound' was crystal clear. Christianity, and therefore the proper concern of the churches, was spiritual redemption, individual morality and the promotion of values such as the family, patriotism and self-reliance. It was emphatically not a kind of wishy-washy socialism which advocated a collectivist approach to social and economic problems. From the invisible church Mrs Thatcher might have won a strong but silent 'Hear! Hear!, for her remarks although, as we shall see, the evangelical world has recently abandoned much of its traditional political conservatism and quietism. But for the leaders of the main visible churches, convinced from both their theological training and their personal experience that Christianity has a clear bias towards the poor and oppressed and demands of its followers a commitment to collective action for social and economic reform, her analysis was fundamentally flawed. They were already very uneasy about the morality of the policies being pursued by the Government, and the whole ideology that underlay them. They were also increasingly coming to the view that the clear duty of the churches was to oppose them. The 'sermon on the Mound' followed a budget which gave a £1.2 billion windfall to the very rich by reducing the highest level of taxation from 60 to 40 per cent and an overhaul of social security provisions which reduced the availability of immediate financial help for the poor at a time when the level of homelessness was rising sharply. In a radio interview the Bishop of Durham went so far as to describe the Government's social and economic policies as 'wicked', while the Archbishop of Canterbury told a meeting of the Free Church Federal Council: 'We in the Church of England deeply need and value your support for our maintenance of the ideal of a social consensus and the welfare state. ... In the Free Churches you have a longer tradition of being a "loyal opposition". If we in the Church of England are sometimes so perceived, please help us to get used to this prophetic perception.'

If Margaret Thatcher was only too well aware of the opposition of the Church of England, she may have calculated that her views would gain more support from the other established church north of the border. It was almost certainly no accident that she delivered her Christian apologia in the land of Adam Smith and to a body which has for long held strongly to the Protestant ethic. In many ways the traditions of the Kirk are deeply conservative and it espouses many of the Victorian Liberal values that Mrs Thatcher revived. But, as in the Church of England, its ministers and activists, though not always its congregations, had come to feel increasingly out of sympathy with what she was doing. In 1981 the outgoing Moderator of the General Assembly, Dr William Johnston, described the Government's monetarist policies as 'immoral and blasphemous' because they had the effect of increasing unemployment. The 'sermon on the Mound' was greeted with polite Presbyterian rebuke, characteristically restrained and subtle but none the less crystal clear in its message to the Prime Minister. At the end of her speech the Moderator of the General Assembly, Professor James Whyte, presented her with a report called *Just Sharing* which looked for 'the beginnings of a renewed Christian social vision rooted in the neighbour'. He later wrote: 'As I listened to the theology of the Prime Minister, I heard much about the importance of the individual, a little about the family, but nothing about those other communities which give us our sense of where we belong. If a government has a defective view of human nature and doesn't understand what makes us tick, then it is liable to exercise power in ways that are quite insensitive to the things that are important to us and that influence us – our sense of community, our sense of belonging.'

Other major denominations responded to Mrs Thatcher's speech in similar terms. A public letter to the Prime Minister from the chairman of the General Synod's Board of Social Responsibility declared that 'justice and generosity apply to governments as well as individuals' and pointed out that 'wealth acts as a barrier to the Kingdom if it encourages total self-reliance and independence, tempting people to believe that they are masters of their own destiny.' The Methodist Church Conference declared its 'sense of outrage' at the way in which the Government's policies were increasing the wealth of the rich 'at the expense of the poor'.

The widening rift between the Government and the churches worried Margaret Thatcher considerably and she made several attempts to heal it. In 1987 she asked Michael Alison, MP, formerly her Parliamentary Private Secretary and the Second Church Estates Commissioner, to organize a dialogue between leading Christian thinkers and her own advisers, including Professor Brian Griffiths, the head of her policy unit and a committed Christian. The group chosen for this discussion was heavily weighted in favour of supporters of the Government's approach and the book which resulted from it, *Christianity and Conservatism* (Hodder & Stoughton, 1990) is strongly critical of the churches, the Church of England in particular, for being very keen to tell the Government what to do but very bad at actually doing anything about their own problems of falling membership and declining moral standards. It also includes the characteristically trenchant observation from Lord Hailsham that 'their function is to save souls and preach the Gospel, and they should get their priorities right before they offend the consciences of their neighbours by public utterances such as some of those made by the Bishop of Durham'. Towards the end of 1988 David Jenkins was one of a number of bishops invited to Chequers by Mrs Thatcher. Few details of the meeting have leaked out although, not surprisingly, it seems that the bishops emphasized their worry about what they took to be the attack on public morality involved in the Government's economic and fiscal policies, while Mrs Thatcher expressed her feeling that the Church was largely failing to stem the decline in private morality which she regarded as one of the main problems facing the country.

Just how great the gap between Government and churches had become was shown in 1989 when a Cabinet minister called on the church to develop a theology of success. Speaking soon afterwards to a gathering of diocesan clergy in Manchester Cathedral Dr Runcie responded: 'Where in the New Testament is success a criterion for godliness and grace? What do you do with the crown of thorns and Christ's shed blood when you create a theology of success?' Some commentators believed that Conservative MPs were trying to get their own back on the Church of England when they threw out a measure which had been passed overwhelmingly in the General Synod permitting the ordination of men who had been divorced and remarried. In October 1990 an advertisement for the Labour party appeared in the *Church Times*. Under the heading 'An open letter to all Christians from Eric James', the prominent Anglican cleric, who is a chaplain to the Queen and preacher to Gray's Inn, wrote 'As a Christian, I am very unhappy with this government's record. Those who need help don't get it. Greed and selfishness are shamelessly encouraged.' In the same month the Trade and Industry Secretary Peter Lilley, a member of St Peter's Church, Vauxhall, defended the Government's policies to a gathering of senior clergy in Southwark Cathedral. His remarks that capitalism could harness the greed and selfishness arising from the fall of man for the good of society, and his attacks on socialist clergy for being out of touch with their congregations, were met with stony silence. By contrast John Smith, Labour Shadow Chancellor and an elder in the Church of Scotland, received rapturous applause when he said that in his experience the Church was much more in touch with the people than the Government was. The verdict of a recent book on the Kirk, *Sermons and Battle Hymns* by Tom Gallagher and Graham Walker (1991), that 'by the end of the 1980s the national Church and the State found themselves

further apart than at any point since the dawn of political democracy in Britain' could equally well have been applied to the situation
south of the border.

How far has the rift between the churches and the Government
shown any sign of healing since the replacement of Margaret
Thatcher and Robert Runcie? There is no doubt that John Major
presents a more acceptable face of Conservatism to the churches
than his predecessor, not just because his policies are perceived to
be less socially divisive and his instincts more consensual, but also
because he is much less concerned with establishing that what he
does has a clear moral and Christian basis. But it would be wrong
to conclude from this that all is now sweetness and light between
Church House and Downing Street. The Gulf War of 1991
provoked, if anything, more opposition from the churches than the
Falklands conflict of 1982. Although there was some admiration for
the restrained and low-key way in which Mr Major conducted
himself throughout the conflict, many church leaders were profoundly unhappy about the decision to engage in the war and the
nature of the bombing inflicted on Iraq. Their reluctance to talk
in terms of victory and their unease about a thanksgiving service
brought strong criticism from sections of the Tory party and the
public. Bill Walker, Tory MP for North Tayside, was incensed
by the comment of Michael Hare-Duke, Bishop of St Andrews,
Dunkeld and Dunblane, that there was no real winner as a result
of the conflict and responded 'It's about time the bishop and other
churchmen who kept getting things wrong paid some attention to
the well-being of their parishioners instead of making high profile
sallies into political areas.' The Bishop of Durham's remark that a
victory parade would be 'obscene' prompted a correspondent to
The Times to note that 'A fine victory for British arms and the
tumbling of a Third World aggressor do not accord with the spirit
of the modern Church of England. The rejoicing in the village pub
will find no echo in the synod chamber. Is it pastor or flock that is
out of step? Perhaps the rows of empty pews suggest the answer.'

This last comment touches on an important point that we need
to establish before we can assess how far Government–Church
relations have been affected by the replacement of Robert Runcie
by George Carey as Archbishop of Canterbury. Is it simply the
leadership of the churches, and especially of the Church of England,
that is out of sympathy with the Government, or are their members
also broadly opposed to the policies and outlook of contemporary

Toryism? I have already suggested that the Anglican episcopal bench of the 1980s, many but not all of whose members are still in post, represented the acme of liberal theology in the Church of England. It almost certainly also stood for a more collectivist and interventionist approach to economic and social questions than the membership of the Church as a whole. There are many reasons for this – one of them undoubtedly the pressure from the growing bureaucracy of Synod commissions and working groups, all producing reports urging action on this or that social problem. As we have noted, the main churches, and particularly the two established churches, now have policies on every conceivable current issue – this is partly a response to the incessant demands of the media for a quote or statement on everything that comes up in the news, and partly a consequence of having democratic structures of government and assemblies that cannot avoid the temptation to be deliberative as well as legislative. It may well also be an aspect of the traditional British heresy of Pelagianism, which tends to reduce Christianity to a matter of moral concern, and suggest that the road to heaven lies in having a strong social conscience and a sense of concern for human material needs. Bishops in the Church of England have a long tradition of speaking up on social and economic issues and criticizing governments for their failings in the areas of social justice and equality. While it would be uncharitable and unfair to suggest that it is an easy way to avoid facing up to more difficult spiritual issues closer to home, there is no doubt that speaking out on political and economic matters does provide a welcome distraction from worrying about falling congregations, leaking roofs and unbelief among the clergy. David Samuel, director of the conservative and evangelically inclined Church Society, may have a point when he says that 'in the absence of a clear spiritual message, the Church's leadership tends to fall back upon a social gospel with a vaguely left-wing stance'.

I suspect that the particular political and social outlook of the Anglican bishops of the 1980s may also have had something to do with the lingering sense of public-school guilt which was alluded to in Chapter 1. Certainly most of them shared an upper-middle class, public school, Oxbridge, academic background which was very different from that of Margaret Thatcher and other representatives of the new Toryism. To that extent the change in archbishops may be significant. George Carey carries no public-school guilt around with him. His background is, indeed, very similar to that of John Major and to some extent he is temperamentally closer to the conviction politics of the modern Conservative party than was the more patrician figure of Robert Runcie. He was, however, quick to dispel any hopes that the Tories may have had that he would be a less outspoken critic of Government policy than his predecessor. Within a few months of taking office he annoyed ministers by linking riots on Tyneside with social deprivation and unemployment and attacking two key planks of Government education policy, the encouragement of schools to opt out of local authority control and the stress on vocational training.

But it would be wrong to suggest that the growing rift in relations throughout the 1980s was simply or even largely a matter of the personalities involved at the top, and that the change which has taken place here will lead to a new mood of harmony. In so far as it can be judged, the political outlook of the clergy as a whole is broadly in line with the views being expressed by church leaders. A survey of Church of England clergy in 1986 found that half supported the centre party alliance, with 34 per cent backing the Social Democrats and 16 per cent the Liberals, a quarter supported the Conservatives and 16 per cent described themselves as Socialists or Labour party. The disappearance of the Social Democratic party will obviously have affected this balance, but all the available information suggests that the majority of Anglican clergy still support centre or left-of-centre parties and only about a quarter describe themselves as Conservatives. Polls of clergy in the other main denominations would probably produce similar results, although a survey of the political views of those found in the pews on a Sunday morning would show a much greater Conservative bias. A poll conducted by *Scotland on Sunday* among the 1,250 commissioners to the 1991 General Assembly of the Church of Scotland, a group made up equally of ministers and elders, showed that 34.5 per cent supported the Conservatives, 32.9 per cent the Liberal Democrats, 15 per cent Labour and 8 per cent the Scottish Nationalists. I suspect that if these figures had been broken down, the Conservative support would have been found to be concentrated almost entirely among the elders, with the ministers being markedly more left-wing. The gap in political views between clergy and congregations is particularly striking in the Church of Scotland, where many members are wholly out of sympathy with what they take to be the left-wing views of the influential Church and Nation Committee, and with the Church's strong line in favour of devolution and a separate Scottish Parliament. But the gap also exists in the Church of England. In an article in the *Yorkshire Post* in October 1988 a country rector in North Yorkshire wittily and accurately characterized contemporary Anglican preaching as 'rather like *Guardian* readers talking to *Telegraph* readers'.

But one should not underestimate the extent to which even the *Telegraph* readers in the pews have been radicalized and politicized since 1979. This has very little to do with the impact of liberation theology or of buzz-words like *kairos* that have been flying around in academic circles and ecumenical gatherings. It reflects rather a gut sense of injustice and unfairness about much recent social and economic policy. This was brought home to me when I read a letter in the May 1990 edition of the parish magazine for the Bride Valley group of parishes in West Dorset. It was written by a woman in the quiet and prosperous town of Beaminster who had been moved by a feeling of anger over the injustices of the Poll Tax to 'take up her cross', and had found herself for the first time in her life taking part in a demonstration in London where she rubbed shoulders with members of the Militant Tendency and the Socialist Workers' Party. She concluded: 'I believe that politics is too important to leave to politicians, and opposition far too important to leave to the groups I saw in London. Christians should be at the forefront of calls for reform, not hiding and wishing it would go away!'

Although the immediate cause of that woman's anger and political agitation, the Poll Tax, has now been removed, I suspect that the sense of injustice and unease which she and thousands of other church-goers have experienced over the last decade will not go away. The fact is that profound disquiet about what is happening to our society as a result of the dominance of the profit motive and the values of the market is not confined to left-wing bishops in the Church of England and the socialist-inclined Church and Nation Committee of the Church of Scotland's General Assembly. Nor is this disquiet simply directed at the present Government. It is part of a much deeper and more widespread unease felt among Christians and non-Christians alike about the spiritual and moral values of a culture which seems to put an increasing premium on success, profit and consumption. Understandably, people look to the churches to provide a set of counter-values, and they do not look in vain. I think that one of the most significant achievements of Robert Runcie's period as Archbishop of Canterbury was his articulation of this deep sense of unease in the country and his persistent and serious questioning of the ethic which has given rise to it. He did so perhaps most forcefully when he said, in an interview in 1989 in the magazine of the Institute of Directors, 'These are days when the simple dictates of profit and self-interest are recognised as the dynamics of industrial success – but to regard these as the sole dynamics of society is fatal.' He went on to warn of a new breed of Pharisees, 'the successful who regard their success as a sort of blessing or reward for righteousness. This can lead to judgements being made about the unsuccessful, the unemployed, the poor and the unintelligent which are both uncharitable and untrue. I'm thinking of the sort of attitude that suggests that the unemployed do little to help themselves, that if only you have the determination and drive you can get on in the world. Those attitudes lead people to be dismissive of the value of their fellow human beings. Those attitudes harden our hearts. They create barriers between us and God.'

It is that kind of language, deeply prophetic, deeply Christian and deeply humane, that we are surely and rightly going to hear more of from the churches in the future. We are likely to hear it from all the churches, visible and invisible. If the 1980s was the decade of the Anglican bishops against Mrs Thatcher, the 1990s look like being the decade in which all the Christian churches speak out about the way in which our society is moving. Significantly, it began with the Roman Catholic Church, which throughout the 1980s kept a much lower political profile than the other main churches, issuing a clear denunciation of the capitalist ethic underlying modern society. A report entitled *The Root of All Evil* argues that it is almost impossible to be a City money-maker and comply with the demands and ethics of Christian morality. More generally, it questions the whole philosophy of basing values on money-making and materialism. Roman Catholics have long had a more systematic and clearly thought-out corpus of social ethics than the Protestant churches, and the tradition of Catholic social teaching is undergoing something of a revival. A conference held in Liverpool in July 1991 to mark the centenary of Pope Leo XIII's encyclical *Rerum Novum* brought together 400 people from every diocese in England and Wales and has resulted in a much greater interest among Catholics in the whole field of social and economic ethics. It seems safe to predict that the Roman Catholic Church will be much more active than it has previously been in this area, not least because of the growing political and economic integration of Europe where it is easily the dominant religious presence. Already, as we have seen, Catholicism has given EEC bureaucrats one of their favourite phrases in the principle of subsidiarity. As the dangers of overcentralized and depersonalized institutions become increasingly apparent, we are likely to hear further elements of traditional Catholic social teaching being preached, on the importance of respecting and protecting local communities and societies.

Of course, pontificating in reports and statements about the ills of society and the failings of government is one thing: actually trying to live by your principles is quite another. Critics of the churches feel that they should examine the morality of their own activities before they criticize others. I predict this is going to be an increasingly hot topic in the next few years. Richard Harries, the Bishop of Oxford, set the ball rolling by launching an abortive assault in the High Court on the investment policy of the Church Commissioners. He would like to see ethical factors playing a much bigger part in decisions about the management of the Church of England's £2,500 millions worth of property and stock market investments. The Commissioners already have a policy of not investing in South African companies or in companies whose main business is in armaments, gambling, alcohol, tobacco, newspapers or television. However, as a charitable body charged with raising revenue for the Church, and responsible for 40 per cent of clergy stipends and 100 per cent of their pensions, they have a statutory duty to raise the maximum potential revenue from their investments. Richard Harries would like to see a change in the law so that ethical considerations could override purely financial ones. Others feel that the present policy of seeking maximum returns on investments is essential if the Church is to maintain a presence in less-favoured areas. In the words of Bill Westwood, Bishop of Peterborough, 'The Church Commissioners pay for Christian religion to be in Tottenham, in Toxteth and in the worst corners of our country. I'm grateful that the Church Commissioners have that money to keep us in being. They deliver us from the suburban captivity of the Church into which the General Synod has fallen.'

There are other areas of their affairs where the churches could be accused of not practising what they preach. The occupation of prestigious city-centre offices like Church House in Westminster and the Church of Scotland's imposing headquarters in George

Street, Edinburgh, seems slightly at odds with proclamations about a bias to the poor and sermons on the evils of symbols of power and status. Demand for the two established churches to move into more modest premises is likely to grow. So is pressure on the Church of England to use its considerable holdings of agricultural land in a more environmentally responsible way. At present most of the land held by the Church Commissioners and by diocesan glebe committees is being either rented out to large farmers or sold off to developers. But, once again, the hands of the Church are tied by the law, which insists that it must get the maximum return from its assets.

Although there is an inevitable gap between what the churches preach and what they practise, there is also a genuine attempt to live out the social gospel. Indeed, one of the most impressive features of church life in the last decade or so has been the espousal of a definite bias towards the poor, not just as an easy slogan but as an active commitment which has meant costly sacrifice. The Church of England's *Faith in the City* initiative did not only result in a report criticizing the Government (and incidentally spurring it into taking a number of initiatives in inner-city areas): it led the Church to set up its own Urban Fund, which has raised £18 million for inner-city renewal projects. Much of the money was raised from more affluent country and suburban dioceses and showed the Church's own clear commitment to redistribution of wealth and tackling inequality. In many of our most depressed urban areas the churches are in the forefront of schemes of renewal and regeneration. The remarkable work achieved by Christians of different denominations joining together in Liverpool under the inspiring leadership of David Sheppard and Derek Worlock is perhaps the best-known and most spectacular example. An Anglican vicar in the notorious Toxteth district of the city, scene of rioting in the early 1980s, described in the *Guardian* the extent to which it has given the churches a political role and made them the main focus of hope in the city: 'I think of it as community theology; it's not necessarily religious. There's a political void, not a moral one. A void that friendly, astute and relevant clergy can get into. Politicians, national or local, don't rate at all in Toxteth: the clergy do.'

One of the main reasons why clergy 'rate' in depressed urban areas like Toxteth is that they are often the only professional people who actually live there. Doctors, social workers and teachers may

come in to work during the day, but often travel home to more
gentrified areas in the evening. Clergy, however, live in the community and are accessible twenty-four hours a day. The strain, the
frustrations and the sense of irrelevance can be horrendous, but
the very fact of just being there in the midst of so much depression
and suffering shows the churches witnessing to the very heart of
the Christian Gospel. In the aftermath of the riots which took place
in several inner-city areas in the mid-1980s Clifford Longley wrote
a typically perceptive piece in *The Times* (14 October 1985) about
the remarkable change in the social and political outlook of the
churches:

> Ten years ago the churches would have been looking for some place
> to hide, not for nettles to grasp. Somewhere along the line they
> have lost their habit of looking over their shoulders at 'respectable'
> middle-class, right-of-centre, church-going Britain. They have
> become almost reckless in their disinterest in pleasing that con-
> stituency. But it would equally be true that they are innocent of any
> hope that the alienated communities of the inner cities will flock to
> church in gratitude.
>
> The religion being represented through the presence of the main-
> stream churches is no opiate. It has nothing so powerful to offer.
> Inner-city clergymen know all about hopelessness, as it is the beset-
> ting temptation of their own ministry; they have the freedom of
> those with nothing to lose, on the other hand.
>
> In fact, just 'being there', pointless as it might seem to a secular
> world, has become an end in itself. The clergy in those situations
> tend to suffer from a restless search for a 'theology' which will justify
> their existence and tell them what to do with it; but there is no such
> external package of ideas waiting to be discovered (in Latin America,
> for instance) which will give them a new sense of commission.
>
> The only useful theology will arise from their experience, which is
> the experience of just being there, doing their thing, being 'irrelevant'.
> And it confronts all the values of the world. They are the only people
> in the inner city with no ulterior purposes whatever, no profits
> to make or careers to advance, no prospect of full churches, no
> manipulative aims whatever. They are as meaningless as monks in
> a monastery.
>
> They will not stop riots nor provide the unemployed with jobs
> and dignity, nor will they convert Handsworth and Brixton. But
> they make each church presence in the urban desert a deep pool of
> mystery, whose whole meaning is to be found in its existence, not its
> purpose.

I have quoted this passage at some length because it seems to me to sum up very well what the churches are achieving simply through their presence in areas of deprivation. Perhaps this is indeed the most effective kind of social and political statement that they can make – it is also one of the hardest. There is much sense in what Hugh Montefiore, former Bishop of Birmingham, has written: 'The Church has been so taken up with raising money for its Urban Fund that the major issue seems to have been put on one side, the spiritual dilemma of the Church in the inner city. One hopes that the Decade of Evangelism will give it a boost, but of that, as yet, there is little sign. The inclination of radicals to "let be" and to concern themselves simply with welfare and politicisation gets us nowhere, nor does the crude Evangelical preaching of Christ as the answer for all problems. Some of the finest clergy I know live and work in the inner city; and the Church needs to encourage them to tell us what they think the answers may be.'

There is also a good deal of church involvement with the social and economic problems of rural areas. The Church of England's report *Faith in the Countryside*, published in September 1990 by the Archbishops' Commission on Rural Areas, showed clearly that poverty and social deprivation are not only to be found in the inner cities. Like *Faith in the City* it was not simply a catalogue of demands for more public spending and Government action, but also called for more initiatives by the Church itself. One problem which it clearly identified is the increasing difficulty faced by low-paid agricultural workers and other local people in affording properties in rural areas as house prices are driven up by affluent city workers and the demand for retirement homes. As a substantial landowner the Church is in a position to do something about this problem, and a number of dioceses are already abandoning the principle of securing the maximum possible return on their assets and making plots of glebe land available for low-cost housing for renting by local people.

The Church of England is not, of course, alone in responding to injustice and deprivation with practical help as well as through prophetic utterances. The Church of Scotland has a long-standing tradition of combining political radicalism with active social concern. Its Board of Social Responsibility runs the largest voluntary social work organization in Scotland with a network of old people's homes, drug and alcohol dependency centres, residential schools and hostels for the homeless and mentally handicapped.

Although it has sadly run into difficulties largely through over-stretching itself, the scheme for training unemployed people which was centred on Buckhaven Parish Church in Fife was the largest of its kind in the country and helped to rejuvenate a particularly run-down area. The Roman Catholic Church is actively promoting projects in many inner-city areas, like the credit union in Toxteth, Liverpool, which helps over 200 unemployed people living on state benefits to manage their money and avoid falling into serious debt and has become a model for other similar schemes throughout the country. The historic Free Churches also have a strong commitment to living out the social gospel. At Laurence Hall in Plaistow, East London, for example, the Baptist Church runs a community centre which offers hostel accommodation for the homeless, employment projects and advice services for those caught in the poverty trap.

The newer and more evangelical churches which make up what I have called the invisible church are also increasingly involved in social and community action. Together with the Afro-Caribbean Evangelical Alliance the Evangelical Alliance runs an employment consultancy, Evangelical Enterprise, to stimulate job creation in inner-city areas. Many of the house churches in and around London support the Oasis Trust which helps the homeless. This kind of activity represents a remarkable change of perspective over the last few years. There is, of course, a strong historical tradition in Britain of evangelical involvement in social and political action, epitomized by the activities of William Wilberforce and the 7th Earl of Shaftesbury. But for much of the twentieth century evangelicals have tended to be quietist and conservative in terms of political and social attitudes, seeing their role as preaching the Gospel of individual repentance and conversion, rather than political campaigning or tackling social and economic injustice. Recently, however, there has been a much greater emphasis on the social gospel in the evangelical camp. A fascinating two-day debate organized by the Evangelical Alliance in September 1990 produced heated exchanges over the conflicting claims of 'kingdom theology' and a Gospel of individual conversion. But at the end even those on the conservative side were happy to affirm that social and political action is an implication of the Christian faith and part of Christ's will for his people.

Some of the credit for this revival of evangelical commitment to the social gospel should perhaps go to Mrs Thatcher. In the summer of 1990 she met Clive Calver, director of the Evangelical Alliance, and Gordon Holloway, director of the Shaftesbury Society, the largest of the evangelical social work agencies. According to press reports, she told them she was 'fed up with woolly, liberal clergymen. Let's see what the evangelicals can do.' Following the meeting the Government published its White Paper on *Care in the Community* which urged local authorities to farm out services to Christian charities. The Evangelical Alliance has received Home Office grants for work with immigrants and young offenders in Birmingham and London, and £500,000 of Government money to help the homeless has gone to fund Shaftesbury Society projects. It would be wrong, however, to suggest that leaders of the evangelical churches are working hand-in-glove with the Government and that they agree with its overall philosophy of privatizing care and dismantling elements of the Welfare State. Relatively few of them are Tory supporters – Holloway votes Labour and Calver Liberal Democrat. One of the main results of their increased involvement in areas of social and economic deprivation, much of which has been in conjunction with black churches in the field of homelessness and unemployment, has been to radicalize the invisible church and make it increasingly critical of Government policies.

Although they are undoubtedly concerned about economic and social matters, it is more specifically religious concerns that have really brought the newer and more evangelically inclined churches into political activism. There is a distinct difference of emphasis here between the visible and the invisible churches. While the former campaign primarily on economic and social issues, and especially on poverty and injustice both at home and abroad, the latter tend to concentrate on subjects which have a more overtly religious and moral flavour, like Sunday trading and abortion.

Opposition to Sunday trading is almost certainly the issue which has produced the most effective Christian lobby and commands the widest support across both the visible and invisible churches. It is spearheaded by the Keep Sunday Special Campaign, a highly professional pressure group run from the Cambridge headquarters of the Jubilee Centre, a small Christian Research Group formed in 1983. When the Government introduced legislation in 1985 to allow unrestricted Sunday opening of shops in England and Wales, a massive lobby was organized by both the mainstream churches and the newer evangelical ones. The Church of England's General

Synod voted by 427 votes to 6 to oppose the bill, and the Jubilee Centre organized a mass 'write-in' of letters to MPs. Four days before the bill's second reading in April 1986 the Archbishop of Canterbury, the Cardinal Archbishop of Westminster and the Moderator of the Free Church Federal Council met the Home Secretary and expressed their united opposition to Sunday trading. This was almost certainly the first time that the leaders of all three major parts of the visible church had together lobbied a Government minister. In the event, the bill was defeated in the House of Commons by just 14 votes, with 70 Tory MPs defying the three-line whip to vote against it. The Government withdrew its proposals, but the issue of Sunday trading remains very much alive, not least because of the constant flouting of the present restrictive laws by shops and markets. In the face of the threat of new legislation the Keep Sunday Special Campaign continues, supported by several major retail chains and by the shopworkers' union, as well as by opinion polls which suggest that around three-quarters of the population believe it would be a shame if Sunday became just like any other day.

An even more high-profile and emotive campaign has been mounted with rather less success by several churches against Britain's relatively liberal abortion laws. Led by two well-organized pressure groups, LIFE and the Society for the Protection of the Unborn Child (SPUC), the anti-abortion movement receives considerable backing from both the Roman Catholic Church and many evangelical churches and groups. This showed itself most strongly when David Alton introduced his Private Member's Bill in 1985 to reduce the time limit on abortions from 28 to 18 weeks. Massive lobbying culminated in a rally at the Royal Albert Hall organized by the evangelical pressure group CARE (Christian Action, Research and Education) and addressed by Cardinal Hume, and the presentation of a petition to the Prime Minister with over a million signatures. In the event the bill was talked out at report stage, but the formidable Catholic–Evangelical coalition built up to support it remains intact and strongly committed to a tightening of the abortion laws. It was, indeed, in action again in 1990 to oppose the Human Fertilization and Embryology Bill.

Complex issues of medical ethics like abortion, *in vitro* fertilization and experimentation on embryos reveal a clear split, with the mainstream Protestant churches on one side and the Roman Catholics and newer evangelical churches on the other. On the whole the former, led by the Church of England bishops and the main committees of the Church of Scotland's General Assembly, are prepared to back scientific and medical opinion and to support research on human embryos and the termination of pregnancy in certain circumstances. Evangelicals and Roman Catholics tend to see these matters in much more black-and-white terms, and regard any experimentation with embryos or removal of foetuses from the womb as contrary to God's law.

To some extent the same split is apparent on other sensitive moral issues such as homosexuality. This has been a particularly vexed question for the Church of England because of the number of homosexual clergy within its own ranks, but on the whole, and in common with most of the mainstream Protestant churches, it takes a broadly liberal and tolerant view. Few Anglicans would probably want to go as far as those in the American Episcopal Church who now perform 'marriage ceremonies' for homosexual couples, but there is a growing acceptance of homosexuality as a valid form of sexual orientation. The official attitude of the Roman Catholic Church and of the newer evangelical churches tends to be rather harder, although there are growing gay and lesbian groups within both communities pressing for greater acceptance of homosexuals.

This difference of approach was reflected in reactions to the arrival in Britain in the mid-1980s of the terrible scourge of Aids which at first afflicted predominantly the homosexual community. A number of leading Christians talked of the disease in terms of a plague sent down by God to punish sinners. James Anderton, the Chief Constable of Greater Manchester, who had moved from Methodism to Catholicism via Anglicanism, attracted a lot of publicity with his observation, which he claimed had been dictated to him directly by God, that the victims of Aids were 'swirling around in a cesspit of their own making ... people with dirty, filthy minds engaged in dirty, filthy acts.' An article by Cardinal Hume in *The Times* in January 1987 was equally judgemental and condemnatory, if slightly less colourful in its language. 'Aids', he wrote, 'is but one of the many disastrous consequences of promiscuous sexual behaviour. Promiscuity is the root cause of the present epidemic. It has always been sinful; it is rapidly becoming suicidal. We are, then, dealing with an intrinsically moral issue and not simply one of public health. No campaign against Aids can ignore or trivialize the moral question. ... Even in the short term a moral reawakening is society's best hope. The fact to be faced is that all of us in society have to learn to live according to a renewed set of values. That will not be easy. How can any appeal for faithfulness and sexual restraint be heeded when there is on all sides explicit encouragement to promiscuous behaviour and frequent ridicule of moral values? Society is in moral disarray, for which we must all take our share of blame.'

The reaction of leading figures in the Church of England to the Aids epidemic was very different. They leaned over backwards to avoid sounding moralistic or judgemental, and deliberately eschewed words like sin. Their call for compassion and getting alongside the victims was matched by the active involvement of many clergy, some but by no means all of whom were themselves homosexuals, in counselling and befriending Aids sufferers. As the disease has spread and brought other groups within its terrible grasp a number of the new invisible churches have also become involved in helping its victims. This has, indeed, been one of the most striking and impressive features of the evangelicals' recent rediscovery of the social gospel. One of the specialist hospices for Aids patients, the Mildmay Mission Hospital in East London, is funded and run by evangelicals. So is the charity ACET (Aids Care Education and Training) which trains volunteers from churches of different denominations to give practical help and care to sufferers in their homes. The director of ACET, Dr Patrick Dixon, an elder in the Ealing Fellowship, a house church which has grown into a 110-strong group, comes under fire both from fellow-evangelicals who feel that the organization's approach is not sufficiently evangelistic, and from those in the gay community who find it too churchy. He responds: 'There is only one answer to a torrent of words and that is the action of unconditional love; the willingness of Christians to do what many others are not willing to do; to go into homes, to wipe the bottom of someone who is dying; to wipe the sick off the floor; to help someone to get comfortable in bed; to take someone by the hand and stay with them at a time when they are feeling angry or lost.'

Such transparent compassion and sensitivity towards the suffering goes a long way to explaining, I think, why the new invisible churches in Britain have not developed the kind of hard 'moral majority' mentality found among similar groups in the United States. Some commentators do feel that, with the resurgence of evangelical Christianity in this country and the advent of pressure groups campaigning for stricter moral codes and seeking to reverse the permissive society, we are witnessing the growth of a movement similar to that which played such a key role in American politics in the 1980s. An article in *The Times* in January 1987, for example, provided a 'who's who in the drive for moral resurgence', listing recently-formed pressure groups like the National Campaign for the Family, the National Council for Christian Standards in Society and the Conservative Family Campaign alongside longer-established groups like SPUC and CARE. It suggested that together they constituted a strong political lobby and quoted Graham Webster-Gardiner, chairman of the Conservative Family Campaign, as saying that he would like to see every candidate in general elections declare his position on a variety of moral issues from abortion and homosexuality to Sunday trading and religious education in schools. He also pointed out that 'There are two million believing Christians prepared to consider their vote'.

It is doubtful, however, whether these kinds of pressure group will have any significant impact on electoral behaviour in Britain. The situation is very different in the United States where levels of church-going are much higher and issues of religion and morality have a much greater public profile. American presidents undoubtedly gain votes from being regular church attenders and identifying with Christian causes. I am not at all sure that the same is true of British politicians. Indeed, I suspect that Mrs Thatcher was rather too like a preacher for many people's tastes. Her recitation of St Francis' prayer of reconciliation on the steps of No. 10 Downing Street when she was first elected Prime Minister somehow sounded slightly false and unsuitable to many British ears. Yet Ronald Reagan's easy evocation of the name of God in his television broadcasts and President Bush's reliance on Billy Graham as a domestic chaplain and counsellor during the Gulf War struck a clear chord with the American people. I suspect that John Major has got it just about right in the eyes of the British electorate, in being mildly sympathetic to Christianity without being too enthusiastic about it. It is said that his wife and children go off to church on Sunday mornings while he catches up on the newspapers – not unlike the behaviour of most British husbands.

It is interesting, and at first sight perhaps rather strange, that the British politician who is most clearly identified with the new moral majority-style pressure groups and the evangelically-led political campaigns should be a Liberal MP and a devout Roman Catholic.

But it is perhaps not so strange when we reflect that the great majority of clergy identify with the centre parties in British politics, and that of all the traditional mainstream churches, the Catholics have been by far the most active in this area. David Alton has, of course, been particularly associated with the anti-abortion movement, but he has also taken up other issues which concern the emerging Catholic–Evangelical coalition seeking to challenge the permissive society and introduce a stricter and more Christian moral code. In the words of one of the main journals of the invisible church, *Leadership Today*, 'he unites Christians – both Catholic and Protestant – in a way that few church leaders could achieve'.

One of the most intriguing products of this new coalition, in which David Alton has been a prime mover, is the as yet little-known Movement for Christian Democracy. Founded in the summer of 1990, its steering group includes Alton, another Roman Catholic MP, Ken Hargreaves (a Tory) and representatives from the Jubilee Centre, the London Institute for Contemporary Christianity, CARE and the Evangelical Alliance. The declaration that launched the movement begins by asserting that 'Christ's call summons us to follow him into every area of life, including the realm of politics' and that Christians have a clear duty to help shape the character of the nation. It goes on to mention issues as diverse as crime, poverty, homelessness, international debt, the Third World and the environment, and to signal its support for democracy, social justice, respect for life, reconciliation, active compassion and wise stewardship. A bundle of slightly more specific policy proposals includes the promotion of a culture of thrift, encouraging an appreciation of the family and the 'institution of life-long marriage', employee participation in decision-making, and decentralization of government.

This stirring call for the application of Christian values in society, with which few inside or even outside the churches would surely much disagree, is expressed in an urgent, almost millenarian tone with which some might feel a little more uncomfortable. In an address to a students' rally, for example, David Alton described Britain as 'a nation in peril' and talked of 'the collapse of Christian values'. Already the movement has shown that it does not intend to be just a talking shop. One of its first actions was to ship over 60 tons of emergency food-aid for Moscow. Early issues of its newsletter also report action to help families in debt by establishing money management courses based on local churches, lobbying on Sunday trading and embryo research and forging links with European Christian Democratic parties.

Britain is, of course, unusual in Europe in not having any political parties based explicitly on Christian principles and church affiliations. In most of the rest of the Continent there are Christian Democratic parties, often having strong links with the Roman Catholic Church. The Movement for Christian Democracy clearly states that it does not see itself becoming a new political party, although coincidentally with its launch the Reverend Dick Rogers, a long-time campaigner on human rights and Third World issues, announced the formation of a new political party to be known as the Christian Democratic Union. Those behind the Movement are almost certainly right to reject such an option – without proportional representation, it is hard to see an overtly Christian party making any real headway. They have, however, said that they will endorse certain candidates at forthcoming general elections. A special committee will be formed to decide which sitting MPs and candidates should be supported, and those chosen will receive a letter of endorsement which can be used in their election material. They will also receive help from Movement members in their campaigning. A note in the newsletter says 'it is expected that the Movement will be able to endorse Christian candidates from across the political parties. The process will provide an important boost for candidates and should strengthen the representation of Christians in the next Parliament.'

It is no accident, and no great surprise, that the pressure for this much more positive lobbying and almost aggressive assertion of Christian values in public life should be coming from Roman Catholics and evangelicals in the newer churches. In many ways it can be taken as a reflection of, and a reaction to, the relative impotence of the two main established churches (and the historic Free Churches that once made the Nonconformist Conscience so powerful a force in the land) in influencing policy and public life over the last 20 or 30 years. Yes, the Church of England and Church of Scotland produce an endless stream of well researched reports on everything from sustainable energy to sanctions against South Africa. Yes, the Speaker's Chaplain still begins every day's business in the House of Commons with prayers. Yes, archbishops have audiences of the Queen, bishops speak in the House of Lords and MPs sit earnestly through the debates on Church and Nation day at the General Assembly of the Church of Scotland. But much of this seems largely symbolic. The national churches have kept a central role in the pomp and pageantry of politics but have lost any real share of power.

Roman Catholics and those in the invisible churches, by contrast, have no experience or expectation of being involved in the ceremonial of state, but a much keener desire to be where real power lies and real decisions are taken. Alone among any denominational yearbook, the *Roman Catholic Directory* lists all MPs and peers who are church members. As has already been noted, they form what is almost certainly the largest single committed church grouping in Parliament. Roman Catholic bishops have no great interest in sitting in the House of Lords but they can be highly effective lobbyists. Thomas Winning, Archbishop of Glasgow, recently used the front page of his archdiocesan magazine *Flourish* to mount a strong attack on the Labour party's 'stringent pro-abortion policy' and to urge Catholic voters to check the pro-life credentials of election candidates before casting their votes. An editorial in the same paper sounds a clear warning to the Labour party, which has traditionally taken the lion's share of the significant working-class Catholic vote in west Scotland, and asks; 'has Labour taken the Catholic vote for granted for too long?' Evangelical groups are equally keen on effective lobbying and political influence. CARE, the evangelical pressure group which serves the booming house church movement, produces pamphlets on how to get onto a school board and how to become a local councillor. One can, I think, fairly safely predict that it is with the highly organized campaigning lobbies of the new Catholic–Evangelical alliance that most of the initiative in Christian political and social involvement will lie in the coming years. With their almost set-piece confrontations between Mrs Thatcher and the bishops and carefully staged events like the 'sermon on the Mound', the 1980s gave the established churches a last illusion of power and influence. Ironically, they owed this to the fact that the Prime Minister they criticized so much actually cared what they said and wanted their support. In the foreseeable future at least, the churches are almost certainly going to have to deal with political leaders who are not so bothered about them. Christian involvement in political and social affairs is likely to become less confrontational, better organized and a good deal more subtle. It may well also become more effective.

6

The clergy

Brother clasps the hand of brother,
Stepping fearless through the night

One of the most marked differences between the two kinds of
church that I have characterized as making up the ecclesiastical
geography of modern Britain is in their attitude towards ministry
and leadership. The invisible churches almost entirely eschew the
idea of an ordained clergy. They may well have full-time paid
leaders in the form of pastors, teachers and evangelists, but these
are almost invariably lay people who are not regarded as set apart
in any way and who do not dress any differently from other
members of the congregation. The visible churches, on the other
hand, while talking a good deal about utilizing the talents of the
laity and recognizing the ministry of all the people of God, remain
firmly wedded to the principle of an ordained clerical class.

With their distinctive uniform, indeed, the clergy are one of the
most visible manifestations of the visible church. The popular
perception of them still probably owes more to Trollope and television series like *All Gas and Gaiters* than to the realities of modern
clerical life. There are certainly colourful characters still to be
found, especially in the Church of England where eccentricity and
eclecticism have yet to be stamped out by the march of managerial
conformity. There are vicars who ride to hounds, parson poets like
the estimable R. S. Thomas, and cathedral deans who still sweep
out of evensong wearing mortarboard and cassock and scurry
across the close to their lodgings for sherry in a way that could
come straight out of the Barchester novels. But for every one of
these old-style clerical figures there are many more whose homes
are not rambling rectories but modest suburban semis, who spend
hours hunched over their Amstrads and who are more familiar

with the jargon of non-directive counselling and group therapy than with the classics or the natural history of their parish. The traditional idea of a clergyman having charge of a single benefice is also becoming an increasing rarity as more and more parishes are being linked or united and churches are responding to falling manpower and social changes by creating new kinds of team, community and specialized ministries.

It has been estimated that altogether there are some 39,000 ministers of religion in Britain – considerably more than the number of doctors, which is around 26,000. But the number of full-time clergy in the mainstream traditional churches has fallen sharply throughout the twentieth century, reflecting a lack of vocations and severe financial problems as well as the overall decline in membership. The Church of England has suffered a drop in its complement of stipendiary clergy from 25,235 in 1901 to 10,500 in 1990, and a further 10 per cent decline is predicted over the next 15 years. In the Church of Scotland the number of parish ministers has dropped from 2,200 to 1,250 over the last 40 years. Admittedly, in both churches there has been a rise in the number of part-time clergy who combine parochial duties at the weekend with working in a non-church job through the week: there are now more than 2,000 such non-stipendiary clergy in the Church of England. The use of part-timers is likely to increase significantly over the coming years.

Although financial problems make it very difficult for the mainstream churches to increase the number of clergy, there are signs that more candidates for ordination are now coming forward than has been the case for some time. Within the Church of England, for example, 773 candidates came forward in 1990 of whom 334 were accepted for training for the stipendiary ministry, as compared with figures of 753 and 308 in the previous year. The Church of Scotland is also experiencing a slight increase in candidates for ordination. In 1990 113 applicants for the full-time ministry attended selection schools, of whom 69 were accepted for training.

The Roman Catholic Church has also suffered a loss of clergy and now has a very high proportion of elderly priests. But unlike the main Protestant churches there is little sign of an upturn in vocations. In 1990 there were just 86 entrants into formation for the secular priesthood in England and Wales, compared with 104 the previous year. In fact, the situation with regard to vocations here is better than in many other countries. Only Malta and Ireland have a higher ratio of priests to baptized Catholics within the population. Ireland has its lowest level of priests for 50 years, and in France the number of priests is now smaller than the number of known fortune-tellers.

One might think that falling numbers would have led the main denominations to pool their resources and recognize the validity of each other's orders. In fact, this has signally failed to happen: an outside observer might be forgiven for thinking that the only respect in which the clergy have come closer is in their manner of dress. It used to be the case that the width of a clergyman's dog-collar provided a good guide to his theological persuasion and denomination. The broader the collar, the lower was the church-manship of its wearer. Nowadays, however, the thin plastic strip which tucks into the collar of a clerical shirt and was once only worn by High Anglicans and Roman Catholics is favoured by clergy of all denominations. This may perhaps have something to do with the fact that, as the Archbishop of Canterbury has testified, it can be fashioned *in extremis* out of a British Rail plastic cup or a washing-up-liquid container. There are still certain sartorial touches which distinguish the clergy of different denominations. Church of Scotland ministers, for example, have a particular pen-chant for blue clerical shirts. But on the whole I suspect that a better rough guide to denomination might nowadays be based on different drinking habits. In my experience Anglican clergy, on the whole, are bitter drinkers and have largely resisted the drift of the rest of the population towards lager. Roman Catholic priests tend to prefer something sweeter and stronger, while Free Church and Church of Scotland ministers are more likely to be teetotal – although there are not a few in the Kirk who will take a dram, and the Methodists have recently reversed generations of total abstinence by voting to allow alcohol at their annual conferences.

Failure to agree on the subject of ministry has been the biggest stumbling block in the path towards closer union between the main churches. Talks between the six major Protestant denominations in Scotland which went on from 1967 to 1985 produced agreement on both baptism and the eucharist. But, as the final report on these multilateral conversations reflected ruefully, 'seventeen years of discussion have proved to us that the theology of ministry and ordination is the most difficult and contentious problem of all, requiring an amount of attention that seems disproportionate'. It went on, despite the difficulties, to recommend that the participating churches accept each other's ministries. But this has failed to happen. The problem is that episcopal churches like the Church of England and the Scottish Episcopal Church refuse to accept as valid ordinations which have not been conducted by bishops, and so do not recognize ministers in the Church of Scotland or other reformed churches as properly ordained. The Roman Catholic Church, in its turn, does not accept the validity of Anglican orders.

At the root of this problem is a serious theological disagreement about what ordination means. The highest view is taken by the Roman Catholic Church, which sees the essence of priesthood as the performance of the sacrifice of the Mass, where the priest stands at the altar *in persona Christi*. Reformed churches like the Church of Scotland and the English and Welsh Free Churches take a much lower view of ordination, eschewing the concept of priesthood and seeing ministers essentially as preaching and teaching elders. Anglicans, as always, are somewhere in the middle, and are also more heterogeneous in their attitudes, some taking a high Catholic and sacramental view of the priesthood and others being much closer to the reformed idea of the ministry of the word.

Debates about the theology of ministry lie behind some of the most difficult and contentious issues currently facing the mainstream churches – most notably the vexed question of celibacy in the Roman Catholic priesthood and the ordination of women to the priesthood in the Church of England. All the indications are that the two churches are responding in very different ways to what is a fundamental challenge to their traditional patterns of ministry – the Roman Catholics by vigorously reasserting the historic character of their priesthood and refusing to make any compromise with modern trends, the Church of England, in common with the other Anglican churches in the British Isles, by moving with the times and preparing to make a major change in its conception of ministry.

Although the debate over women priests in the Church of England has generated more passion and more media interest, the dilemma facing the Roman Catholic Church is probably more serious. Not only is the Church failing to recruit new priests at anything like the rate needed to replace those dying or retiring, but it is also losing a large number of its existing clergy through resignation. Worldwide a total of 100,000 men have left the priesthood over the last 20 years, and there is no doubt that the major reason for this exodus has been failure to keep the vow of celibacy.

The position in Britain may not be as bad as it is in the United States, where more than 20,000 out of 48,000 priests have resigned their orders over the last 20 years and where a recent study suggests that nearly half of those remaining are breaking their vow of celibacy on either a temporary or a permanent basis, but there is no doubt at all that priests here, too, are deeply worried about the celibacy rule. A study of Roman Catholic clergy in the diocese of Middlesbrough in 1990 found that 70 per cent confessed to feeling lonely and to being worried about their own sexuality, while more than 60 per cent said that the vow of celibacy was a matter of concern to them.

Over the last few years some of Britain's best-known Catholic priests have left the priesthood in order to get married. They include Bruce Kent, the former general secretary of CND, and Adrian Hastings, Professor of Theology at Leeds University. There is growing pressure in this country as elsewhere for the celibacy rule to be relaxed and the ordination of married men permitted. One of the leading advocates of this reform is the Catholic psychiatrist Jack Dominion, who believes it would elevate sexuality to its rightful place in Christian life and end centuries of negativity on the part of the Church towards it, as well as opening up the ordained service of God to many more people.

But although the Pope has agreed to accept into the Catholic priesthood married Anglican and Lutheran clergymen who have transferred their allegiance to Rome, he has made it very clear that there can be no compromises over the principle of celibacy for Roman Catholic priests. This view was shared by the Synod of Bishops which met in Rome in October 1990 to discuss the whole idea of the priesthood. It reaffirmed the rule of celibacy on the grounds that 'it consecrates the priest in an intimate union with Christ the bridegroom, who so loved his bride, the Church, that he gave up his life for her'. In other ways, too, the Synod responded to what it acknowledged was a 'deep crisis' in the priesthood by reasserting a deeply traditional and conservative line. While accepting that many priests felt misunderstood, isolated and de-moralized it attributed the serious shortage of new recruits not to any factors within the Church but rather to outside influences such as secularization, eroticism and the degrading of family life. Going back to a pre-Vatican II conception of the priest as a man apart, it re-emphasized the importance of celibacy and the quasi-monastic isolation of the seminary. The idea that either in their training or in their ministry priests should work more closely with lay people or with ministers from other denominations was firmly rejected. In the words of *The Tablet*: 'Confronted with a crisis, the bishops refused to make the slightest accommodation to it. They set out in uncompromising terms an ideal of Roman priesthood, and laid it before the world as an inspiration worth aiming at. It is a high-risk strategy which compels admiration but which cannot be welcomed without reserve.'

Although the current line from Rome is clear and uncompromising, the demands from many British Catholics for a change of attitude towards the priesthood are unlikely to go away. But the main focus of interest at least for the next few years is undoubtedly going to remain on the Anglican priesthood and in particular on the merits and the consequences of ordaining women. This is not a new issue – as long ago as 1975 the General Synod agreed that there was no fundamental objection to the ordination of women to the priesthood, but in 1978 a motion to bring it about was defeated. For the next 10 years the subject was kept in a rather uneasy state of limbo but at last in 1987 the General Synod voted to proceed with legislation enabling women to be ordained as priests. The final measure is expected to come before the Synod in 1992 or 1993, when to be carried it will need a two-thirds majority in each of the three houses.

No other issue currently facing any of the churches in Britain arouses such strong passions. It has split the Church of England into bitterly opposed factions which adopt tactics more usually associated with political pressure groups. On one side stands the Movement for the Ordination of Women, whose members regularly demonstrate with placards outside church meetings and services; on the other, the 5,500 strong Women against the Ordination of Women (WOW) and the Cost of Conscience movement which claims the support of up to 4,000 clergy. George Carey had an early taste of the strength of feeling on the issue when he let slip in an interview with the *Reader's Digest* some months before his enthronement that 'the idea that only a male can represent Christ at the altar is a most serious heresy.' In the face of a storm of indignation and protest he was forced to make a substantial retraction of his remarks.

What are the main arguments deployed by the proponents and opponents of women's ordination? The case in favour is based primarily on arguments of sexual equality and simple justice. If women feel called to the priesthood, as many clearly do, surely they should be allowed to exercise their vocation, particularly when there is a shortage of recruits to the clergy. Already there are female deacons in the Church of England conducting marriages and baptisms and officiating at funerals. When around 70 per cent of the Church's membership is female it seems particularly unfair not to allow women to exercise the full functions of ministry and celebrate the sacrament of communion. Women priests are already an established feature in several churches within the Anglican communion, notably in Australasia and North America. Even in the relatively conservative province of New Zealand, where the first women were ordained in 1977, there are now about 100 women priests and a female bishop, Penelope Jamieson, who was consecrated in July 1990 as Bishop of Dunedin – and, in the words of Charles Tyrrell, canon of Wellington Cathedral, 'the roof hasn't fallen in'.

Supporters of women's ordination are also moved by deeper theological and psychological considerations. Many argue from the doctrine of the Incarnation that Jesus Christ took on not just male flesh but all human flesh, and so any argument that he can only be represented by men is spurious. They also point to the fact that his ministry was directed especially to the marginalized and the oppressed, a condition in which women have traditionally found themselves. Perhaps even more telling is the argument that the qualities most needed in priests are those traditionally regarded as feminine, such as empathy, sensitivity, gentleness and intuition. This has been a main theme of the highly effective and emotive literature put out by the Movement for the Ordination of Women. A four-page broadsheet headed 'Will the church be safe in these hands?', for example, asserts, 'Our church is crying out for a woman's touch. Compassion and strength – Christian virtues – and, in today's world, qualities which are desperately needed. They are the qualities which people used to find in our church. Yet today to many people our church seems aloof, cold and remote, out of touch with the day to day reality of the lives they lead.'

The argument of those on the other side are more historical and theological. They point out that the historic ministry of the church is traced back to Jesus' choice of twelve men to be his disciples. This choice, they maintain, was not simply a matter of chance or cultural conditioning but, in the words of Graham Leonard, the former Bishop of London, 'because in the order of creation head-

ship and authority is symbolically and fundamentally associated
with maleness'. Traditionally, the mainstream churches of both
East and West have not ordained women. It is not on the agenda
of either the Roman Catholic or the Eastern Orthodox churches,
and is a relatively recent phenomenon in the Protestant world
initiated only a hundred years or so ago by the tiny Universalist
Church of the United States of America.

For Anglo-Catholics, the main group opposing women's ordination within the Church of England, the thought of this threat to
the historic ministry which Anglicans have consistently claimed to
share with the Roman Catholics and Orthodox looms large. They
fear that in voting to ordain women as priests the Church of
England would be taking a unilateral decision that would put it
out of step with the rest of the universal Catholic church and
severely prejudice relations with the two other major worldwide
churches. Anglo-Catholic opposition to women's ordination also
rests on a strongly sacramental understanding of ministry. The
priest is pre-eminently the one who represents Christ in the sacrifice
of the eucharist, standing at the altar *in persona Christi*, and therefore must be a male. For evangelicals, the other group in which
opposition to women's ministry is found, though to nothing like
the same extent as among Anglo-Catholics, the argument is much
more Biblical and rests on such texts as 1 Timothy 2.12: 'I permit
no woman to teach, nor to hold authority over men; she is to keep
silent.'

Underlying these arguments there is a deeper, hidden agenda.
To a large extent the issue of women priests has become the main
battleground for the clash between liberals and conservatives. For
its supporters, women's ordination is the key to liberating the
church from its suffocating slavery to hidebound tradition, patri-
archalism and hierarchical rule and making it much more like what
it was originally intended to be by Jesus. Opponents see it rather
as the ultimate expression of the whole package of woolly liberal
thinking that has dominated the church since the 1960s. It is
American-inspired, it owes much more to sociological than to
theological arguments, and it is the hallmark of a church which
allows itself to be ruled by trend rather than tradition and picks
up every passing secular fad.

There is no doubt, too, that this issue has stirred up so many
passions because it touches so clearly on the question of sexuality.
There is a good deal of unresolved uncertainty, guilt and fear

among most Christians about the whole matter of sex, and the Church of England is no exception. Graham Leonard, one of the leading episcopal opponents of women's ordination, honestly admitted the confusion he would feel in wanting to embrace an attractive women priest. It is hard to avoid the conclusion that part of the opposition to women priests among Anglican clergy is fear of the opposite sex. Recent surveys have shown that more than a quarter of Anglo-Catholic clergy in the Church of England are bachelors, as against less than 5 per cent of Evangelicals and liberals. For a significant proportion of these men, opposition to women priests is almost certainly bound up with anxieties about their own sexuality. A detailed study by a psychologist, Dr Ben Fletcher, published in 1990 under the title *Clergy Under Stress*, estimated that around 15 per cent of Church of England clergy are homosexual. The highest concentrations of these clergy are in London and other large cities, which tend to be the places where opposition to women priests is greatest.

Thanks to the interest of the tabloid press, the issue of homosexual clergy in the Church of England is almost as well publicized as the debate over women's ordination, but in fact it is of considerably less moment. It achieved prominence in the General Synod of November 1987 when the Reverend Anthony Higton, a leading Evangelical, called for the removal of practising homosexuals from the Anglican priesthood. The Synod settled for a compromise motion proposed by the Bishop of Chester which stated that Christians should be exemplary in all spheres of morality, including sexual morality, and that homosexual genital acts 'fall short of this ideal'. To some extent this issue proves another battleground between liberals and Evangelicals, with the former arguing for tolerance and acceptance of homosexual clergy in permanent committed relationships, and the latter seeking the removal of all homosexual priests. After the 1987 Synod debate there were fears of a witch-hunt developing, and Dr Fletcher's study of homosexual priests found that they suffered from a considerable degree of stress, in several cases amounting to clinical depression. The whole question of homosexuality among the clergy will not go away, and inevitable occasional scandals will continue to feed the media's appetite for anti-clerical sensationalism. However, it is unlikely to assume major importance or to lead to a serious split within the Church.

The same cannot be said with such certainty about what look

like being the final stages over the debate on the ordination of women. It seems highly probable that the necessary legislation will go through Synod in the next year or so. What will happen as a result to the considerable number of clergy who oppose women priests is less easy to predict. In order to accommodate them a number of concessions have been proposed, such as allowing bishops presently in office to ban women priests from their dioceses and to refuse to sponsor them as ordination candidates, and giving parishes the right to persist in refusing to accept women priests against the views of their bishops. In spite of these concessions, however, the Cost of Conscience movement has prepared detailed plans for what has been called 'guerilla war in occupied territory'. In the event of the passing of legislation for women's ordination, a system of alternative episcopal oversight would be put into operation whereby clergy opposed to the new arrangements would regard themselves as under the jurisdiction not of their own diocesan bishop but of the nearest bishop opposed to women's ordination.

An exodus of large numbers of Anglican clergy to the Roman Catholic Church seems unlikely; economic considerations will probably force them to stay within the Church of England. As one of those involved in the Cost of Conscience put it to me, priests may be uneasy about being in communion with ordained women priests, but 'most will want to stay in communion with the Church Commissioners'. The thought of losing home, salary and pension will probably keep many within the Anglican fold. Certainly the Roman Catholic Church could not afford in its present condition to take on many more ex-Anglican priests and pay them at the level to which they have been accustomed. What seems more likely is the formation of a number of breakaway Anglican churches. An umbrella group for such churches already exists in the shape of the Traditional Anglican Communion, an American-based alliance of Anglican traditionalists. The communion has its own primate, Archbishop Louis Falk, who heads the breakaway Anglican Church of America. He has already visited Britain to confer with opponents of women's ordination.

The worst that could happen to the Church of England as the result of the ordination of women would be the creation of a large and disaffected group of clergy encouraged by sympathetic bishops to operate outside the established diocesan structures and effectively forming a church within a church. But it is equally possible that after the initial fuss and bother much of the opposition may gradually subside. Certainly there is evidence to suggest that the great majority of church-goers would not be much disturbed. In a detailed survey of rural parishioners in five dioceses in 1990 only 11 per cent indicated that the ordination of women would negatively affect their view of the Church of England, while 27 per cent said it would make them more positive in their attitude. The majority, 55 per cent, said it would not affect their views one way or the other, and the remaining 6 per cent were undecided. Out of a total of 333 respondents, only two said that they would leave the Church of England in the event of the ordination of women to the priesthood. Rural parishioners seemed to be much more worried about the prospect of greater use of lay people for taking services – 91 per cent of those questioned said they would accept communion from a woman priest but only 29 per cent were prepared to accept the administration of the chalice by a lay person.

Looking further ahead, it may even be that women will one day become dominant among the clergy of the main Protestant churches in Britain. Half of the new ministers ordained between 1985 and 1990 are female. The highest proportion of women are found in the Salvation Army (60 per cent of commissioned officers) and the Afro-Caribbean churches (39 per cent of pastors). Overall in Britain, however, women make up just 8 per cent of ordained ministers. Within the Church of Scotland, where women have been eligible for ordination to the eldership since 1966 and to the ministry since 1968, there are still only around a hundred female ministers, less than a tenth of the total. Among students in training, however, the proportion is nearer a third. Over the last few years a small but significant group of younger evangelical ministers has emerged who are strongly opposed to women elders and ministers. The 1991 General Assembly declared by an overwhelming majority that ministers or Kirk sessions refusing to ordain women elders on the grounds of their sex were in clear breach of the law of the Church and should be disciplined. Despite this ruling, it seems likely that Scripturally-based opposition to the ordination of women on the part of evangelical clergy will continue to grow in the Kirk, although it is very far from constituting anything like the same challenge to authority as that posed in the Church of England.

Another trend within the Church of Scotland which may become increasingly marked in other denominations is the emergence of ministerial couples, where both husband and wife are ordained and either working jointly in a parish or engaged in complementary forms of ministry. Counting students and probationers in training, there are now 33 such couples in the service of the Kirk. The development of such joint ministries may play some small part in diminishing the sense of isolation felt by many parish clergy. So too may the increasing trend, as yet largely confined to the Church of England but likely to spread to other denominations, towards team ministries. The clergy are the only caring profession who still work predominantly on their own rather than in groups. This can lead to considerable loneliness. A heartfelt article written by a West Yorkshire vicar which appeared in the *Church Times* in March 1991 under the title 'The dark side of rural ministry' could equally well have come from the incumbent of an inner-city parish. It spoke of the isolation and loneliness of the clergyman's life, and went on: 'Being unused is another part of the onus. Months can pass, perhaps even years, when no one approaches the rural priest for "ghostly counsel and advice". They call for the banns certificate or because they cannot find a relative's gravestone. They call because they need a key to the boilerhouse or because they were three magazines short this month. But parishioners rarely call because they face a crisis and want your pastoral guidance ... Preaching to small numbers can also dampen enthusiasm. Seeing the same seven or seventeen there every Sunday makes it difficult to retain an appropriate sense of authority and detachment in the sermon.'

There is no doubt that stress is a growing and worrying feature of clerical life in all the major churches. It shows itself in a rising incidence of nervous disorders and marital breakdowns in a profession which is traditionally associated with emotional stability and steadiness, and in the phenomenon of ministerial 'burn-out', where clergy exhaust themselves and seek early retirement from their parish duties. There are many reasons for this – the problems of being in a job which is seen as irrelevant and unimportant by the majority of the population, the increasing workload brought about by the falling number of clergy, and the poor financial rewards. For those ministering in inner-city and deprived urban areas there are the added strains of having to deal with intractable social problems and seeking to maintain a Christian presence in the face of massive indifference and even hostility. The rural ministry has its strains as well. Many country clergy now look after anything up to half a dozen parishes single-handed and are accustomed to what has become known as 'the Sunday gallop' as they dash round trying to fit in services in as many churches as possible. The record appears to be held by one Anglican incumbent who has on occasion taken 15 services on a single Sunday.

The workload of clergy has steadily increased over the last 50 years, as their pay and status have diminished. In 1931 more than a third of all parish priests in the Church of England had flocks of fewer than 500 to care for. Now over 90 per cent of livings hold more than 1,000 people and some have more than 10,000. A recent survey of parish clergy found that they worked on average 56.6 hours a week, with some putting in as many as 116 hours. Very few manage to get a regular day off in the week to compensate for working on Sunday, and Saturday is often taken up with weddings and sermon preparation. Clerical pay has fallen progressively behind that of other professions. This year (1992) the minimum stipend for Church of Scotland ministers is £13,284. About 500 of the Kirk's 1,300 ministers are on the minimum stipend and most of the rest are paid only slightly above it. Church of England clergy are rather worse off – their average stipend last year was just £12,080. It is true that clergy receive a free house, but this can be a doubtful advantage and it is less and less likely to be the gracious and commodious residence that it once was. Both the Church Commissioners and the General Trustees of the Church of Scotland have a policy of wherever feasible selling off old vicarages and manses and building more modern and less spacious clergy houses. A recent correspondent to the *Daily Telegraph* blamed this trend for bringing about the decline of the great British tradition of large clerical families with children of high academic calibre. 'In cities and villages throughout the land', she reflected sadly, 'the old, rambling vicarages, former symbols of substance, now sport commuter Volvos in the drive, ruched chintz curtains at the windows and a sign saying "The Old Rectory" on the gate. On the other side of the walled garden huddles the new vicarage, a mean, modern dwelling hardly big enough to house a pewful of visitors, let alone a quiverful of children.'

The increasing strains of the job are felt not just by the clergy but also by their spouses. In the past ministers' wives were more prepared to act as unpaid secretaries and assistants and there was also often full-time domestic help in the vicarage or manse. Nowadays many clergy wives are driven by economic necessity to go out and work themselves, and often they want to maintain their

own careers and not subordinate their lives totally to those of
their husbands. There are also particular stresses involved in being
married to someone who is constantly responding to other people's
emotional demands. Not a few clergy wives end up feeling that it
is the parishioners rather than themselves who are married to
their husbands. Writing in the *Guardian*, one described their lot in
graphic terms: 'You stand alone, answering the door to the mad,
the bad and the con man as well as to the genuine seeker of pastoral
services. In the old days you shared this type of commitment
with doctors and teachers, but today doctors are mainly in group
practices and carefully guarded by receptionists and teachers generally live away from their schools. Only the vicarage is a 24-hour
door-answering service, without appointments. I began to dread
the endlessly ringing telephone and doorbell, when there are no
office hours and everyone calling at mealtimes "because they know
you'll be in". One of the things I hated most was having my home
used as a parish hall – all that moving of chairs; the doorbell ringing
twenty times before the meeting; the wet umbrellas dripping on
floors; mud or snow on carpets.'

The Church of England's *Faith in the Countryside* report has
recommended that clergy wives should be paid out of central
Church funds at the rate of around £2,000 a year. This suggestion
has, however, been seen by many as a slight on the many voluntary
workers in parishes who give their time and talents to the Church
without any thought of reward. It is hard to see how the increasing
strains on clerical marriages are going to diminish unless there is
a radical change in the working patterns of parish ministers and
the expectations that are made of them. It may well be that there
is something to be said for celibacy among those who are working in
particularly stressful areas of ministry, such as inner-city parishes.
Certainly the *Faith in the City* report found that there were often
considerable problems for the wives and families of clergy in urban
priority areas. Significantly, it also found that 26 per cent of those
working in such areas are single, compared with only 13 per cent
among the Anglican clergy overall.

The problems of stress and burn-out are undoubtedly going to
be a major concern for all the mainstream churches in the coming
years. New pastoral structures are being developed to help those
clergy who are under strain. In the Church of England, for example,
the Society of Mary and Martha has been set up by a Church Army
captain in Dunsford, near Exeter, specifically to provide a shoulder

for distraught clergy and their spouses to cry on. It is currently
receiving around twenty calls a week, many of them about marital
problems. The Church of Scotland is in the process of setting up
support groups in each presbytery and appointing ministers who
will have specific responsibility for providing pastoral care for the
pastors. There are also increasing moves in all the main churches
to devolve more functions, including the conduct of services, to the
laity. Within the Roman Catholic Church there is now a large body
of eucharistic ministers who can administer communion elements
consecrated by a priest. The Church of England has nearly 9,000
lay readers who are qualified to distribute the elements at communion and conduct funerals. George Carey has said that he would
like to see a service being held at the same time in every parish
church in England every Sunday morning. He sees it as an essential
part of being the national church. If this bold and welcome proposal
is to be implemented, it will mean the extensive use of readers and
other lay people to lead worship on a regular basis.

In a way, of course, these developments further diminish the
status of the ordained clergy and call into question whether they
are really needed at all. The *Faith in the Countryside* report found
that in many cases the absence of a resident clergyman actually
encouraged growth and confidence within local parishes. It quoted
one group of parishes which had indicated to its parent diocese
that it did not want a new resident incumbent, merely access to the
services of a clergyman for 10 hours a week. A number of parishes
testified to a common experience that the life of the church was
enhanced rather than diminished during a period of vacancy. One
churchwarden seemed to speak for many when he observed that
'we all slowed down again after the arrival of the new rector'.
Another pointed out that 'within the lifetime of some of the people
in this place, the vicar has changed from being the person who
distributed money to those who were the chief charge on the
community, to now being the chief charge on the community itself'.

The report went on to note how far the whole role and *raison
d'être* of the ordained minister have been called into question. As
it points out, 'Many pastoral tasks have been taken over by other
professions within an expanded state sector and by new voluntary
bodies dealing with social welfare and counselling ... Within the
community of the Church itself many of the tasks previously done
by the clergy are now performed by the laity, with bishops granting
authority for preaching, teaching, administering the sacrament,

visiting the sick, and burying the dead. With this welcome development of the liturgical and pastoral work of the laity, there has come
also a questioning of the role of the ordained ministry.' The report
goes on to observe that clergy 'find themselves trapped between
the realities of modern multi-parish ministry, the traditional expectations of the laity and a perception of priesthood which was
formed during the period of their own training ... Much of the
evidence presented to the Commission still assumed that the priest
is the person who should be an exemplary performer of all kinds
of ministry, and a model of perfection. Whether the expectations
are implied or made explicit, they are a recipe for disaster and
many clergy have suffered seriously from their attempts to meet
them.'

Those remarks will strike a chord with parish clergy in all the
main churches. One of the greatest obstacles towards creating a
genuine ministry of the laity is the expectation that so many people
still have of the ordained minister as a man of God who is somehow
set apart and more holy than the rest of humanity. It is an expectation supported by much theological training and preparation for
ordination, which still encourages the view that it is a highly
individualistic vocation and not a collaborative venture in which
minister and people go forward together. Much effort is now being
directed by the churches to formulating a new concept of ordained
ministry which emphasizes its enabling role and locates it within the
wider ministry of the whole church. Members of the Archbishops'
Commission on Rural Areas had a stab at defining this new animal
when they said in *Faith in the Countryside* that the ordained minister
'should be the one who is trained to hold the breadth of vision and
to share in it with the whole body committed to his charge ... in
practical terms, this points to guiding and enabling people to
minister within the broad vision of mission, without falling into
the trap of feeling responsible for doing everything themselves.'

In its practical and systematic way the Church of Scotland has
tackled the question of what the role of the clergy should be today
by producing a job description for ministers. A report to the 1990
General Assembly suggested that this should embrace seven areas:
the ministry of word and sacrament, encompassing preaching
and teaching in and through the congregation; personal study
and spiritual growth encompassing regular theological reading and
study for its own sake; pastoral work in the congregation and
parish; mission to the parish; community involvement; involvement

in Presbytery and General Assembly; and organization and administration. It also suggested that while they may well find it very hard to adhere to, ministers should at least take a 40-hour week as a base-line and should make sure that they work into their weekly programme adequate time for relaxation and for spouse and family.

Interestingly, the proposed job description makes much of the need for ministers to spend time preparing their minds for the work that they have to do – perhaps more than a similar document from the Church of England would. Training for the Church of Scotland ministry is considerably more demanding intellectually than for Anglican orders. It is carried out entirely in the four ancient Scottish universities and the normal requirement for ministers is still a four-year arts degree followed by a three-year divinity degree. Those who bemoan the fact that the standards of education are falling among the clergy and that there is no longer any room for the scholar-parson might reflect on this extract from the Kirk's proposed job description about the importance of the minister's study: 'It should not be seen merely as the production line for conveyor belt sermons. When preparation for the worship of Sunday has been completed, escape to the "real world" is not inevitably the order of the day, because for the minister who is true to his or her calling the study, worship preparation apart, is part of the real world and must be seen as such. The systematic and wide-ranging reading that rightly belongs there, the private prayers and reading of the Scriptures in which ministry must be steeped, the committed pursuit of new insights into the mysteries of the faith, the continuing stimulation of mind and heart will all the better enable the minister to preach the Gospel and, human frailty accepted, to live the Gospel. Whether a parish has ten souls or ten thousand, here is its priority.'

So far there has been no suggestion that this job description should become the basis of formal agreements between kirk sessions and new ministers on their induction to parishes. But there is increasing pressure within many churches to follow the practice of other professions and make the system of appointing clergy much more systematized and ordered. There is talk of a more formal contract of employment for clergy, and the new Archbishop of Canterbury has let it be known that he would like the Church to adopt a much more managerial and business-like approach in the deployment of its personnel. It is likely that this could well herald the end of the present rather haphazard system by which Church of England clergy are appointed to parishes. Out of a total of 16,000 parishes, the Church itself holds the patronage of only a third. Another third are still in the hands of private individuals, predominantly peers and squires, 20 per cent belong to patronage trusts, most of which are pushing a particular party line, 7 per cent belong to universities, and 7 per cent to the Crown. The Prime Minister and the Lord Chancellor between them are the patrons of 700 livings. Some livings are advertised but many are not and are still filled on the basis of personal recommendation and through the old boy network. There is increasing consultation with parochial church councils about the sort of incumbent wanted locally, but the methods of appointing clergy remain very varied and somewhat quirky.

Whether the Church of England will model any new clergy appointments system more along Free Church or on Roman Catholic lines remains to be seen. Other Protestant churches tend to give a much greater say to congregations. The process which the Church of Scotland uses for appointing parish ministers is much like that used by political parties for selecting parliamentary candidates. When a vacancy occurs in a parish it is advertised in the press and a vacancy committee is formed which goes round hearing those who have applied for the charge (and others whose names have been recommended) preach in their own churches. A short-list is drawn up and those on it are asked to preach again before a larger committee who afterwards interview them on everything from their views on baptism and blood sports to whether their wives would be willing to preside over meetings of the Woman's Guild. Generally a sole nominee is then chosen to preach before the congregation of the vacant church, after which all those who wish to have him or her as their minister sign a call. Once in a charge a minister is fairly safe from removal until reaching the retirement age of 70. Induction to a charge used to be *ad vitam aut culpam*. Now presbyteries have the right to dissolve the pastoral tie between a minister and his congregation if relations have clearly broken down, but this happens relatively rarely. Interestingly, it has most recently been used to remove two strongly evangelical ministers, one who was refusing to ordain women elders and another who was disturbing parishioners by the strength of his anti-abortion views.

The Roman Catholic Church, by contrast, puts all parish

appointments firmly in the control of bishops who have total power to decide who goes where and when they move. I happened to visit the Bishop of Dunkeld when he was in the middle of a reshuffle of his clergy in Dundee. He was able to tell me exactly who would be going where before any of the individuals involved had themselves any idea that they were in for a move. There is growing unhappiness among Catholic clergy at the ease with which they can be moved around without any consultation, and there have been a number of cases recently of protests and appeals being lodged against the decisions of bishops. Unlike their counterparts in the Church of England, Roman Catholic priests have no security of tenure in their parochial appointments.

The days of the Anglican parson's freehold look to be numbered, however. There is considerable pressure for an end to the practice that has given Church of England clergy a post for life, irrespective of how diligently or how indolently they perform in it, and for the introduction of a more flexible contract of employment similar to that prevailing in nearly every other profession. Those in favour of the abolition of freehold argue that it will help boost flagging congregations and raise morale in parishes where lazy and inept clergymen have lingered on for decades. In a recent synod debate an archdeacon described clergy who remained anchored to one benefice as 'a ball and chain on the body of Christ'. But others argue that the parson's freehold, like academic tenure, allows clergy to say and preach what they feel without fear or favour and without having to think all the time what the bishop or parishioners want. They fear that its replacement by a contract will diminish the spirituality of a priest's calling and encourage a view that he has to be measured in terms of productivity. One correspondent to *The Times* asked, 'Will competence be judged on the ability to raise money, create a mutual admiration society of the like-minded, twang a guitar or twirl a thurible?'

Significant changes are already occurring in the pattern of clerical recruitment. The old stereotype of the clergyman as someone who pursued a boyhood vocation, took orders straight after leaving university and then often stayed the best part of his life in a single parish is now an increasing rarity. Most ordinands are now coming into the church as a second career. Over 60 per cent of Anglican ordinands are over 30, while the average age for Church of Scotland ministers completing their training is 39. This trend towards older entrants to the ministry has many implications, not least in leading to much shorter periods of pre-ordination training and producing a more affluent clergy, many of whom will have been used to owning their own houses before coming into parishes. In common with so many other sectors of society, the clergy are also becoming increasingly mobile, often staying for only five years or so in one parish before moving on.

Many would say that the clergy are becoming not only older but also greyer, and that the new managerial style with its emphasis on efficiency audits, performance reviews and contracts of employment will rob the British churches of the great crop of saints, scholars and eccentrics that has been one of their great glories. 'Give a reasonably educated, middle-class Englishman a modest income, a house in the country and job security for life and see what he will do', Thomas Hinde begins his *Field Guide to the English Country Parson*: 'He will do remarkable things. He becomes a world authority on spiders; he invents a theory of history which makes Druids a tribe of Phoenician pre-Christian Christians; he plants 5,000 rose bushes in his garden and the surrounding countryside, runs his own foxhound pack, makes his rectory into a monastery, collects folk songs, breeds winning race horses or green mice, rides from Land's End to John o'Groats … There seems no limit to the variety of his interests, or the obsessiveness with which he pursues them.'

It is certainly hard to imagine Gilbert White of Selborne, George Herbert, Francis Kilvert, Sabine Baring-Gould or Charles Kingsley having either the time or the space to exercise their literary talents and pursue their scientific interests in the modern Church of England. They would be too busy dashing round their multi-benefice parishes, attending committee meetings and sitting in their cramped studies tapping out children's addresses and agendas on their word-processors. A certain spaciousness and graciousness have undoubtedly gone out of clerical life. So to some extent have both the capacity and the inclination for scholarship. This is only partly a result of falling educational standards among the clergy. It is also because, thanks largely to television, there is much less premium put by either society or the churches nowadays on high literary standards in worship and preaching. The sermon as a finely honed work of art, incorporating carefully chosen classical and literary references and representing the product of many hours' labour by the minister in his study is largely a thing of the past – even, I am sorry to say, in the Church of Scotland, where more care and attention are still lavished on this aspect of worship than in most other churches.

It is true, too, that in the church as in other professions increasing bureaucracy and the demands of administration have produced a style of leadership which is managerial rather than inspirational. The present bench of Anglican bishops are often accused of resembling a group of managing directors or senior civil servants and lacking much of the colour and the spirituality of their predecessors. Yet maybe this is to over-romanticize the prelates of the past. Many who wear the purple today would probably agree with Archbishop Tait's comment made more than a century ago, that 'a bishop is a man in a chronic state of perspiration'. Bishops and other church leaders are all too aware of how easy it is in their highly pressured lives, rushing from one meeting to another, to lose sight of their uniquely spiritual function as those who above all have responsibility for the church's growth in holiness.

The churches are not being taken over by a new breed of clergy–managers who see their ministry as a career rather than a vocation. There are still a good number of gentle, kind, sensitive and saintly souls to be found in vicarages, presbyteries and manses up and down the country. Not a few of them display the stubborn spirituality of the Anglican priest looking after a single rural parish who responded to a request to help in the adjoining five-parish benefice and join the Sunday gallop, 'I'm not here to rush about. I'm here on call and I'm here to pray.' Although they often feel demoralized, tired, undervalued, put upon and taken for granted, there are still many parish clergy who are deeply satisfied in their ministries and who are seeking as best they can to live out the Gospel, mediate Christ's love and forgiveness and stand for what is decent and honourable. New patterns of Christian ministry are bound to evolve, based on more of a team-centred approach, using more part-time clergy and involving more lay leadership and participation on the model of the invisible churches. But for at least the foreseeable future ordained parish clergy, often working on their own, are likely to remain the backbone of the life and witness of the main churches.

7

Education and the young

One the earnest looking forward,
One the hope our God inspires

The churches still have an enormous stake in education. Nearly a quarter of all maintained schools in England are Church of England schools. Overall, in England, Scotland and Wales around 1,700,000 pupils attend either Church of England or Roman Catholic primary or secondary schools. Many of the private fee-paying schools which educate a further 600,000 children have chaplains and strong church affiliations. There are 12 Church of England and 8 Roman Catholic colleges of higher education specializing particularly in teacher-training. Most universities, polytechnics and colleges of higher and further education have full-time chaplains.

Many young people are also exposed to the influence of the church through their membership of uniformed organizations. The Boys' and Girls' Brigades, with about 140,000 members, are closely tied to local churches and built on strict Christian discipline. The much bigger Scout and Guide movements, which between them involve three-quarters of a million young people in Britain, have strong historic links with the churches although they are not specifically religious organizations nor exclusively Christian in membership. High among the promises which all scouts and guides make, renewed annually often at parade services in church on or around 23 April, is 'to do my duty to God'. Many local groups meet on church premises and scouts and guides are encouraged to join their local church or place of worship and attend it regularly.

The influence of these and other organizations may partly explain why church attendance among children has held up rather better than among adults. The MARC religious census found that the proportion of English children attending church in 1989 (14 per cent) was the same as it had been 10 years earlier. It was also slightly higher than the proportion of church-goers in the adult population (10 per cent). However, the survey also revealed that the overall number of children regularly attending church dropped during the 1980s from 1.4 to 1.2 million. There is still a significant level of occasional church-going among young people. A recent Gallup poll of teenagers found that 64 per cent never go to church, making organized religion a considerably more popular activity than politics, in which 82 per cent said they never participate.

These overall figures, however, hide a marked difference of success between the visible and invisible churches in attracting young people. Within the mainstream denominations membership of Sunday Schools, Bible classes and youth groups is at a lower level than at any other time this century. The average age of those involved in these organizations is also considerably lower than it used to be. Although there are still a fair number of primary school children in Sunday Schools, most lose any regular contact with the churches when they reach secondary school age. Figures recently released by the Church of Scotland show that between 1979 and 1989 membership of Bible classes for 12–17 year olds fell by over 40 per cent and youth fellowships by 50 per cent. In many churches teenage youth groups have ceased to function. The situation is broadly the same in the Church of England, the Roman Catholic Church and the historic Free Churches.

Among the newer denominations that make up the invisible church, however, youth attendance and membership are booming. The MARC census found that child attendance in independent, predominantly evangelical churches and fellowships in England had rocketed from 93,000 in 1975 to 132,700 in 1989 – an increase of nearly 40 per cent. Groups like the Jesus Army and events such as Spring Harvest and Greenbelt attract a predominantly teen-age and young adult following. A growing number of parents involved in the new evangelical churches and worried about the lack of Christian emphasis in the state education system are setting up their own private Christian schools. It may well be that as a result of this trend there will eventually be an extensive network of private evangelical schools in Britain on the model of those found in the United States.

For the time being, however, the dominant religious influence in education remains the traditional mainstream churches, and particularly the Church of England. Out of roughly 23,000 maintained primary and secondary schools in England, over 5,000 are Church of England schools. They provide education for just over 800,000 children, or 12 per cent of the total school population. Church schools are instantly recognizable by their titles and from the diocesan coat of arms that is usually displayed on their name-boards. Whether they differ from other schools in terms of ethos and curriculum is more difficult to say. With its broad and tolerant outlook, the Church of England is reluctant to make its schools too 'churchy' or too denominational. There is often little or no requirement on either teachers or pupils to be practising Anglicans. Indeed, one Church of England primary school in Manchester even has a Muslim headmaster, who converted from what he describes as 'loose Christian sympathies' out of admiration for the gentleness, kindness and strong moral standards of Islam.

Successive education acts have guaranteed the survival of church schools, which owe their origins to the period before state involvement in education when the churches were the main providers of schooling. Nowadays virtually all their funding comes from public sources. There are two main types of Church of England school. About 2,000 are voluntary aided, which means that the Governors, representing and appointed by the Church, are responsible for 15 per cent of the capital costs, and the state for 85 per cent. The Governors are also responsible for interviewing staff and for religious education. Nearly all the schools in this category are primary schools, although there are about 100 secondary schools. Voluntary aided schools are allowed to impose conditions for admission, such as church membership, although in practice this is often interpreted broadly. The Church has much less say in the running of the other 3,000 schools. They are voluntary controlled schools in which the local education authority meets all the costs and also employs the teachers. Parents can request denominational religious education but this rarely happens. There is also a small handful of schools where a special agreement exists.

Opinions are strongly divided within the Church of England about the usefulness of maintaining this extensive network of schools. Some feel that they are outmoded and that the Church should not be involved in denominational schooling. Others feel that they are not nearly denominational enough and that the Church is too reticent about nurturing young people in Anglicanism, with the result that a whole generation is growing up without any knowledge of or allegiance to the national church. But the schools also have their stout defenders, like the Bishop of Southwark, Ronald Bowlby, who sees them as 'a valuable bulwark against the steady erosion of Christian faith. It would take a long time to put any adequate alternative in their place.' The contribution of the schools to strengthening the Church varies enormously from area to area. Recent research by Leslie Francis suggests that in voluntary aided rural primary schools a high emphasis is often placed on church-related education, local clergy are generally actively involved and pupils are encouraged to participate in Sunday Schools and take part in the life of the local church. In inner-city areas, by contrast, Church of England primary schools are often at the forefront of multi-racial and multi-cultural education and go out of their way to cater for other faiths. The school in Spitalfields, for example, has Muslims and Hindus queuing up to join it. At the secondary level, Church schools often have a reputation for being better and more disciplined than other maintained schools and often have large waiting lists as a result. In some people's eyes they have become 'independent schools on the rates' and have been largely hijacked by the middle classes.

The Roman Catholic Church is the only other church involved in the state school system on any significant scale. There are about 30 Methodist schools but they all come into the controlled category and the Church has little direct say or influence in their running. By contrast the great majority of the 2,788 Roman Catholic maintained schools in England, Wales and Scotland, which educate a total of 135,000 pupils, are voluntary aided. This means that while the Church has to fund 15 per cent of any new building or capital work, it also retains control of curriculum, staffing and overall ethos and policy through the Governors, the vast majority of whom are appointed by diocesan bishops. On the whole Roman Catholic schools operate a tighter admissions policy than Church of England ones: it is quite common for admission to be restricted to baptized Catholics and to be dependent on a letter of recommendation from the local parish priest. They are also much more committed to providing denominational education and less embarrassed about making the whole ethos of the school distinctively Christian. A document issued in 1990 by the Bishops' Conference of England and Wales and the Department for Catholic Education and Formation, under the title *Evaluating the distinctive nature of a Catholic school*, lays down unequivocally that 'the Catholic school is essentially different and distinct from other institutions in both its philosophy and its practice. Above all its ethos is synonymous with and inseparable from its curriculum.' Each school is encouraged to draw up a mission statement and to look at its aims in respect of general ethos, local environment, admissions policy, religious education, worship, relations between school, parish and home, pastoral care, curriculum and staff.

On the whole Roman Catholic schools coexist happily with Church of England schools and fit in well to the general pattern of state education in England. The two churches have even started establishing joint schools, one of the first of which was the Bede Comprehensive School in Reigate. In Scotland, however, the picture is rather less harmonious and the whole question of separate Roman Catholic schools is a major political issue. This is only partly because of the greater strength of Protestant–Catholic antipathy north of the border. It is also a consequence of the fact that in Scotland the Roman Catholics are the only church to be involved in running schools. The Church of Scotland has a strong historic commitment to education, and for long actively pursued the policy of John Knox of establishing a school in every parish, but in 1872 it handed over all its schools to state control. Ministers generally act as chaplains to the schools within their parishes and regularly visit them to take assemblies, but the Church strongly advocates a non-denominational system of education with schools being open to all irrespective of religious belief. There is considerable unease within the Kirk and more generally in Scotland that the continued existence of separate Roman Catholic schools perpetuates religious division and bigotry and promotes the kind of sectarian spirit which is seen so clearly in Northern Ireland, where only 2,300 children out of a total school population of 340,000 attend integrated schools.

The issue is particularly acute in Strathclyde, which covers Glasgow and much of the west of Scotland. It is here that most of the Catholic schools are concentrated, 252 primaries and 54 secondaries which educate nearly a quarter of all children in the region. Falling school rolls have put pressure on the Church to close some of these schools or amalgamate them with local non-denominational schools, but these options have been fiercely resisted by the Catholic hierarchy in Scotland. There was a major row in 1991 when refusal to integrate a Catholic school in the Cranhill area of Glasgow with its non-denominational neighbour led to the closure of both schools and forced pupils to make bus journeys to schools in other areas. The insistence of bishops on maintaining separate Catholic schools is causing the region considerable expense at a time when finance is tight. In one case, in the Easterhouse district of Glasgow, a Roman Catholic and a non-denominational school share the same building but each has its own staff, its own office and its own telephone number. Pupils share the dining-hall and the playground but are taught everything separately, with a considerable duplication of teaching resources. Overall, Strathclyde Region has estimated that it costs between £50 and £130 more per year to keep a pupil at a Catholic school than at a non-denominational one.

Further disquiet has been provoked in Strathclyde over a recent change in the staffing policy of Catholic schools. Since 1918 the Church has been able to block appointments to teaching posts in voluntary aided schools. A change in the law in 1989 now allows it to veto promotions as well. There is evidence that the Church is using this power to block the promotion of able teachers in Catholic schools because they are not regarded as sufficiently good Catholics. Both the Regional Education Committee and the main teachers' union, the Educational Institute of Scotland, are extremely unhappy about the fact that a parish priest is asked to verify to the Catholic representative on the education committee that an applicant for promotion is in good standing with the Church. As a result, they claim, good teachers who happen to be divorced or who are infrequent in their attendance at Mass are finding promotion denied to them.

As pupil numbers continue to fall and financial pressure increases on local authorities to close and merge schools, the debate over the continued survival of denominational schools in Scotland is likely to intensify. Much will depend on how keen Catholic parents are to see their children educated in Catholic-only schools. The evidence here is conflicting and probably reflects different religious perceptions and traditions in the east and west. Aberdeen's one and only Roman Catholic secondary school was closed down in 1975 because of falling rolls. As a substitute, Catholic teachers of religious education were appointed in three non-denominational schools and arrangements made for Catholic pupils to have separate RE lessons. A recent survey of parents found that while most Protestants said they were quite happy not just with separate RE lessons for Catholic pupils but also with visits to the schools by local priests, opportunities for Mass and confession on the premises

and even with extra-curricular activities like Pro-Life cells, there
was only minimal support among Catholics for these facilities.
Indeed, the take-up for the separate Catholic RE lessons has been
very small, suggesting that many Catholic parents are not particularly wedded to the idea of specifically denominational religious
education. However, the mood in Glasgow and the west may be
rather different. Bishops insist that Catholic parents there do want
denominational education for their children and this is certainly
borne out by the experience of one of the most strongly Catholic
secondary schools on the south side of Glasgow, St Ninian's High
School in Eastwood. Here biology and geography lessons focus on
contraception and population control from a specifically Catholic
point of view, crucifixes hang in every classroom, there are prayers
every morning and a daily Mass at lunchtime. The school is full
and regularly has to turn down would-be pupils from other parts
of the city.

The demand for a rather different kind of denominational education is becoming an increasing issue for several English local
authorities and also posing a new dilemma for the churches. So far
Jews have been the only non-Christian group to receive public
money for schools. There are just 22 Jewish schools within the
maintained sector, all of which are voluntary aided. There is now
increasing pressure from those of other faiths, and particularly
from the growing Muslim community, for similar treatment. So
far this has not been forthcoming – an application by the Islamia
School in the London Borough of Brent for voluntary aided status
was turned down in 1990 – but pressure for separate state-main-
tained schools for those of other faiths is likely to increase. A recent
report for the Commission for Racial Equality, *Schools of Faith –
religious schools in a multi-cultural society*, argued strongly for the
law allowing voluntary aided status to be applied equally to all
faiths. At present, it says, a set of double standards is operating.
Christian schools are described as 'denominational' while Muslim
schools are regarded as 'separate' or 'segregated'. In a multi-faith
society, this is unacceptable.

So far many Muslim parents, including imams, have been happy
to send their children to Church of England or Roman Catholic
schools. Indeed, they have often preferred these to other maintained schools because of their perceived moral ethos and single-
sex nature. But this may be changing. In 1990, Muslim children
were withdrawn from a Church of England primary school in

Salford which has a strong commitment to multi-faith education. A combination of factors seems to have caused this exodus. The Education Reform Act of 1988 apparently alarmed some Muslim parents by putting increased emphasis on the Christian nature of school worship. At the same time the Salman Rushdie affair and the influx of more militant Muslims from Libya into the area seem to have led to the emergence of a more distinct Islamic consciousness. Initially the Muslim children at the school were withdrawn from assemblies and religious education lessons. Then their parents demanded that faith teaching in Islam should be provided on the school premises by a Muslim. It was the refusal of the Governors and staff to agree to this which led to the withdrawal of 29 pupils. It is too early yet to say whether this experience is being repeated in other parts of the country, but it does suggest that increasing tensions may develop between church schools and non-Christian communities.

In fact, leading figures in the two churches principally involved in running schools are backing the establishment of new faith schools within the maintained system. Both Michael Adie, Bishop of Guildford and chairman of the Church of England Board of Education, and David Konstant, Roman Catholic Bishop of Leeds and chairman of the Education Committee of the Bishops' Conference, have said that the Government should seriously consider extending voluntary aided status to schools for Muslims and children of other minority faiths. There is considerable caution on the part of the Department of Education, however, not least because of the feeling that the creation of separate schools for ethnic minorities would hamper race relations. There is also a widely held view that in a pluralistic and largely secular society such as Britain has become, the state should not be involved in actively supporting schools run by particular religious bodies and in maintaining a system which encourages the separated development of those of different faiths. It is not difficult to see why both the Church of England and the Roman Catholics back the claims of Muslims to have their own voluntary aided schools: it may well be that their own claim on public resources to finance denominational education will come under increasing attack. For the moment, however, it does not look as though there is any serious threat to the continued existence of church schools.

A large part of the reason why these schools, and Church of England schools in particular, are reasonably safe is, of course, because they are not really engaged in the business of proselytizing and evangelism. For a growing number of parents, indeed, they are not nearly Christian enough. One of the most striking developments in the whole field of religious education over the last decade or so has been the establishment of a considerable number of private Christian schools which are strongly evangelical in ethos and often closely tied to the house church movement. There are probably more than 80 such schools now in existence. Many of them are members of the Christian Schools Trust whose chairman, David Freeman, is head teacher of Kings School, Witney, Oxfordshire, a typical example of this new phenomenon. Kings School was founded in 1984 by members of the Oxfordshire Community Churches, an evangelical grouping bringing together one Baptist and four independent charismatic congregations. They were unhappy at the lack of Christian and moral teaching in local schools, including Church of England schools. The school now has more than 170 pupils aged between 5 and 17 who follow a curriculum which is Biblically based and strongly American in influence. The teachers are recruited through a national network of community churches. Parents pay fees according to their means. They are told that it costs £100 a month to educate each child and are provided with guidelines as to what contribution would be appropriate, based on different levels of income.

While increasing demand for more specifically Christian education is most clearly showing itself in the creation of these new private schools, it is also said to have been one of the factors behind the recent boom in independent education. Certainly most of the traditional British public schools have strong Christian roots and still put a premium on attendance at chapel services and education in Christian moral values. Whether this is the main reason why more parents are digging deep into their pockets to send their children to them is another matter, but it is undoubtedly the case that one of the attractions of independent education for many is its traditional Christian ethos. Even parents who are not themselves church-goers are keen that their children should be exposed to Christian influences and to the experience of regular worship.

The whole subject of public schools is rather a vexed one within the churches, and particularly in the Church of England. As has already been pointed out, a high proportion of Anglican clergy were themselves educated at independent schools and feel varying levels of guilt about their privileged upbringing. Perhaps because considerably fewer of its priests had a public-school education, the Roman Catholic Church is much less embarrassed about its involvement in private education and talks proudly of the 224 independent Catholic schools which educate a total of 70,000 pupils. The Church of England's stake in the private education sector is much bigger. There are very nearly 1,000 Anglican clergy working as chaplains in independent schools and the Church supports these establishments in other ways as well, as the *Faith in the City* report pointed out:

> It has been said to us, on more than one occasion, that far from reflecting a bias to the poor, the Church's involvement in education might reveal a bias towards the 6 per cent of young people who attend private schools. Many private schools employ chaplains. Many schools in the private sector invite bishops to their prize days and Confirmations, and clergy to preach, conduct retreats and take part in festive occasions, or to be involved in the management of schools. All involvement in such an important field as education must be a priority of bishops, clergy and lay people; but it has been put to us in evidence that many of them, especially bishops, spend a disproportionate amount of their time at the schools attended by 6 per cent of the population of the country, and rarely visit the schools which educate the other 94 per cent.
>
> The bishop's diary may symbolize a deeper and wider problem. The evidence from many sides is that private schools in Britain have been divisive of the nation to an extent far beyond their apparently small numerical importance. We readily recognize the long tradition of Christian education and the ethic of service to others which is part of the history of independent schools. Moreover, some of us have great loyalty and respect for private schools. But few of us would deny that their separate life exacts a heavy toll from the maintained schools ... Nor can it be denied that the Church of England has been implicated in this process of division and inequality in the upbringing of children.

The ties binding the Church of England to the world of independent education have been very strong. Of the twelve Archbishops of Canterbury since 1862, six have been headmasters of public schools. A majority of the clergy have been through the independent system and a good number of them choose it for their own children – according to *Faith in the City* 38 per cent of clergy working in the urban priority areas send their children to independent schools. But things are changing. The appointment of

George Carey, the first non-public school, non-Oxbridge primate
this century, may well herald the development of a more classless
leadership in the Church. The proportion of those currently training for the priesthood who were at public schools is probably down
to about a third. Public-school religion is itself changing. It is less
confident and triumphalist. *The Public School Hymn Book* has
undergone a discreet change of name to *Hymns for Church and
School*. There is more gentleness and less militarism and muscular
Christianity – you no longer hear the kind of sermon so brilliantly
caricatured in the 1960s film *If*, where a chapel full of boys in
uniform preparing for the annual Combined Cadet Force field day
was told by the chaplain, 'Jesus Christ is our commanding officer'.
Historically, of course, the role of independent schools was to turn
the sons of trade into Christian gentlemen. They have produced a
particular kind of Anglican character, often deeply imbued with
ideals of service and sacrifice and also, like Betjeman's Wykehamist,
broad of Church and broad of mind. They will probably remain
one of the most fertile recruiting grounds for both clergy and
committed laity in the Church of England. They sometimes appear
to be almost the last bastions of traditional Anglicanism, and
perhaps part of their role is to preserve this now rather threatened
species from extinction. But they are also an important source of
new ideas in the fields of worship and religious education.

It may be that distinctions between private and state education
are going to become less sharp as more maintained schools opt out
of local authority control under the terms of the 1988 Education
Reform Act. A number of church schools have already chosen to
take this route, despite the strong opposition to opting out on the
part of both George Carey and Basil Hume who have spoken
out against this aspect of Government education policy. Clifford
Longley has argued in *The Times* that the churches would, in
fact, gain considerably by opting out their own schools *en bloc*
from local authority control and establishing a confederation of
Christian schools responsible for educating a quarter of the
country's children. There are signs that the Roman Catholic
Church in Scotland may be contemplating such a move but it
is too radical at least for the immediate agenda of the Church of
England.

There are other features of the Education Reform Act which
have, at least on paper, strengthened the Christian element and the
influence of the churches in education. Its provisions in the field of

religious education mark a clear departure from the whole approach of the last 20 years, which has been strongly pluralistic and multi-faith, emphasizing the study of comparative religion rather than the primacy of one particular creed. Both in the Act, and even more explicitly in subsequent comments by the Education Secretary, the Government has clearly signalled that it expects there to be a distinct bias towards Christianity both in the RE classroom and in the school assembly. The Act specifically prescribes that there should be a daily act of collective worship in schools 'either wholly or mainly of a broadly Christian character'. But in practice this is difficult to enforce. Many schools dropped daily assemblies during the 1970s and there is little evidence that they have been revived on a large scale in the last few years. The extent to which acts of worship are taking place, and even more the extent to which they are overtly Christian in character, depends very much on the commitment of individual head teachers.

The 1988 Act has given religious education a rather ambiguous place in the new national curriculum. It is recognized as a basic subject but not as a foundation subject, which means that it is not assessed and is inclined to get squeezed out of the timetable. In fact, the Government was quite prepared to put RE in as a foundation subject but the Roman Catholics objected because it would have meant putting control of it into the hands of the Secretary of State. Denominational control has been retained – the Act laid down that each local authority must establish a standing advisory council on RE made up of church representatives – but at the cost of marginalizing the subject, especially in the 14 + age range when the demands of other, examinable subjects threaten to squeeze it out of the timetable.

The Act also lays down that RE lessons should reflect the fact that 'the religious traditions in Great Britain are in the main Christian, whilst taking account of the teaching and practices of the other principal religions represented in Great Britain'. This represents a significant shift of emphasis away from the comparative religion approach which critics had come to feel left British children with a smattering of knowledge about Buddhism, Hinduism and Islam but often virtually no knowledge of the Christian heritage of their own land. Evidence of this was provided in a *Songs of Praise* programme from Belfast in February 1988 when a Protestant girl was asked if she had learned anything about Roman Catholics in her RE lessons. She replied that she had learned a lot about Hindus and Muslims but nothing about Roman Catholics. A further sign of how little people now know about basic features of the Christian faith came in a *Sunday Express* poll in 1991 which found that 34 per cent of respondents had no idea why Easter was celebrated. In fact it is doubtful how far the insistence of the 1988 Act on a distinct Christian bias in RE lessons is actually being followed in schools. Many of those teaching the subject are thoroughly schooled in 1960s ideas of comparative religion and are unhappy about the new stress on one particular faith. In December 1990, 89 MPs from all parties signed a Commons early-day motion tabled by Michael Alison warning that the terms of the Act are not being carried out and that many education authorities are continuing to produce multi-faith syllabuses.

There is likely to be growing pressure for more distinctly Christian religious education in schools, not just from parents associated with the newer evangelical churches and house groups but also from within the mainstream churches. Writing in *The Times* in February 1988, for example, John Miller, Schools Religious Education Officer for the Anglican diocese of Guildford, argued that 'RE should set out to offer to pupils a Christian foundation for life. It should present to boys and girls, for their careful and critical study, confident teaching about the Christian dimension for life: love the Lord your God; about the Christian ideal for life: love your neighbour as yourself; about the Christian standards in life: honesty, self-control, compassion and forgiveness; and about the Christian demands upon life: humility, self-sacrifice and service to others.'

In the 1960s and 1970s such remarks would have been regarded as crossing over the boundary line between religious education and religious instruction. In the rather different climate of the 1990s, with the Government having signalled a clear return to a bias in favour of Christianity, the churches are becoming less cautious about their own involvement in education and bolder in their calls for a more evangelistic approach. This does not mean that RE is in danger of returning to an uncritical diet of Bible stories and credal affirmations. We are not about to witness the reintroduction of the catechism and learning prayers by rote. There is, rather, much highly imaginative work being done both intellectually and pastorally by those involved in religious education. The new religious studies syllabus for the higher grade examinations in Scotland, for example, offers 16-year-olds a chance to get to grips with some of the issues facing Christianity in the contemporary world, including the growing gap between rich and poor, gender roles and relationships and ecology and stewardship. It also covers challenges to Christianity from humanism, science and Marxism. Another example from Scotland indicates the initiatives being shown by some school chaplains. David Anderson, minister of Gorgie Parish Church in Edinburgh, has a caravan permanently parked in the playground of the local secondary school where he holds 'open house' every Friday lunchtime. Pupils come with a variety of practical and personal problems and to ask questions about matters of faith and belief.

Alongside such imaginative and informal new ways of working, the churches also need to remain committed to a more traditional and formal educative role. There is an understandable reluctance on the part of many clergy and church workers to appear old-fashioned and didactic: Sunday School syllabuses are becoming more and more project-orientated and 'user friendly', and confirmation classes ever shorter and less concerned with formal instruction in the faith. But the church does have a fundamental responsibility to teach the great objective doctrines of Christianity – the Incarnation, the Resurrection, the Atonement, the mysteries of the Trinity and everlasting life. Without a grounding in these essentials of the faith, there can be no real foundations on which to develop a sure moral sense and system of values. If the churches withdraw from this particular teaching role, and there are signs that they are doing so, no one else is going to take it up and we will be left with a generation with no real understanding of Christian belief.

The churches, and the wider Christian community, also have a very considerable responsibility to promote the spiritual dimension in education. This is particularly important at a time when both at school and in higher levels, the emphasis is increasingly intellectual, vocational and technical. As curriculums and syllabuses become ever more crowded there is less room for lessons which do not have a narrowly instrumental purpose and which are concerned with broader discussion and with imparting values. Education as a whole is coming to be regarded as another commodity in the market place, a highly competitive industry whose products can be valued in terms of exam results and vocational qualifications rather than as a process of nurture and development which cannot be measured in terms of its contribution to the gross national product. In one of his last major speeches as Archbishop of Canterbury Robert Runcie expressed his concern to members of the Headmasters' Conference that education was coming to be seen as 'nothing more than the acquisition of knowledge and skills which will enable pupils to achieve material success. We end up with minds as sharp as razors and about as broad.' One of the most valuable contributions that the churches can make to British society in the coming decade is to reassert vigorously the Christian understanding of education as the inculcation of a sense of personal worth and service to others and as a lifelong pilgrimage of discovery and growth in faith.

There may well also be a much wider and more diffuse educative role for the churches to take on in the coming years. As the brutalizing and dehumanizing values of commercialism and the mass media increasingly pervade our society, we need badly to increase the influence of every agency which can act as a counterweight and spread a little sweetness and light. With the philistines and barbarians no longer just standing at the gates but occupying the very citadels of power and influence, I find myself more and more drawn to Matthew Arnold's vision of the churches forming a clerisy standing for the maintenance of culture and order. This need not be an élitist exercise – much of the most effective educational work can be done at the grassroots level with ministers, congregations and small groups quietly but clearly witnessing to values other than those of rampant consumption, sensationalism and slavery to style and image.

The assumption of such a role would, of course, involve an enormous broadening out of the churches' aims and concerns far beyond what is normally understood by evangelism. But in a decade in which Christians have been enjoined to look outwards and share the message of their faith, it seems to me a wholly appropriate and exciting task in which to be engaged. In a sermon at Oxford University in September 1991 Douglas Hurd, the Foreign Secretary, suggested that the church's job is to infuse charity, gentleness and wisdom into modern society. It is a massive and difficult task but one that might give the churches a new purpose and vigour. It could hardly be more vital.

– 8 –

The church of the air

Clear before us through the darkness
Gleams and burns the guiding light

For most people in Britain today the most powerful source of religious influence is not the church down the road but the television set in the corner of the living room. More than 60 per cent of the population watch a religious television programme at least once a month – six times as many as attend a church service in the same period. The 'electronic church' may not yet have reached the level of influence here that it has in the USA where tele evangelists apparently effect miracle healings over the airwaves and collect millions of dollars from viewers every week. But with the deregulation of broadcasting and the growing impact of satellite and cable channels, many people believe that we are on the verge of an explosion of religious propaganda over the airwaves of a very different kind from anything previously seen in this country.

At present, religious broadcasting in Britain is very much weighted in favour of the traditional visible churches and the broadly liberal values which they espouse. Indeed, it could be said to be one of the biggest allies they have, giving them a much higher public profile than their actual numerical strength really justifies. This is not just because of the televising of major events like the enthronement of the Archbishop of Canterbury, the Church of Scotland's General Assembly, the thanksgiving service for the Gulf War and royal occasions where the pomp and ceremonial of the national churches are shown to best advantage. The regular output of both BBC and ITV conveys the message that the traditional mainstream churches are the main purveyors of religion in Britain and that they are in very good heart. Most Sunday mornings around 11 o'clock ITV carries a service of morning worship from a church somewhere in Britain which is watched by more than half a million people. Every Sunday evening around seven million people tune in to *Songs of Praise*, the flagship programme of the BBC religious broadcasting department, to watch hymn-singing from packed churches and listen to interviews about people's faith. *Highway*, the ITV programme which goes out at the same time which also features sacred music from churches and inspirational interviews, has similar viewing figures. The fact that a quarter of the British population chooses to spend the early part of every Sunday evening watching what is essentially a church based act of worship says much for the survival of a strong residual folk religion in our national culture. If we are, indeed, a post-Christian country, then the tribal chants of the defunct cult that we are supposed to have discarded have a remarkable staying power.

Religious programmes on radio also command large audiences. *Good Morning Sunday*, Radio 2's Sunday breakfast programme hosted by Don Maclean and featuring sacred music, interviews and prayers, is listened to by up to two million people. At the same time a further three-quarters of a million are tuned to the religious current affairs programme *Sunday* on Radio 4. On Sunday evenings on Radio 2 up to 750,000 make a date with Roger Royle for *Sunday Half Hour*, the hymn singing programme which was started in 1940 for British troops serving abroad. An even longer-running programme, the *Daily Service*, which began in 1926, regularly attracted up to half a million listeners when it was broadcast at a quarter to eleven every weekday morning on Radio 4 although this figure will almost certainly have dropped following its recent move to ten o'clock on long wave only.

An important part of the audience for these programmes, and especially for broadcast services of worship, is made up of the house-bound and elderly who are not able to get to church. But although this section of the population is growing, its size is not enough to explain the high viewing and listening figures for religious programmes. Audience research suggests that they appeal across the spectrum. As I have already mentioned, BBC current affairs bosses were taken by surprise when a poll of listeners revealed *Thought for the Day* to be one of the most popular elements in the *Today* programme on Radio 4. The graph recording the daily pattern of listening on Radio 4 showed a significant move upwards when the *Daily Service* came on in its old 11.45 slot on both long wave and VHF. It is both sad and surprising that the decision was taken to move it in September 1991 to long wave only, albeit with the addition of a new daily programme following it and consisting of a reading from the Bible.

In general the response of channel controllers and schedulers in both the BBC and ITV to what is clearly a lively and growing demand from listeners and viewers has been an increase in religious output. Radio 2's very popular *Pause for Thought* has recently been given two night-time slots, aimed at the half million or so listeners who are tuned to the network through the small hours. On Radio 4 documentaries and features made by the religious broadcasting department are increasingly being put out in peak weekday morning slots and not consigned to the traditional 'God-slot' late on a Sunday evening. In 1990 Scottish Television launched a very lively religious magazine programme called *Eikon* which is screened early on a weekday evening. The same company's religious documentaries, which have recently featured such subjects as the history of the Free Church of Scotland and Gaelic psalm singing, also get prime transmission time. Indeed, in Scotland as a whole significantly more air-time on both television and radio is given to religious broadcasting than in England. Both Scottish and Grampian Television put out mini-sermons immediately after *News at Ten* under the respective titles of *Late Call* and *Reflections*. BBC Scotland gives substantial coverage to the Church of Scotland's General Assembly, with half-hour programmes on both television and radio every evening throughout Assembly week. Radio Scotland has its own *Thought for the Day* slot every weekday morning and a five-minute programme of prayer every evening at five to ten. It also has a strong commitment to religious current affairs and worship programmes and is not frightened of tackling serious theological issues in a deep and challenging way.

It is, of course, thanks to a Scot that religion has so honoured a place in British broadcasting. If their Latin is good enough, visitors to Broadcasting House in London can get a flavour of the avowedly Christian aims which lay behind the foundation of the BBC by casting their eyes to the inscription above the lifts in the entrance hall. Translated, it reads:

This temple of the arts and muses is dedicated to Almighty God by the first governors of broadcasting in the year 1931, Sir John Reith being director-general. It is their prayer that good seed sown may bring forth a good harvest, that all things hostile to peace or purity may be banished from this house, and that the people inclining their ears to whatever things are beautiful and honest and of good report, may tread the paths of wisdom and righteousness.

Stern and unbending embodiment of the Presbyterian conscience that he was, Lord Reith ran the BBC as though it were an extension of the church and took it for granted that it should be a strongly Christian organization. The first question he often put when interviewing prospective staff was, 'Do you accept the fundamental teaching of Jesus Christ?' R. S. Lambert, being interviewed for the editorship of *The Listener*, tried to avoid a direct answer by saying 'I might accept the teachings of Christ if I could be really sure what they were', to which Reith replied curtly: 'Everyone knows where they are to be found – in the Bible and in the teachings of the Churches.' When Russell Twisk was being interviewed for the same job in 1981 the first question he was asked was 'How do you propose to get more science into the paper?'

Reith stamped British broadcasting with a firmly Christian ethos and gave organized religion a uniquely privileged place within it. Characteristically, he complained that the churches had failed to appreciate 'how accidental and odd it was that, from the very beginning, and against indifference, ridicule and opposition, the Christian religion and the Sabbath were given positions of privilege and protection in the broadcasting service, which – circumstances having been otherwise and as might have been expected – no protest or petition by the churches could have secured for them.' He felt the churches had lamentably failed to follow up the opportunities given to them – if they had, 'there might have been a national revival on a scale hitherto unimagined'. His comments were to a considerable extent confirmed by what happened in his own homeland when a serious attempt was made to harness the power of radio for evangelistic purposes. In 1950 the Scottish Home Service was taken over for a Radio Mission which sought nothing less than the conversion of Scotland. A similar venture was tried two years later. Both had little impact, largely because of indifference and lack of follow-up on the part of the churches.

The mainstream churches in Britain have, indeed, taken a long time to come to terms with broadcasting and to see it as a potential ally rather than a threat. It is perhaps understandable that in the early days of radio clergymen were unhappy about people listening to acts of worship on headphones. In 1923 permission to relay the

Armistice Day service and a royal wedding from Westminster Abbey was refused by the Church authorities on the grounds that 'the services would be received by a considerable number of persons in an irreverent manner, and might even be heard by persons in public houses with their hats on'. This kind of attitude persisted for a long time. As recently as 1968 the Church of Scotland issued a report deeply suspicious of broadcasting and talking of 'a deliberate strategy of cultivated immorality and conscious abdication of ethical responsibility by the big television corporations, and especially by the BBC'.

Nowadays, of course, the mainstream churches would be only too delighted to get their message into public houses. Indeed, both the Church of England and the Church of Scotland have even started experimenting with advertising on independent local radio. Where once they were highly suspicious of the medium, they are now embracing it with alacrity. The Church of England seconds clergy to serve as religious producers on local radio stations and in 1990 appointed Eric Shegog, former head of religious broadcasting at the Independent Broadcasting Authority, to lead a communications team in Church House which will train priests how to perform well in front of cameras. The Church of Scotland, which was the first of the main denominations to provide itself with broadcasting equipment, now has a highly professional audiovisual unit which makes television programmes for ITV and Channel 4 as well as in-house videos. The Roman Catholic Church has well-equipped radio and television centres in England and Scotland. Many of the newer evangelical churches are also actively engaged in making video and audio cassettes and are preparing for the time when they will be able to make programmes for transmission in a deregulated broadcasting system.

Unfortunately for the churches, this new-found enthusiasm for using the media as a tool of evangelism is no longer shared by those running the main broadcasting stations. Certainly in the hierarchy of the BBC there is no one now who shares Reith's view of the Corporation as an arm of the church and an agent for national religious revival. *Thought for the Day* may still offer clergy the opportunity to express strongly held convictions – though they cannot be too opinionated, as Eric James discovered in September 1990 when he was taken off the list of contributors for being too avowedly partisan towards the Labour party. But it is impossible to conceive of it ever being described nowadays in the way that its predecessor, *Lift Up Your Hearts*, was in the *Radio Times* as 'early morning prayers, little services aiming only at converting each listener's home into a shrine for a moment or two before the day's work begins'.

The gradual departure from the Reithian concept of religious broadcasting can be traced through the utterances of successive director generals of the BBC. In 1948 Sir William Haley could still say: 'We are citizens of a Christian country, and the BBC – an institution set up by the state – bases its policy upon a positive attitude towards the Christian values. It seeks to safeguard those values and to foster acceptance of them. The whole preponderant weight of its programmes is directed to this end.' Twenty-five years later Sir Charles Curran talked rather of the moral neutrality of broadcasting in a 'post-Christian era' and said 'It is not our job to adopt a particular morality and then to try to persuade everybody else to follow it'. The reports of the various government committees on broadcasting set up over the last 30 years also signal a clear retreat from Reithian certainties. In 1960 the Pilkington Committee could still be told by the BBC that the objectives of religious broadcasting were to reflect the worship, thought and action of those churches that represent the mainstream of the Christian tradition in Britain, to show what is most relevant in the Christian faith to the modern world and to reach those outside the churches. When the BBC gave evidence to the Annan Committee in 1977, the objectives had shifted to 'reflecting the worship, thought and action of the principal religious traditions represented in Britain, recognising that these traditions are mainly though not exclusively Christian, seeking to present to viewers and listeners those beliefs, ideas, issues and experiences in the contemporary world which are evidently related to a religious interpretation or dimension of life and also seeking to meet the religious interests, concerns and needs of those on the fringe of, or outside, the organised life of the churches.' In 1988 a further significant shift of policy was indicated when the BBC's Central Religious Advisory Council dropped the word 'churches' and replaced it with 'major religious groupings'.

This change of emphasis away from churches and mainstream Christianity to principal religious groupings and traditions underlines a significant shift in broadcasters' perceptions about the role of religious broadcasting. It is a shift from evangelism to exposition, from proclamation to reflection. Lord Reith was an unashamed 'proclaimer' who believed that religious broadcasting should be

openly exhortatory and aim to encourage Biblical principles and
Christian beliefs. His successors today are very definitely 'reflectors'
who want to avoid any whiff of proselytizing in religious programmes and aim rather for carefully balanced and strictly neutral
analysis of what is happening in this particular area of human
experience. The Annan Committee laid down clearly that 'religious
broadcasting should not be the religious equivalent of party political broadcasts'. A document produced for the BBC's General
Advisory Council in 1990 spells out even more sharply the departure from the Reithian position: 'It is no longer possible for the
religious broadcasting department of a public service broadcasting
authority to be the mouthpiece of the churches or any other interest
group. The BBC is not a church. The daily service can no longer
be introduced by a continuity announcer saying "our prayers are
taken" as if the whole BBC were at that moment on its knees.'
BBC producers' guidelines lay down that 'guests invited to take
part in religious programmes, while explaining their beliefs and
provoking discussion about them, may not use the opportunity to
evangelize on their behalf'. Similar rules have until very recently
governed independent radio and television. A programme made
some years ago by the Salvation Army and bought by ITV companies was withdrawn shortly before transmission because it was
judged by the Independent Broadcasting Authority to contravene
guidelines that 'no religious broadcast should attempt to prose-
lytize, that is to make converts'.

As this shift in perspective has occurred, religious broadcasting
has also lost some of its status and no longer commands the air-
time that it once did. I recently came across a copy of the *Radio
Times* for Good Friday 1955. There were only five hours of television transmitted that day, of which two and a half were devoted
to religious programmes, including an hour-long portrayal of the
Passion play in mime, a live relay of a Billy Graham rally and a
series of Biblical pictures performed by the Norwegian Ballet. On
Good Friday 1991 BBC 1 was on the air for eighteen hours, yet
just one and a quarter hours of off-peak time were given to religious
programmes: there was a worship sequence from Wells Cathedral
at 11 in the morning and a 15-minute dramatic enactment of the
events leading up to the crucifixion at 11.05 p.m. In the peak mid-
evening slot which Billy Graham's rally had occupied in 1955,
Terry Wogan hosted the competition to choose the British entry
for the Eurovision Song Contest. Old hands in the BBC, and

particularly in BBC Scotland where for many years religion was one of the biggest and most productive departments, fondly recall the days when the outside broadcast vehicles, or scanners, were said to have stained-glass windows because they were so often in use to record church services. It was not uncommon in the 1950s and 1960s for three worship programmes, including *Songs of Praise*, to be transmitted live or recorded over a single weekend. Now sport is king and recordings of *Songs of Praise* have to be squeezed in to Monday and Tuesday evenings so that they do not conflict with Wednesday evening football matches and preparations for weekend sporting fixtures. Religious programmes now make up just 2 per cent of the total output of BBC television and account for just 2 per cent of total costs – a small proportion considering the substantial audiences that they gain.

But although it may have lost the favoured status that it once had religion is still accorded considerably better treatment on radio and television than it might be thought to warrant in a supposedly secular society. The fact that the BBC and ITV still have well-staffed religious broadcasting departments and have not simply amalgamated this area of programming into current affairs or documentary features, says much for the continuing commitment of broadcasters to religion as a separate and important subject in its own right. Within these departments, the bias remains overwhelmingly Christian. Despite the shift in emphasis from proclaiming the Gospel to reflecting the varieties of faith in a pluralistic society, religious broadcasting still gives a very favoured place to Christianity. Although there are occasional contributors from other faiths, most notably Rabbis Lionel Blue and Jonathan Sacks, Radio 4's *Thought for the Day* is generally presented by an ordained minister from one of the mainstream Christian churches. Similar slots on independent and BBC local radio are often even more overtly Christian, as in the *Pause for Thought* slot on Radio 2's breakfast programme, which with a regular audience of two million has the biggest listenership of any religious programme on radio.

There has been much lobbying of the BBC from representatives of other faiths, particularly from Muslims who claim that with a following of more than a million in Britain they should receive more air-time. In fact, BBC television does broadcast Muslim prayers during the month of Ramadan, but there are difficulties in finding Muslim speakers for programmes like *Thought for the Day* because of the number of factions within the Islamic community.

Attempts have been made to feature the worship of non-Christian faiths – an example was the *Festival* series which occupied the *Songs of Praise* slot during the summer of 1990 – but they have not been particularly successful. The strong bias in favour of Christianity also extends to religious current affairs programmes. An analysis of the output of Radio 4's *Sunday* programme during 1989 found that out of 568 items broadcast, just 52 – less than 10 per cent – were on non-Christian subjects. They included 11 features on Islam, 11 on Judaism, 5 on Hinduism, 3 on Buddhism, 2 each on Sikhism and Shintoism, and 18 items dealing with religious cults and fringe groups, humanists and religious superstition. Scottish Television's *Eikon* programme has made a deliberate effort to include items on non-Christian faiths and cults, but these still form a minority of its content.

The present religious broadcasting output of the BBC and ITV is not only predominantly Christian in its subject matter – it is also heavily weighted in favour of the traditional visible churches. It is true that *Songs of Praise* is making increasing forays into the world of the new evangelical churches and has regular programmes from Spring Harvest and the March for Jesus. *Highway*, however, remains largely committed to traditional parish churches and robed choirs. Ten years ago the BBC, largely for financial reasons, took the decision to abandon televising church services on Sunday mornings. *This is the Day*, the worship programme which replaced them, and which still goes out live every Sunday morning, comes from people's homes and could easily have become a televised expression of the growing house church movement. In fact, relatively few of those who take part in it are from the new churches and its presenters are drawn largely from the old-established denominations. It represents an interesting and commendable attempt to create a distinctive style of worship for television and to involve viewers more than if they were simply watching a conventional church service, but its one-to-one interview format does not reflect the group approach of the house church movement. Leading figures in the new churches are seldom if ever accorded spots on *Thought for the Day* or *Pause for Thought*. Radio worship may have been changed over the last few years to reflect the growing impact of new music and more contemporary language, and Radio 4's *Daily Service* in particular has been revamped, with much less emphasis on the immaculate enunciation and crystal-clear diction of the BBC singers and much more use of amateur choirs and groups performing contemporary songs, but it is still very uncommon for the Sunday morning service on Radio 4 to come from anywhere other than a church of one of the main established denominations.

This bias reflects the background and the preferences of those working in religious broadcasting. They are predominantly themselves drawn from the traditional mainstream churches and are often out of sympathy with the strongly evangelical ethos of the invisible churches. This is also true of the members of the Central Religious Advisory Council, which advises both the BBC and independent broadcasting companies. In his *Crockford's* preface, Garry Bennett noted that the religious broadcasting departments of the BBC and ITV provided one of the most fertile recruiting grounds for the ultra-liberal bench of bishops appointed during Robert Runcie's period as Archbishop of Canterbury. In fact, there are very few Anglican clergy in the higher echelons of religious broadcasting. The present head of religious broadcasting in the BBC is a Presbyterian minister from Northern Ireland, and the Head of Religious Programmes for BBC Television is a layman. Although there are a fair number of Anglican clergy working in local radio, those in the national networks are predominantly lay and include a good sprinkling of Nonconformists and Catholics as well as several agnostics without any church affiliations.

Garry Bennett was undoubtedly right, however, in suggesting that the ethos of contemporary religious broadcasting is strongly liberal. This is particularly true of the BBC. In the independent sector there are rather more evangelicals and proclaimers around, and this is reflected in a difference of programme content. Independent programmes tend to lean more towards the world of schmaltz and show business. They aim to comfort and console rather than to challenge, and have a high entertainment factor – this approach reached its peak in the 1960s with *Stars on Sunday* but it still clearly informs *Highway*. The BBC on the whole eschews this approach, although its radio religious broadcasting department has for some years cherished the idea of making a soap opera in the belief that 'there is ample material for a light-hearted exploration of quite serious issues without relying on the obvious stereotypes of camp clergy and vicarage tea parties'. If the fault of religious programmes on independent radio and television is to be oversentimental and emotional, the BBC tends to err in the other direction by producing programmes which almost completely lack a spiritual dimension. Religion is treated as a phenomenon and the hard-hitting factual documentary approach employed, with the result that programmes of a devotional or reflective nature are few and far between or, like the admirable *Seeds of Faith*, consigned to the dark recesses of the night.

There is, in fact, a growing reticence on the part of the BBC in particular, especially discernible in radio, about using broadcasting as a medium for worship or spiritual meditation. The decision to relegate the *Daily Service* to long wave is the most recent and the most serious result of this attitude. It is becoming increasingly hard to find on the BBC's mainstream radio channels the spiritual food that radio provides better than any other medium – public worship of God in prayer, hymn and sacred music together with more intimate and personal reflection and meditation. Programmes incorporating this kind of material are still being made, often with great care and sensitivity, but they tend to be given unfavourable transmission slots like *Seeds of Faith* or the consistently inspiring Sunday sequence which is tucked away on Radio 3 at six o'clock on Sunday evenings.

Perhaps I may be permitted to ride a personal hobby horse briefly here. When I was appointed Head of Religious Programmes at BBC Scotland in 1990 I caused some eyebrows to be raised when I stated clearly that as far as I was concerned religious broadcasting is a form of ministry. By that I do not mean that its purpose is narrowly evangelistic, but it does seem to me that the whole justification for giving it special status as a separate department, and not simply subsuming it within current affairs or documentary features, is because religious broadcasting is not like any other kind of programme-making. It should not simply be trying to inform or entertain an audience, but rather to reach out and touch people's souls – seeking to move, to comfort and to challenge them and to help them on their pilgrimages of faith by pointing them towards the numinous and the eternal and giving them a glimpse of glory. I am well aware that this sounds very portentous and high-falutin'. I am also well aware of the limitations of television in particular as a medium for exploring the transcendent and touching the spiritual in humankind. There are many extremely talented and committed people working in religious broadcasting, but much of what they produce, particularly perhaps in the case of the BBC, is not really religious, in the sense that it does not try to address the audience in spiritual terms. Many of the programmes in the *Everyman* and *Heart of the Matter* series would fit equally well into *Panorama* or other documentary feature strands. They concentrate largely on social and political issues and, apart from a predictable moral bias in favour of the poor and disadvantaged, often lack any spiritual content or dimension. By contrast, programmes which are clearly religious and do touch a deep spiritual chord often come from other departments – I recall particularly a fine radio documentary on Gerard Manley Hopkins which was the work of the drama department.

Others have also noticed this curious lack of religious content in religious programmes. John Barton, former broadcasting officer for the Church of England, has written in the *Church Times* (15 December 1989) that 'Far too many of the documentary programmes which pass muster in the BBC's religious television output are not religious at all. They are well made and they grapple with important moral issues, but it is quite wrong for the BBC's religious budget to be spent on these substitutes.' Crispian Hollis, Roman Catholic Bishop of Portsmouth, commented in similar vein on entries submitted for the Sandford St Martin awards for the best religious radio programmes in 1990. Summing up the feelings of the judges, he said that many of the programmes which they had heard 'contained elements that were religious, and often came from a religious stable, but were nevertheless more concerned with social and political issues that happened to have a religious tinge'.

The understandable inhibitions about the dangers of proselytizing which perhaps make some of the output of the BBC's religious departments less spiritually based than it might be do not affect the growing number of Christian radio stations and production companies springing up in the newly deregulated world of broadcasting. Most of these are unashamed 'proclaimers', firmly in the evangelical camp and often associated with the new invisible churches. Their enthusiasm can often make for lively programming, albeit of a kind that jars on the ears of those accustomed to *Thought for the Day* and *Choral Evensong*. It was significant that the 1990 Sandford St Martin Award went not to the BBC or one of the established independent local radio stations but to GRF Christian Radio, a strongly evangelical production company based in Glasgow. The judges particularly commended a series of one-minute contributions which it made for Radio Clyde's breakfast show. Entitled *The Resurrection Case*, they sought to unravel the Easter message through the eyes of an American private investigator sent to discover the mystery of the disappearing body from the tomb. The language was direct and punchy: 'This Jesus guy just wouldn't lie down. Pretty impressive for a stiff!' Also commended was a series of 'Morning Thoughts' for Pennine Radio which set the Christmas story to specially-composed 'rap' music.

GRF, which describes itself as 'a Christian radio mission', is the leading example of a network of evangelical production companies which have sprung up over the last decade or so. It is staffed by a group of about twenty volunteers, drawn predominantly from the Baptists and the Brethren but also encompassing members of most other denominations. Thanks to regular donations from prayer partners it is able to afford expensive professional recording equipment. It supplies packaged programmes to Christian radio stations around the world and is also making an increasing number of 'Morning Thoughts' and longer programmes for both independent and BBC local stations. It was also responsible for the first religious advertisements heard on British radio. Made for the Church of England diocese of Lichfield to encourage greater attendance at Easter services and specifically targeted at the 14–25 age group, they were broadcast on Beacon Radio in March 1991. The advertisements were apparently successful in their aim and have subsequently been taken up by the Oxford diocese and a parish church in Newcastle.

Advertising by churches and other religious bodies is one of the many new freedoms introduced by the 1990 Broadcasting Act. Although several of its provisions took effect from 1 January 1991, some have yet to come into force. Religious advertising on television, for example, will not be allowed until 1993. Overall, the Act greatly increases the opportunities for religious broadcasting in Britain. Churches and other religious bodies are now able to own and run local radio stations and cable and satellite television channels. The first religious radio station in Britain went on air on 1 July 1991 in Stoke-on-Trent. Backed by United Christian Broadcasters and funded entirely through donations, it operated for an experimental 28-day period, broadcasting for 18 hours a day with a mix of contemporary Christian music and short Bible teaching features. Further such stations are likely to open up in the next few years. In an increasingly deregulated system where more and more programmes will be made by independent production companies, religious groups will also have much greater opportunities to make programmes for the main national television networks.

The heated debate which took place over the religious provisions of the Broadcasting Act produced a classic confrontation between 'reflectors' and 'proclaimers'. On one side, defending the status quo and arguing strongly against changing the rules to allow church ownership of stations and permit religious advertising, stood the leaders of the mainstream visible churches and the religious broadcasting establishments of the BBC and ITV. They were worried about an abandonment of the carefully achieved consensus which saw the purpose of religious broadcasting as being to reflect impartially on the multiplicity of faith and religious experience in a pluralistic society, and a return to the old Reithian idea of religious broadcasting as proclaiming the Gospel. They were also worried that deregulation would open the floodgates to American style tele-evangelism. Their case was put most forcibly by David Sheppard, Bishop of Liverpool and chairman of the Central Religious Advisory Council which advises both the BBC and the independent radio and television companies. He argued that those churches and religious groups which would buy stations and advertising time would tend to be the more marginal and extreme ones. The broader mainstream churches, stretched to the limit to maintain a ministry across the country, would be unlikely to have the financial resources to advertise or buy a station. He also felt that restriction and restraint were needed to maintain the high quality of religious programmes in Britain and prevent the exploitation of audiences which occurred in other countries where there was a glut of 'cheap, shoddy, exploitative and trivializing religious advertising and programmes'.

Ranged on the other side was a formidable coalition of evangelical pressure groups. They included the National Council for Christian Standards in Society, Christian Choice in Broadcasting, the Evangelical Alliance, the Jubilee Trust and CARE. They were strongly supported by Baroness Cox, the Earl of Halsbury and Lord Orr-Ewing in the House of Lords and Michael Alison and Kenneth Hind in the Commons. Petitions bearing more than 276,000 signatures were handed in to 10 Downing Street pleading for greater freedom for positive Christian broadcasting. They made the point that while Billy Graham could buy air-time on Indian television to spread the Gospel, such an opportunity for Christian evangelism was denied in Britain. The Bishop of Liverpool in particular and the liberal church and media establishment in general were castigated for being wet and apologetic, engaging in censorship and seeking to preserve the cosy cartel which produced social concern programmes of a left-wing political hue but never actually dared to preach the Gospel.

In the event, thanks to the skilful lobbying of the evangelicals and the free market sympathies of the Government, victory went to the proclaimers. During its passage through Parliament the Broadcasting Act was substantially amended to give greater freedom than originally intended to religious bodies wishing to use radio and television for essentially evangelistic purposes. A key clause stating that no undue prominence should be given to a specific religious viewpoint was dropped in favour of a requirement that there should be no improper exploitation of audience susceptibilities or abusive treatment of other people's religious views and beliefs. The way seems open for direct tele-evangelism of the kind seen in the United States. Already Rupert Murdoch's Sky channel broadcasts the American evangelist Robert Schuller's *Hour of Power* every Sunday morning. The first daily evangelistic programme produced in Britain, *Victory with Morris Costello*, which is heavily based on a US original, was launched on the Super Channel satellite station in 1991 though hardly at prime time, being given a half-hour slot at 5.30 a.m.

However, there is as yet no evidence at all to suggest that as a result of the Broadcasting Act American style tele-evangelism with its heavy emotionalism, show business atmosphere and appeals to the audience for money is about to take over from *Songs of Praise* and *Highway* as the dominant form of religious programming on British television. Nor does it seem likely that religious advertising on television will bring about the vulgar commercialism and dangers of exploitation that its critics fear. The Independent Television Commission has drawn up a very tight code which basically limits such advertising to publicizing services, meetings and other events, factually describing an organization's activities and offering publications or promoting the sale or rental of other merchandise. Promotions of the Bible will be allowed but advertisements may not directly promote doctrine or faith healing, offer moral or emotional counselling or denigrate other faiths. Appeals for money will not be allowed unless it can be reliably demonstrated that any profits from television commercials will be devoted solely to the benefit of disadvantaged third parties. Advertisements will not be allowed to play on fear by alluding to any alleged consequences of not subscribing to a particular faith. Testimonials and personal case histories will not be allowed. In an effort to protect children, no religious advertisements can be designed to appeal to the under-18s or placed in or around programmes aimed at that age group.

Predictably, this long list of restrictions has been greeted with dismay by evangelical groups, who point out that young people can be bombarded with adverts for alcohol and Teenage Mutant Ninja Turtle films but are not to be allowed to watch commercials for youth clubs and church holiday schemes. On the other hand, those opposed to religious advertising, like David Sheppard, feel that the safeguards are not sufficient to offer audiences protection from American-style evangelists or the possibilities of cults using the airwaves. It will be fascinating to see how far the new opportunities for religious advertising are actually taken up, and by whom.

Undoubtedly deregulation of the airwaves offers both the visible and the invisible churches considerable opportunities to put their message across using the most powerful medium of communication in the modern age. How many churches will actually take advantage of the freedom to set up their own local radio stations or cable television channels remains to be seen. It is likely to be some of the newer more evangelical groups which pioneer the way in this area, although several of the older established mainstream churches are also well equipped to enter the broadcasting business. Whether many people will actually tune in to such stations is another matter. What is far more important is what happens to religious broadcasting on the main national television and radio networks where most viewing and listening is likely to remain concentrated at least for the foreseeable future. Here the growing proportion of independently produced programmes also offers the churches considerable opportunities. In response to lobbying from all the churches, the 1990 Broadcasting Act has laid down that Channels 3 and 5 must carry religious programmes as part of their public service obligations. It is inconceivable that the BBC's obligation to carry religious programmes, or its substantial commitment to that area of output, will disappear when its charter is renewed in 1996. There will perhaps be more proclamation and less neutral reflection in religious programming, but that may be no bad thing provided it offers some real spiritual nourishment and not just an evangelistic hard sell. As Angela Tilby, a distinguished member of BBC Television's religious department, admits, 'The well-balanced, moderate religious television that the BBC and ITV networks have evolved over the years creates few stars and suffers few scandals. We are mostly at peace within our broadcasting system and backed by the mainstream Churches. Our theology is impeccable, but I sometimes wonder whether it touches the vivid dramas of the soul that the tele-evangelists instinctively tune into.' (*Church Times*, 12 October 1990.)

– 9 –

The future

Onward, therefore, pilgrim brothers,
Onward with the Cross our aid,

So far this book has been largely about the present state of Christianity and the churches in Britain. In this last chapter I want to offer some predictions, and some pleas for the future, keeping in mind the distinction that has been made throughout between the visible and the invisible church and looking especially at likely developments in this present decade of evangelism.

The first prediction which I think can fairly safely be made is that religion will continue to be a major topic of interest both to the public at large and to the media. Indeed, I think one can go further and say that the nineties will be a religious decade. By this I do not necessarily mean that church attendance will increase, although this may well happen in some areas, but that overall there will be a greater awareness of the spiritual dimension in life and a deeper longing for ultimate values and meaning. There are several reasons for this. As we near the end not just of a century but of a millennium, it is to be expected that thoughts will turn to judgement, the last days and the purpose of existence. We are already beginning to hear self-styled prophets speaking in Messianic terms about the end times. The 1990s are proving to be a serious and thoughtful decade – and that is not surprising. Over the last generation or so the mood in Britain has swung in a series of cyclical reactions. The dull, conventional, consumerist fifties were followed by the wild, idealistic, iconoclastic, swinging sixties. The 1980s have been a decade of rampant materialism and individualism, shallowness and secularism. It would be odd if we did not now experience a reaction – a search for deeper values than those of the yuppie and the public relations consultant, a rediscovery of the common interest and a sense that not everything in life can be treated as a commodity and bought and sold in the market.

There are already many signs of a new stirring of spiritual consciousness and a reawakened moral conscience. The business world is showing increasing concern with ethical and moral issues and realizing that it is not simply enough to make profits and beat the competition. Regular attenders at management seminars and inter-governmental meetings even report that the word 'soul' is to be heard on the lips of business executives and civil servants. More and more people are becoming concerned about threats to the natural environment and are beginning to question the wisdom of continuing to worship the twentieth century's trinity of economic growth, scientific materialism and manufactured images. There is less faith that unaided human reason can solve the world's problems and a much greater openness to the supernatural and mysterious.

Of course, it is by no means inevitable that Christianity, and still less the traditional churches, will be the beneficiaries of this new mood. Many of those who are rejecting materialism and searching for new and deeper values are drawn to New Age movements or to the ancient religions of the East. But it would be surprising if at least some of this renewed moral concern and spiritual consciousness did not find its expression through the churches. After all, as we have seen, one of the most notable features of both the visible and the invisible churches over the last few years has been the recovery of their prophetic role, questioning prevailing values and policies and passing judgement on the Government and nation. The Christian voices raised on subjects as diverse as the Gulf War, Sunday trading and the Poll Tax have struck a chord with many people who would never describe themselves as church-goers. As issues like fairness, social justice and care for the environment come more and more to the fore, the exercise of this prophetic ministry is going to become increasingly important and the churches are going to find that they are listened to, and perhaps even looked to for leadership, far beyond their own shrinking memberships.

There is also every reason to hope that the growing thirst for spirituality, particularly among the young, will find at least part of its satisfaction in Christian forms of expression. We have already commented on the upsurge of interest in Celtic Christianity, the strong attraction for young people of the ecumenical religious communities at Taizé and Iona, and the growing popularity of

festivals of praise like Spring Harvest and Greenbelt. Ancient
Christian shrines and holy places are becoming a magnet for the
ever-increasing number of people who are rediscovering the traditional practice of pilgrimage. Iona now receives over 250,000
visitors a year. It will probably be the case that much of this
renewed interest in spirituality will find expression in what might
be called the fringes of the church, leading to a growth in retreats
rather than church attendance, in monastic rather than priestly
vocations and in special events rather than ordinary weekly
services. But it will also enliven regular church worship. We are
likely to see much more variety in services, with on the one hand
more use of dance, mime, banners and the exuberant expressions
of joy and spontaneity found in charismatic congregations and the
churches of Africa and, on the other, a growth in more meditative
kinds of worship with more space for silence and contemplation.

I think we can look forward too to an increasing number of inter-
faith festivals and celebrations and even to joint acts of worship and
witness involving Christians and those of other faiths. In March
1991 the Inter-Faith Network, which represents 66 different groups,
challenged all religious communities to move forward together and,
in the words of Rabbi Hugo Gryn, one of the network's co-
chairmen, 'to learn the complicated language of dialogue and then
to speak it; and to support each other as we build our sometimes
splendid, often modest bits of God's kingdom on earth'. Clearly
this is going to be a contentious issue between liberals and evangelicals and, more broadly, between the visible churches, many of
whose leaders welcome closer relations between the major world
faiths, and the invisible churches, who still see relations with those
of other faiths in terms of conversion rather than dialogue. There
have already been heated clashes over the proper attitude which
Christians should adopt towards Jews. The whole question of
relations with other faiths is likely to remain very sensitive and to
loom increasingly large on the agenda of all churches.

Another potentially divisive issue arises from the growing integration of Europe. January 1993, as we know all too well, will see
the creation of a single European market. But it is not just in
economic and political terms that the significance of national
boundaries is diminishing and Europe is becoming more and more
of a single unit. The implications of closer European integration
are considerable for the major churches in Britain. For Roman
Catholics it spells the end of centuries of isolation and being

perceived as a minority and alien church. Continental Europe is an overwhelmingly Catholic community. Pope John Paul II has already talked in terms of the moves towards closer European integration paving the way for a revival of medieval Christendom. He has also hinted that the Roman Catholic Church will become the soul of the new Europe, a prospect that fills extreme Protestants with alarm. In fact, closer links with the Continent also provide exciting possibilities for several British Protestant churches to discover their roots and forge new alliances. The Church of Scotland and United Reformed Churches are likely to develop closer relations with Reformed churches in Switzerland, France, Germany and the countries of the old Eastern Europe. The Church of England in some senses stands as the major British denomination most likely to be isolated as a result of these developments. For largely historical reasons its links have been much closer with America and the Commonwealth than with continental Europe. Its most natural bedfellows are the Lutheran churches of Germany and Scandinavia. The desirability for closer relations with this group has, indeed, already been recognized: in February 1991 the General Synod committed itself through the Meissen Declaration to a new bond of unity with the Lutheran Church in Germany.

What is happening in the former Communist lands of Eastern Europe is also going to have an influence here. The kind of Christianity which is being embraced so enthusiastically there and filling churches in a way virtually unknown in the West is very different from the enlightened liberal faith of the mainstream British denominations. It is for the most part mystical, authoritarian and deeply conservative. It is also often allied with extreme nationalism and racialist sentiments. The 'green' holistic teachings of Eastern Orthodoxy and its colourful and mysterious liturgies are making an increasing appeal to many in the West, but there are other less attractive aspects of the religious fervour in these newly liberated lands which may also find followers over here.

One of the most striking features of religious life in Eastern Europe has been the number of young people going to church. In the days of Communist rule, of course, this was in part a form of political protest. Church-going became a badge of opposition and even a kind of ritual among the young. It was the 'done thing' to be seen at church. There is conflicting evidence as to how far regular church attendance and worship among the young has persisted since the fall of the Communist regimes. These activities have now lost their cult status but they do still seem to be flourishing, perhaps signifying as much as anything a certain disapproval of the older generation for their lack of spiritual integrity and their willingness to condone a system of brutality and repression. What impresses about the pictures shown on television of overflowing churches in Russia and neighbouring countries is that the congregations are made up almost entirely of the young and the elderly – there are relatively few middle-aged people.

To a large extent the same is true here. Church attendance in Britain is lowest among those in the 35 to 55 age group. It is strongest among the over-60s, who predominantly frequent the older visible churches, and among the under-35s, who largely join the newer invisible churches. It is these latter churches which come nearest to displaying the life and vitality of the booming Christian communities in Eastern Europe and across Africa where congregations are growing so spectacularly. They do, indeed, seem to be the churches of the future. This may be hard for traditionalists to stomach but it is also hard to deny. As one youngish High Anglican clergyman who is certainly no friend to this new movement and what it stands for in terms of worship and doctrine said to me: 'I think we have to accept that it is through the charismatic and evangelical churches that God is now choosing to work and that that is where the growth and action is likely to be in our lifetime.'

But where does this leave the traditional visible churches? Should they now seek to follow the new invisible churches, pension off their ordained clergy, shut up their old buildings and introduce charismatic worship and house groups? Should they throw themselves whole-heartedly into the decade of evangelism and seek to win back the lost generation, the 35- to 55-year-olds, in the hope of recruiting sufficient new members to make up for the older ones who are dying off? Or would it be better simply to call it a day and close down, recognizing that the Spirit is now moving through a different kind of church, and that it is better to die gracefully than suffer the ignominy and the agony of gradual decline into oblivion?

This is where I move from prediction to pleading. I want to argue in the remainder of this chapter that there is still a very important role for the traditional visible churches, for what they stand for and even for what may seem on the face of it some of their most quirky, archaic and damaging features. I say this while accepting and welcoming the fact that most of the Christian growth and dynamism in the remainder of my lifetime will come in the new invisible churches. There is much about these bodies to admire and to learn from – their commitment to sound doctrine and to Biblical principles, their enthusiasm for mission and evangelism, their spontaneity and joy in worship, their lack of clerical hierarchies and bureaucracy, their strong sense of the presence of the Spirit and the supernatural. But there is much too that they can learn from the customs and approach of the older traditional churches. It would not, I believe, do the cause of Christianity any good if the visible church disappeared from the face of Britain and left the task of witness and ministry to its new invisible companion – nor, indeed, if it abandoned its distinctive hallmarks in an attempt to make itself invisible.

Of course it is right for the mainstream churches to see what they can learn from the success of the newer house churches and fellowships. To some extent this is already happening and it is bound to continue. There is likely to be less emphasis on special church buildings and set liturgies, with more congregations meeting in homes and halls for informal group worship. There are bound to be new patterns of ministry involving more use of lay people and part-timers. The charismatic influence will almost certainly grow in the major denominations. But these developments need to come in their own good time and as local circumstances allow. Some churches and congregations will take easily to more spontaneous and participatory worship, but others will not, and should not be dismissed as fuddy-duddy in consequence. It is perhaps worth recalling Jesus' warning about putting new wine into old bottles, and his reminder that in his father's house there are many mansions. The variety and breadth of God's kingdom should be reflected in the churches. Different styles of worship appeal to different personalities and, indeed, to the same personality at different stages of his or her pilgrimage of faith. Spontaneous, informal services which use contemporary language and modern choruses may well be the way to introduce many young people to Christianity. But they can be profoundly alienating for older folk, not just because they are unused to that kind of worship but because at their stage of life's journey there is a need for something calmer and more reflective.

The visible churches are often criticized for appealing predominantly to the elderly. But is this necessarily a bad thing? If their special mission is, indeed, to the older members of society, then they have a role which is growing in importance and scope rather than diminishing. As we well know, the over-60s are making up an ever higher proportion of the population. It is among the elderly that many of the most lonely and vulnerable souls are to be found – those most in need of the churches' spiritual and pastoral care. There are also increasing numbers of highly active and intel- ligent retired people who have the time to think about spiritual matters and the energy to devote themselves to voluntary organ- izations and activities. I know it can be demoralizing for clergy to see the same elderly faces in the pews week after week, but it is far too easy to dismiss the church as simply a geriatrics' club. I for one will not be distressed if the visible churches continue to cater largely for older people, speaking to the deeper concerns about life and death and the increased spiritual awareness which come with advancing age, and harnessing the energies and the time of the active retired in ways that give purposeful activity as well as fel- lowship.

There is a very real sense in which the churches can best serve this older age group, and perhaps also many younger people who would respond to a quieter and more meditative kind of worship, simply by being there. This ministry of presence is of great import- ance. There is a danger that the churches will respond to the decade of evangelism simply by launching a recruiting drive and feeling that they have to go out and convert people. Already there are signs that churches are playing the numbers game and eagerly counting the total of extra bottoms on the pews and new recruits on the Sunday School roll. But is this really what evangelism is about? Do not the churches, and particularly the visible churches, make their most important witness to Christ simply by the fact of being ever-present and ever-available? It may seem a rather dull and unspectacular kind of witness compared with the mass rallies, the sudden conversions and the emotional appeals which the more evangelical invisible churches are inclined to go in for, but it is no less valid or necessary.

The task of evangelism, after all, is not just a matter of enlivening the soul. It also involves convincing the mind – and it is here that the visible churches have a particularly important role to play. At times in this book I have been critical of the liberal establishment in the main churches – in whose ranks I would put myself. I think we have been too intellectual, too frightened of introducing emotion and of letting the Spirit take over. But that said, it is vitally important that the churches do not withdraw from intellectual debate. Some young people, maybe even a majority, are likely to be drawn to Christianity through emotional experience, but many others are more interested in reasoned argument and persuasion. Evangelicals, including many in the newer invisible churches, are, as we have seen, becoming much more interested in theology and in establishing the intellectual case for Christianity. But it is still overwhelmingly within the mainstream visible churches, Catholic and Protestant, that most of the serious thinking is going on about theological issues and about how the Christian Gospel can best be presented to modern scientific minds. In a decade of evangelism that kind of thinking is just as important as the contribution made by those churches which play more on the emotions.

There is another factor which would make me very worried about the invisible churches taking over as the main Christian presence in this country. It relates to their essentially sectarian and atomistic nature. As we have seen, their theology is often strongly individualistic, stressing personal salvation and a personal relationship with Christ. They tend to be anti-ecumenical and strongly opposed to dialogue with other faiths. Their outlook is exclusive rather than inclusive. I do not mean by this that they are not welcoming to the casual visitor or that they put up barriers to those who wish to join them. Far from it, they are often more welcoming than the older established churches, but they tend to stress the importance of going through an initiation rite such as believer's baptism, to draw rigid dividing lines between the saved and the unsaved, and to concentrate more on their own little community than on the wider church.

Many of the visible churches are, sadly, moving in the same direction. As their numbers fall and their influence and status wane, it is tempting for them to become more and more gathered congregations of the faithful, 'holy huddles' looking increasingly inwards to their own concerns. I believe that this tendency should be vigorously resisted. The great strength of the main historic denominations is that they have the capacity to be broad, inclusive churches which can reach the great unchurched majority. Once again we are back to the ministry of presence, with all its possibilities and all its frustrations. The fact that they are constantly available to all comers for the so-called occasional offices of baptism, marriage and burials understandably annoys some clergy and makes them feel they are just being 'used'. As one Church of

Scotland minister rather ruefully put it after conducting a funeral
for someone who never went to church and being handed £10 by
her son, 'many look on church and minister as somehow coming
under the auspices of the National Health Service or the Department of Social Security – a part of the welfare state'. He went on
to ask, 'How long can we continue to provide a free, nationwide
service for rites of passage to all, irrespective of whether they ever
darken our doors or make any contribution to our funds?'

Yet it is surely by providing such a service that the church
witnesses to the unconditional love of Christ and the abounding
and freely available grace of God. I fully accept that there will be
growing pressure to restrict it, not just because of a narrower
theology on the part of some clergy but also because of financial
pressures. It seems quite reasonable for churches to make some
kind of charge for their services in respect of occasional offices: it
would be very sad indeed if they were to pull out of this area
altogether, and restrict their ministry simply to the faithful few
who turn up for worship every Sunday. Not only sad, but also very
damaging. As the Archbishop of Canterbury has so rightly said,
'If we have lots of hoops people have to jump through – for instance
saying we will not baptize your child unless you are a committed
Christian, or we will not marry your daughter because we have not
seen her in church for 15 years – we will become increasingly
irrelevant.'

If the mainstream churches, and especially the established churches, are to retain this ministry of presence and availability to all,
then it is important that as far as possible we preserve the parish
system. Financial difficulties and shortages of clergy will inevitably
mean more linking of parishes and the creation of more team
ministries. This is not necessarily a bad thing, provided that what
is kept is the understanding that the parish church and the parish
clergy are there for everyone and not just for regular attenders or
members. Once that sense goes then the church has really signalled
its withdrawal from the wider community. It is no longer interested
in serving the people or the nation as a whole, merely the gathered
congregations of the elect.

Unlike many in the churches today, I would actually want to go
further on this tack and argue for the retention not just of the
parish system but also of the principle of establishment as it is
applied to our two main national churches. This is an increasingly
live issue and it is worth examining the pros and cons in some

detail. I suspect that the call for disestablishment, and more particularly the disestablishment of the Church of England, is going to be heard repeatedly through the 1990s. It will be argued on the grounds that there can be no possible justification for giving a whole set of legal, economic and political privileges to one denomination which has the active support of just 2.5 per cent of the population. Establishment, so its opponents say, is a barrier to creating an authentic witness in our pluralistic society, an anachronistic relic of the days of Christian imperialism and state religion which should be dispensed with as soon as possible.

Disestablishment first became a substantial public issue in the last century when it was championed by the Liberal party, aided and abetted by the great Nonconformist Conscience. It was held up as a way of freeing the people of God from the grip of Caesar and removing the corrupting influences of political patronage and privilege from religious life. The case for disestablishment was founded on the principle of voluntaryism – the belief that churches should derive their support from the commitment and free gifts of members rather than from either state or private sources. It also owed much to the argument for equality of treatment for all denominations and the feeling that none should be given special privileges.

These arguments remain valid today. The theological agenda for the churches has not shifted: it remains the advancement of the kingdom of God. But the political and cultural climate is now very different from what it was a hundred years ago. One of the greatest threats now to the hegemony and cohesion of our society, and to the values of Christ's kingdom, comes from the drive towards privatization and unrestrained individualism in all areas of life. What we are witnessing is an assault from Government, from commercial pressures and increasingly from a whole new cultural climate on a particular value system which has underlain British society for the last 100 years and on the public institutions which embody it. Its founding father was perhaps Matthew Arnold, the great Victorian poet and prophet who railed against the individualism and philistinism of sectarian religion and argued for the existence of an established church as a guardian of common standards and aspirations. In its extreme form Arnold's vision of a state given a unity and focus by shared religious principles could lead to an ugly nationalism of the kind that developed in Germany. It found very different expression in Britain through the creation of the Welfare State, the development of public education and the establishment of public bodies like the BBC and the National Trust. These institutions embody the idea that there are such things as public morality and a common good and that society is something more than just a mass of competing private goods and interests: they are now under severe threat from privatization, insistence on the primacy of market forces and the profit system, and a growing cultural relativism and pluralism.

In such a climate the continuing existence of established churches becomes very important. It is too grand to talk of them acting as the conscience of the nation, yet there is a sense in which they do still in a whole variety of subtle and complex ways mould our common values and cultural aspirations. It is partly from them that we derive simple but fundamental values like justice, compassion and tolerance, as well as some of those more elusive Arnoldian qualities of sweetness and light. The fact of being a national church, as opposed to just another sect or denomination, presents a unique opportunity both to serve and to bind together the whole community and not just particular groups within it. It allows the Church of Scotland and the Church of England to reach out throughout the countries they serve, speaking to the unchurched as well as the churched, linking privileged and unprivileged areas of society, maintaining a presence throughout the land. At a time when there are so many forces making for fragmentation and polarization in our society, this is not something that should be given up lightly.

It is interesting that the person who has written and spoken more clearly than anyone else in recent years about the importance of maintaining established churches is actually a non-Christian. In his 1990 Reith Lectures Jonathan Sacks, the Chief Rabbi, argued that church disestablishment would mark a sad and significant retreat from the notion that there are some values which we can all share. In his final lecture, he referred to the loss of what the American sociologist Peter Berger called 'the sacred canopy' – that overarching framework of shared meanings that once shaped individuals into a society. 'In its place has come pluralism: the idea that society is a neutral area of private choices where every vision of the good carries its own credentials of authenticity. But pluralism carries an explosive charge of conflicting interpretations ... By dismantling and privatising the concept of a common good it means that no one position is forced to come to terms with the reality of any other. It is no accident that as pluralism has gained ground, there has been a sharp increase in racial tension and anti-Semitism, and an air of insolubility about our most basic moral disagreements. Once we lose a common language, we enter the public domain as competing interest groups rather than as joint architects of a shared society. Communities are replaced by segregated congregations of the like-minded.'

Sacks suggests that in our increasingly atomized society and individualistic culture we have neglected the institutions which sustain communities of memory and character. He puts churches high among those institutions, especially an established church which 'places faith at the centre of our national symbols'. Religion, he argues, gives us a sense of belonging, rescues the individual from isolation and creates community. 'But religion has a larger role to play as well, in charting our shared moral landscape, that sense of common good that we need if our communities are to cohere as a society ... But more than that. If someone invented a religion-detector and passed it over the surface of our culture, the needle would swing when it came to our still strong convictions that compassion and justice should be part of the social order, that human life is sacred, that marriage and the nurture of children are not just one lifestyle among many. When we lack power, we still feel responsible. When we see others suffering, we can still feel pain. These are traces that the Biblical tradition has left deep within our culture: signals of transcendence that can at times move us to otherwise unaccountable acts of conscience and courage.' (*The Listener*, 3 January 1991.)

In some ways it is not surprising that this powerful and eloquent defence of the principle of ecclesiastical establishment should have come from a non-Christian. The established churches, in common with all the mainstream denominations, have a tendency to denigrate themselves and underestimate their influence. Understandably they have tended to become somewhat preoccupied with statistics of decline and do not always appreciate the extent to which they are still admired and respected by a wide section of the community. They also perhaps neglect their role as what the Germans called *volkskirke*, churches which serve the whole people of the country and act as a focus for the strong folk religion which, as we have seen, survives even in a supposedly secular society. The extensive poll undertaken for the book *Britain under the MORI-scope* revealed that two-thirds of the population still describe themselves as belonging to their national church, i.e., the Church of

England or the Church of Scotland. The disestablishment of these two churches would probably sever the remaining links, tenuous as they are, that still bind so many of the great unchurched majority to organized Christianity.

This does not mean that the Church of England should retain its present form of establishment. There is a good deal to be said for it having control over its own affairs and being able to appoint its own leaders without political interference. The Church of Scotland is the established church north of the border but there is no Prime Ministerial say in its appointments, or Parliamentary veto over its deliberations. It is entirely free to order its own affairs through its courts. What it gains through establishment is a unique status and standing in the country, the opportunity to minister to the whole population through the parish system and the chance to mould public values and influence social mores. The Church of England would be well advised to study and consider adopting the Scottish model of establishment. It might also look seriously at the very interesting suggestion made by Dr William Davies, when he took up the post of Moderator of the Free Church Federal Council in March 1991, that the historic Free Churches and the Roman Catholic Church should also become established. Like Dr Sacks this prominent Free Churchman sees perhaps more clearly than many in the Church of England the benefits of establishment. He feels that it binds the church into society and the life of the nation and that far from being ended it should be extended to give a greater role for all the mainstream churches in promoting social cohesion and communal values.

The idea of a new ecumenical established church bringing together all the main denominations is exciting but I fear probably unrealistic, at least in the foreseeable future. But it is not too much to hope that the visible churches will increasingly speak together with one voice on the need for a concept of the common good and of public service in our society. I hope too that they will also continue to witness clearly to the communal nature of Christianity. The invisible church is inclined to encourage a kind of privatized faith which people carry around with them rather like a personal stereo. The visible churches need to guard against espousing a similar creed. The point was well put by Dr Robert Runcie in a sermon to the clergy of the Manchester diocese in February 1989: 'If we are to serve the Kingdom of God I am sure we must not abandon the vision of our Church as a public body, at the service of the whole nation, serving those in the outer court as well as those in the sanctuary; a Church pervasive, guarding the roots and the memories, pointing to eternity amid a time of restlessness, distraction and ephemeral social change.'

There is another very important set of values which the visible churches represent and which is under very severe assault throughout our society. They are values like understatement and reserve, genuineness and honest doubt, gentleness and humility. Almost alone among major organizations and institutions, the mainstream churches have as yet largely resisted the blandishments of management consultants and the burgeoning public relations industry. They have not succumbed to the modern heresy that efficiency, image and style are the most important things in life. They still follow manifestly inefficient practices, like keeping open hundreds of small parish churches with tiny congregations and not concentrating their resources only on the areas where they are strongest. They show a blatant disregard for presenting a clear and successful image, being hesitant and diffident about proclaiming their message of salvation and indeed appearing often to be very uncertain as to what exactly it is. The invisible churches are not generally smitten by these handicaps. They are often highly image-conscious and open to the latest management techniques. I fear there are already ominous signs that it may not be long before the visible churches go the same way. The new Archbishop of Canterbury has let it be known that he would like the clergy to become more managerial in approach and that he will be seeking professional advice on how to improve the church's image. The magazine *Marketing Week* has produced a four-page supplement on the opportunities for marketing the churches under the terms of the new Broadcasting Act, and advertising agencies are queuing up to provide a test campaign. The managing director of one agency has said, 'The church has a much better product than its publicity would suggest'.

It is not, I think, just my old-fashioned puritanical bent that makes me squirm at these words. What the church has to offer is not a product, it is a mystery beyond price and even beyond reason – something deep and holy which cannot simply be packaged and marketed like detergent or breakfast cereals. The whole philosophy underlying advertising and public relations and management consultancy is totally inappropriate to the life and witness of the churches. They are not in the business of creating an attractive brand image or maximizing efficiency. If they were, they would long ago have got rid of their elderly congregations, sacked most of their clergy and turned their large store of ancient buildings into sets that could be hired out for weddings and period parties.

Part of the glory of the church is that it is not in the world's terms particularly effective or stylish or even very useful. When nearly everyone else is being made to be cost-effective and viable it is marvellous to have a profession like the clergy whose con- tribution cannot be measured in financial terms. When other organ- izations are being forced to rationalize and close down small branches because they are uneconomic, it is splendid that tiny churches are still remaining open even when there is only a handful of worshippers left in them. We are back again to the importance of the ministry of presence, of just being there. There is a terrible tendency for all organizations today to feel that they must always be busily doing things and changing things to justify their existence. I am afraid that the churches are not immune from this. There is an understandable but ultimately very damaging feeling among contemporary clergy that they must be constantly proving their relevance. But the fact is that the irrelevance and uselessness of the church are among its most important qualities. There is, after all, nothing more useless – judged by the standards of the world – than a community of monks who spend most of their waking hours in prayer and meditation. Yet the world would be a spiritually poorer place without them. When I talked about the 'uselessness' of the monastic vocation to one of the monks at Pluscarden Abbey in the north-east of Scotland, he gave me an analogy which I think could apply to the whole church. 'We are', he said, 'like one of those great lakes of water in the Highlands that has been dammed up as part of a hydro-electric scheme. In a sense the water does nothing but sit there uselessly. Yet it provides the force to generate the energy which provides heat and light and energy for millions of people. In the same way the church is a powerhouse of prayer, a source of spiritual energy for the whole world.'

Spiritual energy is a difficult quality to discern and define. It is present most obviously perhaps in the hand-clapping, chorus- singing, self-consciously Spirit-filled worship of the charismatics. But it is also there in the atmosphere of quietness and peace which allows us to hear the still small voice of calm. One of the unfortunate results of recent liturgical developments, as we have seen, is that there is now often a lot of talk and action in church services and very few periods of quiet. Silence is a very precious commodity, and an increasingly rare one in our society. There is a place for noise, heartiness and exuberance in the worship of God, but there is also a time for quiet contemplation and waiting on God. Because of their historic liturgies, their choral traditions, their atmospheric and restful architecture, and perhaps too because their congregations are often small and elderly and their buildings half empty or even deserted, the visible churches have a particular contribution to make to this ministry of silence. It is perhaps appropriate to recall that passage in 1 Kings where the prophet Elijah hears the voice of God not, as he expects, in the earthquake, wind or fire, but in the still small voice that follows these mighty works. I wonder whether today we may not also hear the voice of God in the quiet, hesitant, sometimes slightly muddled voices of those churches that do not scream their message in bold and simple language from advertising hoardings and amplifiers.

There are two well-tried Christian concepts which I would like to see guiding the church in Britain into the third millennium. One is the rather neglected doctrine of reserve – the preservation of a sense of reverence and awe in the face of the mystery of God. There is a terrible temptation today, from which I myself am certainly not immune, to want to spell everything out – in contemporary jargon, to 'have it all up front'. A recovery of the essential mystery of Christianity would, I think, be very salutary. The other idea that I would seek to recover and emphasize is that of pilgrimage. The hymn that gives this book its title and chapter headings was not chosen just because of my love of nineteenth-century hymnody. It expresses very well the sense that Christians are engaged on a journey that will have many twists and turns, many setbacks and detours, one which, at least in this life, never quite ends.

On the whole, I suspect that the newer invisible churches would not be terribly happy with either of these ideas. They tend to be 'up front' in their theology and to see God as immediately accessible. They tend, too, to regard Christianity not so much as a long and continuing pilgrimage but rather as a matter of conversion, often dramatic and sudden. There is a sense of confidence and certainty in their position, a feeling that they have already arrived at their destination, that they are saved and that their days of wandering and searching are done.

The prevailing mood in the visible churches is rather different. It seems much less certain and confident, often even rather muddled and confused. There is much searching and agonizing and when conclusions are reached and judgements are made they tend to be very tentative and reticent. Their approach is often characterized by critics as weak and wishy-washy. It is also very human, and I venture to suggest that it is true to the teachings of the One who told us not to judge and who promised that if we go on searching, we will find. Its character was summed up brilliantly by Bernard Levin in a piece which he wrote in *The Times* after attending the debate on homosexuality in the Church of England's General Synod in November 1987:

> I emerged with a wondering but intense admiration for this amazing body. The Church of England, facing for once a real problem, predictably and inevitably fudged it. But in the very act of fudging, it spoke with tongues. It will be denounced, from within and without its ranks, for both cowardice and brutality; but the result was a victory for all the best qualities of this country. The Church is as puzzled, worried, and uncertain as the rest of us; but in a strange way, it gave us all a lead, if only by telling us that to be puzzled, worried and uncertain is the lot of all thinking people, and it is no shame to confess as much. The Church of England – loving, muddled, well-meaning, daft, forgetful, brave, honest and absurd – is certainly not all right. But it is, emphatically, All Right. (*The Times*, 12 November 1987.)

For me one of the finest recent exemplars of this approach has been Robert Runcie. In his enthronement sermon at Canterbury Cathedral in 1980 he stated his own view of the role of the Church: 'The cry is "The Church must give a firm lead". Yes. It must – a firm lead against rigid thinking, a judging temper of mind, the disposition to oversimplify difficult and complex problems. If the Church gives Jesus Christ's sort of lead, it will not be popular.' During his ten years as Archbishop he himself came under considerable criticism, much of it very wounding, for being weak, indecisive and uncertain in his leadership. But, as his son wrote in a moving tribute shortly after his retirement, it is easy to see doubt where there is really ambivalence, indecision where there is forbearance, dithering and weakness where there is thought, pause and reflection. James Runcie admitted that he got so fed up with his father being pilloried in the press that he once implored him, 'Can't you do anything? Can't you be clearer, stronger?' The reply from his father was almost angry: 'I am strong on forgiveness, tolerance. I am clear. Clear in my faith in Jesus Christ. And I believe in authority – the authority of love.' (*Daily Telegraph*, 22 December 1990.)

As we approach the third Christian millennium there are plenty of churches which are full of certainties and confident that their own particular journeys to faith are largely over. But I would venture to suggest that it is in those churches which are yet searching and still feel themselves to be on a pilgrimage that Christ's presence is nearer. Indeed, I would go even further and suggest that the mark of the true church is that it is a suffering church which experiences genuine pain and anguish and bears the burden of the Cross. This may well mean that it will be divided and weak and sometimes even rather bitter. The church as Christians understand it is the body of Christ here on earth – and Christ's body was broken. It is out of that brokenness and pain and suffering and sacrifice that faith grows and the strength comes to continue on the pilgrimage. Just as it is the love which suffers that is the love which saves, so it must be the church that suffers that will be the church that saves. More than 150 years ago, in 1834, on the eve of what was perhaps the greatest revival and spiritual awakening in modern British church history, John Henry Newman wrote:

> The Church is ever ailing and lingers on in weakness, 'always bearing about in her body the dying of the Lord Jesus that the life also of Jesus might be made manifest in her body.' Religion seems ever expiring, schisms dominant, the light of the Church dim, its adherents scattered. Meanwhile, this much of comfort do we gain from what has been hitherto – not to despond, not to be dismayed, not to be anxious at the troubles which encompass us. They have ever been; they shall ever be; they are our portion. 'The floods are risen, the floods have lifted up their voices, the floods have lifted up their waves. The waves of the sea are mighty and rage horribly; but yet the Lord, who dwelleth on high, is mightier.'

The future may look bleak for many churches in Britain just now. But it would be bleaker still if, this side of that great and mysterious consummation which Our Lord has promised when all will be all in him, they ceased to feel that they were pilgrims marching through the night of doubt and sorrow and felt rather that they had arrived at their destination and knew all the answers to the mystery of existence. It is only when the songs of expectation turn to choruses of certainty and the Cross ceases to be an experienced reality and becomes simply a trinket that there is real cause for worry about the future.

> Through the night of doubt and sorrow
>   Onward goes the pilgrim band,
> Singing songs of expectation,
>   Marching to the promised land.
>
> Clear before us through the darkness
>   Gleams and burns the guiding light;
> Brother clasps the hand of brother,
>   Stepping fearless through the night.
>
> One the object of our journey,
>   One the faith that never tires,
> One the earnest looking forward,
>   One the hope our God inspires:
>
> One the strain that lips of thousands
>   Lift as from the heart of one;
> One the conflict, one the peril,
>   One the march in God begun.
>
> Onward, therefore, pilgrim brothers,
>   Onward with the Cross our aid,
> Bear its shame; and fight its battle,
>   Till we rest beneath its shade.

Suggestions for further reading

1. On the current state of the churches in Britain

Peter Brierley, *'Christian' England* (MARC Europe, London, 1991). Presents and analyses results of the detailed church census taken in October 1989.

Prospects for Scotland (National Bible Society for Scotland & MARC Europe, London, 1985) and *Prospects for Wales* (Bible Society and MARC Europe, London, 1983) are also worth consulting.

Eric Jacobs & Robert Worcester, *We British: Britain under the MORI-scope* (Weidenfeld and Nicolson, London, 1990) has a useful chapter on 'Religious Britain'.

David Winter, *Battered Bride? The Body of Faith in an Age of Doubt* (Monarch Publications, Eastbourne, 1988), is a lively account of the church scene in contemporary Britain.

2. On specific churches

William Oddie, *The Crockford's File* (Hamish Hamilton, London, 1989). A vigorous and opinionated analysis of what is wrong with the Church of England.

Adrian Hastings, *Robert Runcie* (Mowbray, London, 1991) is a superbly written and sensitive study not just of its subject but also of contemporary Anglicanism.

Interesting interpretations of the recent history and current state of the Church of Scotland are provided in Tom Gallagher and Graham Walker, *Sermons and Battle Hymns* (Edinburgh University Press, 1991) and Robert Kernohan, *The Protestant Future* (Christian Focus Publications, London, 1991).

Michael Hornsby-Smith, *Roman Catholic Beliefs in England* (Cambridge University Press, 1991) discusses the results of surveys among Roman Catholics in the 1960s and 1970s.

The growth of the new evangelical churches is well explained in Clive Calver, *He brings us together* (Hodder & Stoughton, London, 1987) and Stephen Abbott, *Join Our Hearts* (Marshall Pickering, London, 1989).

3. On the ecumenical movement

Paul Avis, *Christians in Communion* (Mowbray, London, 1990)

Derek Palmer, *Strangers No Longer* (Hodder & Stoughton, London, 1990)

Rupert Davies, *The Church in our Times* (Epworth Press, London, 1979)

Edward Yarnold, *In Search of Unity: Ecumenical Principles and Prospects* (St Paul Publications, Slough, 1989)

4. On contemporary theology

Salvation and the Church. Report of the Anglican–Roman Catholic International Commission (Church House Publishing, London, 1987)

The Nature of Christian Belief (Church House Publishing, London, 1986). Doctrinal statement produced by the House of Bishops of the Church of England in response to issues raised by the Bishop of Durham.

David Ford, *The Modern Theologians: An Introduction to Christian Theology in the Twentieth Century*, 2 vols. (Basil Blackwell, Oxford, 1989)

Daphne Hampson, *Theology and Feminism* (Basil Blackwell, Oxford, 1990)

John Polkinghorne, *Reason and Reality: The Relationship between Science and Theology* (SPCK, London, 1991)

5. On church involvement in social and political issues

Faith in the City: Report of the Archbishop of Canterbury's Commission on Urban Priority Areas (Church House Publishing, London, 1985)

Faith in the Countryside: Report of the Archbishops' Commission on Rural Areas (Churchman Publishing, Worthing, 1990)

Ed. Michael Alison and David Edwards, *Christianity and Conservatism* (Hodder & Stoughton, London, 1990)

6. On ministry

Ruth Edwards, *The Case for Women's Ministry* (SPCK, London, 1989)

Jacqueline Field-Bibb, *Women Towards Priesthood* (Cambridge University Press, 1991)

Ben Fletcher, *Clergy under Stress* (Mowbray, London, 1990)

Index